When we pray, we speak to God, but when we meditate, we allow God to speak to us and guide us. Through meditation, we can also get in touch with our soul: that piece of God that is in each of us and is a storehouse of knowledge and wisdom. It is our inheritance, and through meditation, we can tap into that knowledge, which no books, no science, no teachers, or gurus can teach us.

Books by Shakuntala Modi, M.D.

Remarkable Healings:
A Psychiatrist Discovers Unsuspected Roots
of Mental and Physical Illness

MEMORIES

OF

GOD

AND

CREATION

Remembering from the Subconscious Mind

SHAKUNTALA MODI, M.D.

HAMPTON ROADS
PUBLISHING COMPANY, INC.

6/02

Cover design by Marjoram Productions
Cover art by © Image Ideas, Inc./PictureQuest

For information write:

Hampton Roads Publishing Company, Inc.
1125 Stoney Ridge Road
Charlottesville, VA 22902

Or call: 804-296-2772
FAX: 804-296-5096

e-mail: hrpc@hrpub.com
Web site: www.hrpub.com

If you are unable to order this book from your local
bookseller, you may order directly from the publisher.
Quantity discounts for organizations are available.
Call 1-800-766-8009, toll-free.

Library of Congress Catalog Card Number: 00-102565

ISBN 1-57174-196-8
10 9 8 7 6 5 4 3 2 1

Printed on acid-free paper in Canada

Dedication

I humbly dedicate this book to God,

all the masters, angels, heavenly guides,

all the other Light beings,

and the whole creation.

May it enlighten mankind and

expand its consciousness.

Acknowledgments

There are many people who need to be recognized for their great assistance in preparing this book. First, I acknowledge my patients, through whom I was privileged to receive this information. Their willingness to explore and share this awesome knowledge is greatly appreciated.

My sincere thanks to Joanne Romshak for hours of tedious typing and retyping. She is a God-sent help for me.

I am also grateful to my local editor, Milton Ronsheim, for his corrections and suggestions.

My thanks to Hampton Roads Publishing Company for editing, designing, producing, and promoting this book.

I have to acknowledge my two little grandsons, Devesh and Vikash, for showing me what real, innocent joy is. When things became rough and everything appeared bleak and hopeless from time to time, all I had to do is remember their smiles, giggles, and the joy in their twinkling eyes, and in no time I would forget about what was wrong. They, like all the children of the world, are little angels reminding the grown-ups what real joy is. Thank you for being the light of our lives.

Ultimately, I humbly acknowledge God, all the masters, my higher self, angels, heavenly guides, and all other Light beings for their consistent and enthusiastic participation, assistance, education, guidance, protection, and the gift of this book. I am eternally grateful for this awesome privilege and all the blessings.

Contents

Introduction

The Beginning

For all those readers who have not read my first book, *Remarkable Healings*, I would like to give some background information about myself and how that book and the present one evolved over the years. I am a board-certified psychiatrist and have been in private practice for about twenty-five years. When I was doing my psychiatric residency, I realized there was no single treatment that worked for every patient. Medication works, but not for every patient, and because of the side effects, it can make some patients more dysfunctional than they were before medication. Traditional talk therapy helps only a small percentage of patients. I saw many patients going from doctor to doctor and from hospital to hospital, searching for relief from their symptoms.

During my residency, I strived to learn various treatment methods such as individual psychotherapy, group therapy, family therapy, marriage counseling, psychodrama, transactional analysis, hypnosis, and hypnotherapy. I wanted to use them with patients to suit their needs for healing. Over the years, I used hypnosis and hypnotherapy with good results. Hypnosis allows patients to uncover the underlying subconscious reasons for their emotional, mental, and physical problems. The unresolved problems are brought from the subconscious mind to the conscious mind, and by recalling, reliving, releasing, understanding, and resolving the unresolved traumas and issues, the patient can be free from their long-standing problems, often in a few sessions.

Over the years of my psychiatric practice, I always felt good about the quality of my work and the results I had with my patients. I was able to help them with a combination of different treatment modalities, according to their needs. But still there were some patients for whom I could not do much except use medication and supportive psychotherapy. So I continued to search for ways to help my patients.

About fifteen years ago, one of my patients, Martha, age thirty-four, came to me with severe, long-standing claustrophobia, depression, suicidal preoccupation, and severe panic attacks several times a day, every day. During these panic attacks, she had difficulty in breathing, palpitations, dizziness, feelings of intense fear and apprehension, and a fear of dying. I began to treat Martha with medication and psychotherapy, which helped her somewhat, but her claustrophobia, depression, and panic attacks continued.

During a session, I asked Martha about the last time she had a panic attack. All of a sudden, she became anxious and said, "Doctor, I am having one right now," and she started to gasp for breath. I asked her to close her eyes, focus on her emotional and physical feelings, and allow those feelings to take her back to another time, to the source of her problems when she felt the same way. As she focused on her feelings, she slipped into a self-induced trance state. I thought she would probably remember a childhood incident when perhaps she was locked in an attic, closet, bathroom, or a small room from where she could not come out. Instead, she said she was in a different time, a different life, and a different body as a young girl. "I am in a coffin," Martha cried. "They think I am dead! They are closing the lid. I am afraid to die, but what if they close the lid of the coffin and I do not die? Then what am I going to do?"

I was taken by surprise, but I let Martha continue the story and release the emotions associated with it. When she came out of this self-induced trance state, she looked puzzled but relaxed, and her panic attack was completely gone. During the next session, she reported she was free of her claustrophobia, depression, and panic attacks.

I was pleased with Martha's dramatic cure. None of my patients had ever regressed to another life before. I wondered if any other psychiatrist or hypnotherapist had patients who regressed to former lifetimes. As I searched the medical literature, I found there were many books written on the subject and there were many therapists across the country who were doing what they called "past-life regression therapy." I realized past-life regression therapy is just a continuation of age regression therapy, only it takes the patient back further, into another life, to a traumatic event that caused the problems in the current life. I began to use past-life regression therapy in combination with other traditional therapies and often obtained fast and dramatic success in relieving patients' symptoms.

Another patient, Connie, suffered from asthma, and also could not tolerate anything being close to her neck. Under hypnosis, as I asked her to move back in time to the source of her problems, Connie found herself regressed back to the time of her birth. She reported that the umbilical cord was wrapped around her neck and she could not breathe.

During the next session, Connie told me her asthma was better but she still could not wear anything around her neck. Again under hypnosis, I asked her to go to the source of her problem. She found herself in another time and another life, when she was a man who was hanged. After releasing the emotions and the physical feelings associated with it, Connie was free of her asthma and was able to wear necklaces and button her blouse all the way up to her neck without discomfort.

I found many symptoms in patients that had their source in one or more past lives. Usually psychosomatic disorders, deep-seated personality problems, and immune disorders resulted from past-life traumas. Symptoms such as depression, anxiety, fears, phobias, panic attacks, premenstrual symptoms, sexual disorders, eating disorders, perfectionism, obsessive-compulsive disorder, headaches, fibromyositis, arthritis, other aches and pains, skin conditions, asthma, and allergies often have their origin in one or more past lives. These are described in detail in *Remarkable Healings*.

Another patient, Breana, age fifty, came to me for depression and abdominal pains from which she had suffered off and on for several years. Her physical examination and laboratory tests were normal. She wanted to try hypnotherapy for her abdominal pain. As I asked her to focus on her symptoms and let those feelings take her back to the source of her abdominal pain, Breana found herself in another time and another life when she was a man in 1974. It did not make any sense to me because Breana was fifty years old, so this could not be her "past" life.

As I asked Breana to check and see what was going on, she became emotional and said that the man was the spirit of her father who died in 1974 of stomach cancer, and his spirit was in her. I was very surprised. I tried to communicate with her father's spirit through Breana. He said that after the death of his body, his spirit came in to comfort his daughter because she was sad, but he got stuck in her and could not come out of her. He claimed his daughter was suffering with *his* depression and *his* abdominal pain, from which he had suffered before his death. They were transferred over to Breana. He also said that there are many spirits of other people in Breana, but he did not know them.

I did not know what to do with the spirit of Breana's father. During past-life regression therapy, after the death of their physical bodies in a past life, patients often report seeing angels and their departed loved ones in the bright white Light coming to help them. So I asked Breana's father to look up and tell me what he saw. He claimed to see brilliant white Light, and his own deceased mother in it, wearing a long white robe. She looked young and healthy and not sick or old, as she was before the death of her physical body. I asked Breana's father—and all the other people in Breana—to hold his mother's hands and the hands of the angels who were there, and to go to the Light (Heaven). Breana said her father and the spirits of other people who were inside her went to the Light along with her grandmother and the angels.

After the session, Breana was emotional about seeing her

deceased father and grandmother. She was sad about him leaving, but she felt happy and at peace, knowing that they were not really dead and that they both were in Heaven. She had no doubt about what she saw and experienced during that session. During the next session, Breana reported she was free of her long-standing depression and stomach problems. They were her father's symptoms that were transferred over to Breana after his spirit came into her.

I was surprised to find that spirits of deceased people can come into people and affect them physically, mentally, and emotionally. Many questions ran through my mind. Breana's father and the spirits of other people—were they real or was she fantasizing about her father because she missed him? Maybe this was her way of grieving and letting go of her father? But what about the strangers? If it was all her fantasy, then how was it that her long-standing depression and stomachache were relieved after that session? If the spirits were real, then why was it that none of my patients ever reported them before? Could it be that there were spirits in other patients too, but we had not recognized them? I did not know. All I knew was that my patient was now free of her symptoms after only one session.

Since then, hundreds of my patients under hypnosis have reported finding human spirits inside themselves, separate and distinct from their own soul. These spirits are reported by my patients as the visitors, what we call the attached or possessing earthbound spirits that did not make their transition to Heaven after the death of their physical bodies and that have remained on the Earth plane. These "guest" spirits in my patients could be conversed with through the patients. They often claimed to remain on the Earth because of strong emotions, such as anger, hate, love, fear, jealousy, or the desire to take revenge. They also remained earthbound because of unfinished business, obsessive attachment to a person, place, or an object, or addiction to drugs, alcohol, food, gambling, or sex.

These earthbound human spirits claimed they could enter my patients when the energy fields (aura) around their bodies were weakened when they were physically sick, during anesthesia and surgery, when they had been knocked unconscious, or after an accident. Emotional conditions such as anger, fear, hate, depression, anxiety, and grief can also open a person's energy field (aura). Many human spirits claimed to join my patients when they were using drugs and alcohol or playing video games, listening to loud and disharmonious music, using Ouija boards, doing automatic writing or channeling without protection, sitting in a seance, or playing conjuring games such as "Dungeons and Dragons" and "Demons." I realized that everybody is potentially open for spirit entry because we all get sick; have surgery; accidents; become angry, anxious, depressed and afraid; or use drugs and alcohol. Unfortunately, most people are not even aware of having any spirits in their bodies and auras.

These possessing earthbound human spirits are like cosmic hitchhikers on the road to Heaven. They use humans like a motel, coming in like uninvited houseguests with all their "baggage" of physical, emotional, and mental problems that are transferred over to their hosts. When these spirits are released during treatment, they take their problems away with them, thus freeing the patients of their symptoms.

Another patient, Nick, a thirty-five-year-old man, came to me with frequent migraine headaches, depression, and chronic fatigue, which he'd had since he was a teenager. During a session, as he focused on his headaches, Nick saw a "black blob" in his head; it claimed to be a demon, a disciple of Satan, who sent it to Nick to cause him problems. I was shocked. The only exposure I had had to demons was through the movie, *The Exorcist*, and my patient was not behaving like the character in that film. The only change I saw in Nick when the "demon" spoke through him was a change in the tone of his voice and the appearance of an angry expression and arrogance on his face. Nick normally was soft spoken and polite.

The only logical step, it seemed to me, was to continue the dialogue to find out more about this so-called "demon." It claimed to have entered Nick when he was using drugs and, once in, it caused him headaches by pressing on his brain, blood vessels, and nerves; it also stated that it caused Nick depression and chronic fatigue by siphoning off his energy.

As this demon began to talk, Nick's headaches became very intense. At this point, Nick said the room was filled with a bright, white Light and with many angels, who put a net of Light around the black blob, the demon in his head. It did not like the Light and claimed that Satan told all demons to stay away from the Light because it would kill them or make them disappear.

According to Nick, the angels twisted the net around the black blob and asked it to look inside its core. As the demon reluctantly looked inside, it claimed to find a spark of Light in it, and as it focused on that spark, it began to grow. The demon's darkness began to dissipate until it became a ball of Light in just a few minutes. The transformed being seemed to be shocked and described feeling a peace and joy it had never felt before. It apologized to Nick for causing him problems and thanked me for helping it. According to Nick, the angels said that this transformed being is a being of Light and needs to go back to Heaven, and that they could take the being there.

Nick watched this in amazement. He was surprised to realize that his splitting headache was relieved after the entity was transformed into Light. He also saw angels cleansing, healing, and filling his head with Light where the demon was. The next week Nick reported he was free of depression and headaches and that he was feeling more energetic.

I did not know what to think of that session, but I was glad Nick was free of his symptoms. My mind was filled with many questions. Was the demon Nick described in his head real or a figment of his imagination? Maybe his subconscious mind made up this fantastic story so he would not have to be responsible for his problems. But if it was just his fantasy, how could this cure his headaches and depression? I realized it did not matter. What mattered was that Nick was free of his symptoms. Traditional psychotherapy and medication did not give this kind of dramatic cure.

For the next fifteen years after that episode, hundreds of my patients reported having demons in them that were responsible for their emotional, mental, physical, and spiritual problems. Releasing these demons from them cured their symptoms. I learned that every organ, every part, and every cell of the body can be infested and inflicted by these demons. They claim to cause aches and pain, numbness, weakness, and diseases in every part of the body by pressing, scratching, and squeezing—directly or indirectly—and by using different demonic "devices" created by them for these purposes.

The demons also claimed to be the single most common cause for most psychiatric problems. They claimed to cause depression, anxiety, panic attacks, violent angry outbursts, suicidal and homicidal thoughts and behaviors, sadomasochistic behavior, fears, phobias, hallucinations, paranoia, and delusions. They project their anger, hate, paranoia, arrogance, fear, desire for power and position, and violent sadomasochistic behavior onto the patients, who then act and behave in the same way. They also claimed to cause people to curse, use obscene language, and desire to use drugs and alcohol.

Heavenly beings have often said through my hypnotized patients that these demons are as real as they are, but they are of negative energy and are responsible for most of our personal, marital, social, emotional, mental, and physical problems. According to the angels, doctors, psychiatrists, and all the health professionals should pray daily for protection and guidance, because they do not know what they are dealing with when they work with patients.

My hypnotized patients have consistently stated that these demon spirits have great powers, but with the help of God and heavenly beings, we human beings can be more powerful than Satan and his demons. Demons have only as much power as we give them. In contrast to what most people believe, Satan and his demons operate within limitations.

Under hypnosis, my patients also reported seeing their souls located in their chest area. They described the soul as an immortal energy essence, a part of God in each of us. It empowers the body, which cannot live without it. At the time of death, the body dies, but the soul continues to survive, retaining all its memories. Patients also reported that with mental, emotional, and physical trauma, the soul fragments into many pieces, creating holes in the soul, which in turn cause a weakness of the body and the energy field. This makes a person vulnerable to spirit entry. These soul parts can remain in the body as what we call in psychiatry as subpersonalities, alter personalities, or the inner child. Some soul parts can go to different people. Our husbands, wives, parents, children, and other relatives and friends are the most frequent possessors of our missing soul parts.

Some patients who have been abused claimed that their soul parts are in possession of their abusers, causing them continued fear and emotional turmoil. In these cases, patients are negatively influenced by the abusers' experiences, behaviors, and problems. Patients also claimed that many of their soul parts are in Satan's possession in hell, where demons manipulate a person's thinking, attitudes, and behavior, and cause the person different emotional, mental, and physical symptoms through these captive soul parts.

Patients also reported that they have soul parts of other living people in their possession. These soul parts act as possessing earthbound spirits and influence patients physically, emotionally, and mentally. Treatment is usually at a stalemate until these soul parts are returned and integrated with their rightful owners and all the patient's missing soul parts are brought back and reintegrated with them. This is particularly true in cases where Satan and his demons are the possessors of patients' soul parts.

Discoveries such as these marked the beginning of an exciting journey looking deep into the subconscious for the reasons for mental, emotional, and physical problems. I began to understand that there are several sources of patients' problems, that is, current life traumas, including birth and prenatal traumas; past-life traumas; possession by human, demon, and other spirits; and soul fragmentation and soul loss. By recognizing this, we can understand that any emotional, mental, or physical problem in fact is a disease of the soul. To heal the mind and body, we need to heal the soul, by removing all the possessing earthbound (human) and demon spirits and the soul parts of other living people. Then we need to heal the traumas from the current and past lives by recalling, reliving, releasing, and resolving them and by reclaiming all the lost soul parts from those traumas and integrating them with the patient's soul. By healing the soul, we can heal the physical body of its emotional, mental, and physical problems.

Belief in past lives, reincarnation, and earthbound (human) and demon spirits is not at all necessary, either for the patient or the therapist, for the therapy to work. The only requirement is that the patient be willing to go through the experiences provided by their subconscious mind in order to resolve their symptoms.

After many years of doing this therapy, I examined the charts of one hundred patients whom I treated with spirit releasement, past-life regression, and soul integration therapy, and noted various pieces of information. The conclusions of that research were surprising, if not shocking, even for me. Some of the conclusions were as follows:

- Ninety-two patients had earthbound spirits
- Eighty patients had more than one earthbound spirit
- Fifty patients had spirits of their relatives
- Seventy-seven patients had demon spirits.

A total of 80 percent of the primary symptoms (acute symptoms for which patients came to my office, such as depression and its associated symptoms, anxiety, panic attacks, psychotic symptoms), and 30 percent of secondary symptoms (chronic symptoms, such as chronic arthritis, sinusitis, back pain, headaches, and so forth) are caused by spirits, while 20 percent of primary symptoms and 70 percent of secondary symptoms result from past-life traumas, according to my research.

By releasing the possessing spirits from the patients, most of the acute symptoms were relieved in a few sessions, sometimes just in one session, without much medication or traditional psychotherapy. Also, my research showed that depression and its associated symptoms, that is insomnia, chronic fatigue, poor concentration and memory, and panic attacks, are the most common symptoms caused by the spirits.

Having human and demon spirits in one's body and aura does not mean that the patient is "evil." It is a human condition. Because of our human frailty, everyone is open to spirit entry. We all get sick, have surgeries or accidents, get emotionally upset, take drugs, drink alcohol, or indulge in behaviors that weaken the energy shield around us. As soon as we are born, spirits come on board with us and potentially continue to come in throughout our lives. Nobody is free of this. According to the human and demon spirits, people with a higher life purpose and those who are doing God's work actually are targeted more intensively by the spirits.

Over the years, I have realized that we psychiatrists and other mental health professionals have a limited understanding about the true reasons for mental and physical illness. I have learned to keep my mind open, to ask questions, and to stay away from giving my own interpretations during a session. I understand that the patient's subconscious mind not only has the knowledge of the reasons for their problems, but it can also provide solutions and even healing. After receiving similar information from a cross-section of my hypnotized patients for many years, I felt compelled to write about this mind-bending knowledge. My first book, *Remarkable Healings* was the result.

But the discoveries did not stop there. My hypnotized patients also began to provide astonishing reports of memories of God and the creation, the subject of the present book. This book is the product of the compilation of the knowledge given by many hypnotized people. It answers almost everything we always wanted to know about God and creation, that is, how it happened and why, and everything since then. It is the history of our soul.

This book is only about the normal aspect of God and creation. The next book will be about what goes wrong in the universe and why, that is, the pathological issues.

None of the information presented in this book comes from my religious or cultural background or from any of my personally held beliefs. It is based solely on what hundreds of my patients have consistently reported under hypnosis. One of the most impressive results is the universality of the information obtained. Although most of the people reporting the information come from diverse cultural, religious, socioeconomic, and educational backgrounds, the information they received under hypnosis is strikingly similar and consistent. Even young children and teenagers have given similar information. Their words may differ, the expression may vary, but the basic information is the same, woven of common threads into the same essential themes.

The word "Light" is used synonymously for God, Heaven, and for the emanation of Light coming from Heaven. The letter *L* in the word Light is capitalized to differentiate it from regular, earthly light, and also because patients describe God and Heaven as just pure white Light. Also, throughout this book, I have addressed God as "It" and "He" because that is what my patients called Him.

According to heavenly beings, humans are spiritually ready to receive the new knowledge reported in this book and say it will help us to evolve, transform, and illuminate ourselves and our planet. Understanding the facts about who we are, where we come from, why we are here, and what is our destiny can transform us and take us "Home" to God sooner.

Chapter One

Tapping into the Cosmic Memories

It has been about fifteen years since my patients, under hypnosis, began to recall current and past life traumas, possession by human and dark spirits, and soul fragmentation and soul loss as the source of their emotional, mental, and physical symptoms. They also started to remember some amazing spiritual information, such as who we are, where we come from, why we are here, and what happens to us when we die. Many of my patients even regressed back to the time when they were one with God and there was nothing else, only God. No planets, no individual souls, and no creation whatsoever. Some of my patients regressed back to the time of the creation of their souls, and found it to be the source of their feelings of depression, separation anxiety, feelings of rejection, fears, and inferiority. This is exactly how they felt when their souls were created by God and separated from Him.

My patients also found it to be very profound and therapeutic to remember firsthand that they came from God and are a part of Him. While one with God, they described feeling totally content and peaceful, and had no negative feelings. I began to wonder: if everything was good and peaceful before creation, why did God decide to create, and why we are going through this revolving door of birth and death cycles, as my patients have claimed under hypnosis. Did God also create Satan and his demons, and if yes, why? What is the purpose of all this pain and suffering we go through while on Earth?

Throughout my first book, *Remarkable Healings*, and also in this book, most of the information I received was not only through my hypnotized patients but also through so-called "normal" people, who recalled similar information under hypnosis. Because of our human frailty, every human being is open for spirit entry at one or more times in their lives. So, I also worked with many people who did not have any acute symptoms but who wanted to be free of all the attached spirits within them, to retrieve all their missing soul parts, and to be fully integrated. After cleansing and healing, they can fulfill their purposes without much dark influence.

As I began to ask different questions to people under hypnosis, they were able to receive answers and understanding about various issues as well as a lot of higher spiritual knowledge. Any information and understanding we wanted was given to us by the heavenly beings. Wisdom that was previously given to only a few selected prophets is now given to anybody who desires it and is ready to receive it. According to heavenly beings, much of the information in this book has not been revealed before because we humans were not ready to receive it. But now it is time for us to know and understand this information, for our spiritual growth.

Hypnosis: Looking beneath the Surface, the Subconscious Mind

In my first book, *Remarkable Healings*, I have described hypnosis and other therapeutic techniques in detail. But since everybody may not be familiar with my first book, I will explain hypnosis and how it works in therapy. The general public has many misconceptions and fears about hypnosis based on what they understand from television, movies, and stage hypnosis. For people to benefit from the treatment, we need to dispel the misconceptions about hypnosis. It is important for people to understand what hypnosis is and what it is not, so they can enter into therapy free from fear and with the correct expectations.

Hypnosis is a state of focused concentration where we selectively block out peripheral awareness. To understand hypnosis and how it works, we need to understand our conscious and subconscious mind. The conscious mind is the thinking, reasoning, and problem-solving part of our mind, also known as the left brain. It is the part of our mind that deals with day-to-day functioning. It is the normal state of our awareness. The subconscious mind functions at a deeper level than our conscious mind and is known as the right brain. It deals with memories, intuition, and knowledge.

Normally, our conscious mind, or left brain, is cluttered with our day-to-day thoughts and problems. It is busy and constantly aware of everything that is happening around it. In this state, we cannot bypass the conscious mind and get in touch with our subconscious mind to give suggestions or retrieve information.

The goal of hypnosis is to set aside our constantly chattering conscious mind. One way to do this is to guide people to focus on their breathing and to relax different parts of their bodies. When the conscious mind is calm and quiet and not preoccupied by unnecessary thoughts, it is easy to bypass it and get in touch with the subconscious mind. Here the conscious mind is not asleep or unconscious, but it acts as a passive observer. It is aware of what is happening during a session, but it does not interfere with its doubts, constant analysis, and interpretations.

We achieve a similar state of focused concentration daily, normally and naturally, when we are absorbed in reading a book, watching a movie, listening to music, or driving on a highway (highway hypnosis) when we lose track of time. Similarly, while daydreaming, we are focusing on a person, place, or an event and are not concerned about our surroundings, nor are we distracted by the events near us. In these cases, our concentration is focused on whatever we are doing, and we are not asleep or unconscious. Other times during which we are in a state of deep hypnosis include the moments just before we fall asleep and at the beginning stage of waking up in the morning.

Similarly, when we are focusing on our emotional, mental, and physical problems, we are in a state of hypnosis. Most of the time when patients come to my office, they are suffering with intense emotions, such as anger, fear, or sadness or physical sensations, such as pain, numbness, palpitations, or difficulty breathing, or they use certain words over and over to describe their problems. In these cases, I usually ask them to focus on their emotional, mental, or physical feelings or thoughts and let those feelings and thoughts take them back to another time, to the source of the problems when they felt the same way. This can instantly bridge a present-time conflict to a conflict in the past, either in the current life or in a past life. By recalling, reliving, and resolving the trauma, they are often freed of their problems. This is called "bridge technique."

Thus we can understand that during hypnosis, people are not asleep or unconscious. They are in a state of focused concentration in which they are not aware of or paying attention to what is happening around them. Every hypnosis is a self-hypnosis, just like the different examples of daily hypnosis described above. We go in and out of the state of hypnosis several times every day without any formal induction. In therapy, a therapist only acts as a guide in assisting the patient, who controls the level of the trance and what is being revealed. The patients cannot act against their ethical or moral codes, and they can come out from under hypnosis any time they desire.

Hypnosis itself is not a therapy. It is only a tool that can be used in therapy. It allows therapists to give positive suggestions to help the patient, as in the *directive approach* in therapy. But patients are free to accept or reject any suggestions they choose, and even at the deepest level of trance, they will not accept any suggestions that are against their morals and ethics. In therapy, I usually make a relaxation tape for my patients to use at home with positive suggestions to suit their needs. It usually works well and people feel better, but it is just a symptomatic treatment. What a tranquilizer, a sleeping pill, or a pain pill can do, a relaxation tape with positive suggestions can also achieve in a motivated person. These pills do not cure the problems and neither does the tape. Most posthypnotic suggestions last only for a few hours to a few days.

In the *nondirective approach,* instead of giving suggestions under hypnosis, the reasons for the problems are explored by asking the patient questions. Under hypnosis, I usually ask patients to focus on their symptoms and to allow those feelings to take them back to another time, to the source of the problem. By getting in touch with their subconscious minds, patients not only can find the reasons for their problems, but they can also find the solutions and even healing. After recalling, reliving, and resolving the emotional, mental, and physical residue of the traumatic events, patients can be free of their symptoms without any medication or long-term traditional talk therapy.

With this understanding, we can realize why traditional talk therapy only works as a "Band-Aid" approach and is slow and less effective. During talk therapy, we deal with our conscious mind and knowledge, which is often superficial and based on intellectual interpretations. It is the subconscious mind that holds the understanding and knowledge about the real reasons for our current problems. Thus we can see that the power to heal lies largely with that untapped portion of the human mind, the subconscious mind or the soul.

According to my hypnotized patients, the subconscious mind is, in fact, our soul, which contains all the memories from the beginning of time. Everything that has ever happened to us is recorded in our subconscious mind (soul), from this life and all other lives since the beginning of time. No matter how important or unimportant, happy or sad, traumatic or nontraumatic, exciting or boring, nothing is erased.

The subconscious mind is also the storehouse of our inner wisdom and knowledge into which we all can tap. It is our inheritance. This book is a by-product of tapping into those memories, knowledge, and wisdom. Venture with me into that unexplored territory. Follow me into the case histories of people who, in their journeys into that region, have brought back treasures of knowledge and understanding.

Akashic Records: the Cosmic Library

Over the years, higher spiritual information was received in many different ways. Some people were able to regress to that point in time and recall the information, while others were able to tap the information from the Akashic Records, a place of knowledge in Heaven where all the information about creation is recorded from the beginning of time. "Akasha" is a Sanskrit word that means sky, or ether. People under hypnosis describe the Akashic plane as an etheric place in Heaven, the subtle spiritual essence that pervades everything. They call it "Cosmic Library," "Akashic Library," "Akashic History," "Cosmic Memory Bank," "Cosmic Data Bank," "God's Story," "God's History," and so forth, because God encompasses everything in creation, and everything in creation is God.

All our books are also included in the Akashic library, which contains our personal records since our creation. We can tap into our past, present, and future lives, and other information. We can also tap into other people's lives or receive knowledge about anything in creation that we are allowed access to at this time.

People under hypnosis vividly describe these cosmic libraries. They claim there are multitudes of cosmic libraries in Heaven, almost like a city. If these buildings are in the periphery of the globe of God (explained in a later chapter), they appear more earthly and solid, as on Earth. They contain knowledge needed for people's understanding, like their life or lives they are dealing with on Earth.

The buildings that are closer to the interior of Heaven contain higher knowledge. The celestial types of buildings that are closer to the godheads contain higher spiritual knowledge. People under hypnosis claim there are specialty buildings containing specific knowledge, that is, buildings for art, science, music, mathematics, conventional medicine, energy healing, vibrational healing, magnetic healing, healing with movements (such as yoga and martial arts), sound healing, spiritual healing, prayers, and so forth. There are also buildings for astronomy, architecture, economics, politics, and government. It is like a university with different department buildings.

In those buildings, there is specialized historical knowledge, what we know now and what is to come in the future. People who are living on Earth and those who are in Heaven between lives go there to learn. There are regular classes and training continuously going on in every building. According to different hypnotized people, there are similar building complexes all around the globe of God for other worlds and planets in their sections of Heaven. There is also a library exchange between different Heavens for different planets. Humans, angels, and masters of one planet go to the libraries of other planets to learn and teach. It is our awareness that directs us to the correct building, because we cannot comprehend more than we are able to receive.

Following are some descriptions given by different people under hypnosis about these Akashic libraries and the knowledge available there:

- "I am outside a building in the Light (Heaven). It is a big stone building with pillars, like a sandstone building of buff color. It is all Light. I am wearing a white robe and I do not have a form. I am a spirit. The building has a soft, white Light all around it. There are big steps with pillars leading to a big wooden door almost ten feet tall.

   "Inside the building, in front of me, there is a stand with a big book on it like a dictionary. There are books all around. The room is round. There are bookshelves as far as you can see. There are books everywhere on shelves, all the way around except where the doors are.

   "There are many stories in this building. The ceiling is dome-shaped. The shelves and books look solid, but when you pull them out, they are not solid. All I have to do is think about a book and it is here. I can access it telepathically. There are other people who are here to study. They look like humans, but in their spirit form. There are other beings in white robes, and they look like librarians, here to help."

• "I am at an Akashic library in Heaven. The building is grandiose, made of white marble, and has many stories. The building is not really solid; it is made of Light. The landscape features beautiful gardens with a beautiful array of vibrant colors that are much more intense than any on Earth. There are beautiful bright blue waterfalls all around. Everything is bright and clean.

"The building has huge marble pillars around it. Double doors are made from fine mahogany and oak, and there is attractive hardware on the doors. Inside the circular building are stacks of books. There are benches for seating and tables for using the books. Ceilings are high in this multistoried building and a skylight to all floors adds brightness. One can look up and see all of the stories from below and one is given an awareness of other levels of knowledge. There are many, many bookshelves all around, some going up to the ceiling. There are identification marks or names on all books, but they can be selected merely by thinking about them. There are many such buildings on this plane."

• "I am in a big bright panoramic valley in heaven with a lot of vivid colors in the vegetation, and there is a bright sky. It is all Light. The building looks weightless, made of Light. The building has big gold double-arched doors, and I can see through them. The building is glistening, transparent, and crystal-like, and all the facets are radiating Light. I see people in the building, as well as shelves all around. My guide is here and is smiling. I am in this ethereal, airy place in a crystal building where there is spiritual knowledge. It is brighter in here than outside because it is closer to the godhead.

"There are long, golden chandeliers whose dazzling Lights are reflected off the crystal walls. The building is one huge room. The shelves and floors are made of glass and are not connected to the outer wall. Glass stairways lead up to each floor. There are hundreds of such buildings all around and the understanding comes to me that 'there are many mansions in my Father's house.' Each library is attuned to people at different levels of awareness.

"In the periphery of the globe of God, I see solid buildings you cannot see through. It is like there are groups of cities connected to each building, and the people who live around each have the appropriate level of awareness to use that particular library. People are trying to tap into their Earth lives, learning lessons and understanding where they fit in. At this level people come to understand their lives and have different gradations of spiritual understanding.

"I see a skyscraper. This is for people who are on a fast track. They live a very earthly and busy life, so they go to the skyscraper library to use the elevator to get up and down and find what they need to know. It is faster this way, so they can go back to Earth and get on track with their fast lives again. This is a more practical type of library, but it is at a very earthly level of thinking.

"Your awareness directs you to the building and floor you need to go, because you cannot understand anything more than you are ready to receive. The lowest level has 'lower' knowledge and the higher levels have 'higher' knowledge. All the buildings are at the periphery of the godhead, and it is almost as if the godhead energy is fed into the libraries for those who are asking for knowledge.

"I feel the Akashic Records are the reality of our oneness, our connectedness. We all have access to one another's history, our own history, and our connections as part of God. In the Akashic Records we experience God's infinite intelligence and understanding that we are all part of God's mind."

• "I am in Heaven looking at a large building that resembles a library. It has many levels. The building looks like a castle, except that it has a lot of graceful architecture, more graceful than on Earth. The roof has curved shapes and blue and gold colors. The blue acts as a natural shield. The building is made of a crystalline substance, almost like glass, but it is opaque so you cannot see through it. It is made of a type of condensed energy.

"I am in a room, which is ornate in many ways.

The walls are covered with books, each with a golden binding. There are angels here, and they are six or seven feet tall, with bright faces. Their hair looks like Light and they have Light rays around them. They are wearing white robes with gold belts. The robes are embroidered at the bottom, and they are wearing golden sandals. Their eyes are bright and loving. They are the custodians of the libraries: they access information and also write information down.

"There are various functions and levels of this building from outside in or from lower level to higher level. Each level deals with the knowledge associated with that layer in Heaven. The highest layer, or the deepest inner level, deals with a unique and rare form of knowledge. It is more specialized and more refined.

"There are many other buildings, arranged in a circle. It is like a city of Light. There are buildings concerned with different types of learning. The building for art is pinkish-gold. There are paintings inside and the records of the arts from different civilizations. This building has all the knowledge of art. There are human souls here that have come here to learn about art.

"Paintings inspired by the dark side are not here, only the paintings inspired by Heaven. There are different chambers filled with the paintings of different artists on Earth, at different times, making it like a living museum. One of the inner levels of this building has art forms not yet released in the world.

"There are buildings of greenish-gold color dealing with science. All the buildings have gold, because gold is associated with the wisdom and quality of God. The science building deals with different sciences known on Earth during different civilizations in different parts of the world, but there are some sciences that are not yet known on Earth.

"The science building is attached to the mathematics building. I see the mathematics and music buildings in the center of this city. In the Heaven-world, science and art cross over in an interdisciplinary type of connection. There is science to music and art to music; there is science to mathematics and art to mathematics.

"I see the music building now. I understand there are both mathematics and science to music. Music and mathematics seem to be some of the purest forms of learning. In the music building, different types of music are recorded. As the musical instruments are played on Earth, they draw the Light, and angels and other heavenly beings dance to the music. They intermingle with the audience, which feels spiritually uplifted because of the music.

"However, if the music is negative, demons come around that place. Rock-and-roll music is not from here. The heavenly music is tuned to the natural frequencies of our energy centers (chakras), the seven invisible gateways that are located in the subtle (etheric) body, from the base of the spine to the top of the head. When you hear harmonious music, it vibrates in these energy centers. If the music is disharmonious, it blocks the flow of energy into these centers, and this weakens the aura and allows the entities to come in. Any music, such as classical music, that harmonizes the chakras is good music. There is a plan for other types of music to come in the future, and these have a different quality. There are people who are working on it.

"Singing devotional songs raises the vibrations of a human. It is not just the words, but the emotions and the feelings that open a person to the higher sources. I am hearing devotional songs in different religious traditions, such as *bhajans* [Indian devotional songs], temple bells, the sound of conches—they each have a purifying vibration. There are certain types of sounds such as mantras that affect energy centers, such as syllables *Ram, Rum, Aum.* They heal. There are other higher forms of sounds, some not known to us yet.

"There are different systems of movements, such as yoga with different postures, qigong, martial arts, slow-movement dances, classical dances, all of which produce healing by movements.

"The kind of dancing you see in night clubs is not here in Heaven. The effect of a dance depends on what is the intent in the heart of the dancer. For example, an angel can make the same movements with the hips and the rest of the body, but the intent determines the positive vibrations. Seduction with an intent to harm somebody, to cause them to lose control, to deprive them of something, is a negative act. It is not a healing movement. So it can be great music and a great dance, but if the intent in the heart is negative, then it will have a negative effect. What I see from Heaven is that during positive dances, angels dance with you, but during the negative dances and movements, the demons dance with you.

"I see the astronomy building, which deals with stars, other planets, and the cosmos. There is an understanding of the civilization of other planets here. There are buildings dealing with structural forms (architecture), buildings dealing with marine life, and even building dealing with air. There are lots of buildings for the applied sciences such as physics, biology, and chemistry and for transportation in different time periods.

"One building deals with the science of prayer, invocation, and the religions of the world and their scriptures. I see Catholic prayers. They have certain vibrations that attract Light. I see the Buddhist and the Hindu forms of prayers, that is, the mantras and knowledge of the Vedas and how they invoke the Light. The original knowledge of all the scriptures is here. There is a science to prayers and the invoking of the Light and Light beings. This was well known in the ancient time, but it has been influenced by the dark forces. The opposite of prayers are curses; while prayers invoke Light, curses invoke darkness.

"There are buildings dealing with conventional medicine and different types of healing, that is, energy healing, vibration healing, electric healing, and magnetic healing. There are also buildings dealing with oils and different types of liquids and baths. Souls go through this in between lifetimes for a kind of energy bath or bath of Light.

"Healing is an art and also a science. There is a type of healing in which different parts of the body are restored. The body has blueprints, and these are like a pattern of energy for how the body is supposed to be. Let us say if the liver fails, then the memory of the energy pattern reinforces the original pattern of the blueprint, and around the blueprint there is regeneration of the organ.

"There is a building connected with disease of the soul, with its evolution throughout the time line of its creation, the problems it has had during different lifetimes, and the places and planets where the soul has been. The work here is similar to what you [Dr. Modi] are doing with your past-life regression therapy, spirit releasement therapy, and soul-integration therapy. The healing we are doing right now, removing the dark entities and retrieving and integrating soul parts, is a form of energy healing—removing negative energy and replacing it with positive energy. It is a spiritual healing.

"I see leaders of different countries coming to Heaven to learn how to do their jobs better. There is a section dealing with how governments and organizations function. There are two aspects to the teaching. One explains how things work in Heaven, things without the human element of ego and pride; the other teaches how they work on Earth with the elements of ego, arrogance, and pride, and there are ways for them to function properly.

"There are hundreds of such buildings. There are areas here dealing with pure learning, where classes are held and people are taught. I am looking at the souls that are in these heavenly buildings now, but that are also incarnated on Earth; I see their connecting cords going down from their spirit body here in Heaven to their physical body on Earth. Some of them are awake in their physical body, but quite a lot of them are asleep. It seems that in sleep these people come here for learning and even those who are awake send a part of their consciousness here.

"I get a sense that all of these buildings are different departments in Heaven, and there are specialized beings associated with each building. It is like an office, but the beings do not stay in the same 'office' all the time. They move on as they learn, and go to other higher functions. Some of these are angels and some are different levels of masters. There are similar buildings for other worlds and planets in their sections of Heaven. I see library exchanges between Heavens for different planets. There are different centers of learning, and the masters and humans from here go to the Heavens of other planets, to their learning centers."

The Time Tunnel to the Cosmic Library

People can go to the Akashic library in different ways. They can go there after a past-life regression. My hypnotized patients report that during a past-life regression, after the death of the physical body, the spirit makes its transition to Heaven. There, after reviewing and resolving the issues from that life, the spirit can be guided to go to the Akashic library.

Other times, patients under hypnosis can be taken directly to the Akashic library in Heaven through a time tunnel. Patients under hypnosis describe a "silver cord," a line that connects our soul to God. It is seen as a silver cord, a tunnel, corridor, or a long hallway, depending on whether it is perceived from outside or inside. Through this "cosmic umbilical cord" pass all communications, as prayers, to and from God. My hypnotized patients claim that, when they are traveling through what looks like a time-tunnel, they are really traveling through their silver cord to God. They also go to Heaven and other places in their sleep through the same silver cord. During a near-death experience, when people describe going through a tunnel, their souls are traveling through their connecting silver cord to God.

Patients claim that, when they move through the time tunnel, it is their spirit that is traveling, yet part of the spirit remains in the body to sustain it. People often describe the door leading to the tunnel and the tunnel itself in different ways, depending on what they are doing during that session. If we are doing a past-life regression, people see a door that is similar to the door to their home, in that specific past life, and that is representative of that time period they are about to enter. For example, if somebody lived in a palace in that past life, they will see a palatial door. If somebody is about to go to the Akashic library, they might see a door made up of golden or white shimmery Light; others see a door they are familiar with in this life.

The following are some descriptions given by my patients about traveling through the time tunnel:

- "I see a golden door. I open and go through it, then shut it behind. I go through a long corridor, with no end in sight. At first I seem to move very slowly, and the farther I go, the more I feel as though I am picking up speed. I see worlds passing by. As I get close to the end of the tunnel, the speed gets more intense, and suddenly I begin to feel movement around me before I can discern anything.

    "Suddenly I am aware that there are angels around me. They usher me along. As I reach the other end of the tunnel, there are many angels everywhere. I go through the circle of angels into the Light; it feels like a sunburst. There is a feeling of freedom, as if I have shed the body. It feels good, like a release.

    "I come through the same time tunnel (my silver connecting cord) back into my body. On the way, I can see universes, galaxies, planets, stars, suns, and moons. Angels accompany me to the gate of the tunnel, and my guardian angels go through the tunnel with me. Then I come out through the door and enter my body through my chest."

- "I look at the door opening into the time tunnel, which is really the door or opening in my soul. The door is made of shimmering crystalline light. Through the door, I enter a tunnel of Light. There is no light source, no lamps, but the wall is shining with the Light. I see the bright Lights at the end of the tunnel, and as I step out, I find myself at the Akashic Library."

- "As I open the door and go inside I see a brightly lit room with steps leading into the distance. Everything is filled with golden Light. There is no darkness anywhere. As I go up to the top of the steps, I find myself in the Light (Heaven)."

• "I enter through the door and I see myself in a long, round time tunnel. It has walls that are made of Light. There are different types of doors on both sides of the tunnel. Some are white, while others have colors. There are thousands of such doors, each representing a different past life. The doors are designed according to the time period of the life. Some are twentieth-century style, some are castle doors, some are elegant and well formed, and others are just regular doors. Some doors have a date written on them."

• "My spirit comes out of my head, leaving a small soul part to sustain my body. My spirit looks white and transparent, a ghostlike form. While traveling through the time tunnel, I experience a happy anticipation. I feel like I am flying or floating, somehow touching the ground but not walking.

"The time tunnel becomes transparent as I get closer to the end. At the beginning (farthest from the Light), the tunnel is solid and I cannot see what is on the outside. As I progress, it becomes partially transparent, and as I get closer to the Light, it is transparent and I can see the stars through it. This is an awesome experience. There are millions of stars, and I can see their connecting cords going to God."

• "I open the door and enter the tunnel, which is like a path covered with tall grass. It appears as if the 'grass' is creating the tunnel. As I travel through this time tunnel, it is like walking through the woods or high grass. It is a long tunnel and at the end is something like a shining sun."

• "As I open the door and enter the tunnel, my spirit comes out of my chest. My arms are extended and I fly through the tunnel. My spirit looks gauzy and translucent, like a ghost. As I return from Heaven through the time tunnel, I seem to fly backwards and enter my body again through my chest."

The Cosmic Helpers' Role During a Hypnosis Session

During a hypnosis session, while working with past life regression, spirit releasement, or soul integration, patients often claim there is a great deal of heavenly help from their (and my) angels, guides, higher self, masters, and God. Most of the time I do not see, hear, or sense anything, but for some reason, I have a knowledge and faith that I will be guided in the right direction to help my patients.

Many times I have known things intuitively about the patient's problems or what I need to do or ask next, which often turns out to be true. This never ceases to surprise me, even though I know that a host of heavenly beings is always there during a session to help us and that it is not just the patient and me working alone. It is a teamwork with heavenly beings and God. When I think of this, I melt with humility.

Patients report that during a session, groups of heavenly beings are often present, and they decide what information is needed to heal patients, what they need for their spiritual growth, and what I need to know to help patients. Anything we need as far as information goes is provided. Sometimes patients think they are alone during a session, but when they look around, they see their guides or other heavenly beings somewhere in the background, helping and giving them information.

I have learned to pray for protection and guidance every day and also before sessions. Many times when we get stuck in a session, I pray for understanding or for a technique to get us through the blocks, and sure enough, new ideas and techniques come to my mind. With God, anything is possible. With some patients, we remain stuck, and the understanding we get is that the patient has lessons to learn and is not ready for healing at this time.

The following is a description given by a patient on how heavenly beings help us during a session:

- "There are many heavenly beings assembled here who determine what information to send us. There are seventeen of them here today, including several oversouls and three masters who are not particularly connected to us. They are just the ones who have chosen to do this work. There are three archangels, Michael, Gabriel, and Raphael, who are also part of this group and who are transferring information through me. Of the nine guides who are working with us, two have worked with us before, and one is my future guide preparing for the role.

"They have the rules about what information we should get at this time, what is needed to heal me, what you need for your practice, and what information we both need to fulfill our purpose we have planned in Heaven for the current life. Based on these criteria, they decide what information to give us and how to convey it."

Mechanism of Receiving Information During a Hypnosis Session

During a hypnosis session, whether we are doing a current or past-life regression, tapping the information from the Akashic Library, or receiving information from heavenly beings, patients usually describe having a parallel awareness. They are aware they are in Heaven or in a past life *and* of being in the chair in my office. Sometimes they report forgetting that they have a self here in the chair, but they can hear me and answer my questions.

Some people see events vividly in color, while others see in black and white in their mind's eye. Some people do not see or hear anything but receive the information from within their soul. If they are receiving information through a heavenly being, it comes through telepathic communication through their connecting cords. Sometimes a patient's consciousness can step aside and I can communicate with a heavenly being directly *through* the hypnotized person. The following is a description of how patients receive information:

- "Often, information is transferred through mental communication. Sometimes angels will give information to me through what sounds like verbal speech. On a few occasions, it was done through written information or symbols, and sometimes through pictures. There are channels from the group of souls to the archangels and then from them to me. It is like a golden funnel that turns into a tube as it comes to my head.

"Most of the time during a session, I have a parallel awareness. I am aware that I am in Heaven and at the same time I am also aware of being here in the chair, although occasionally I forget that I have a self here in the chair. In both cases, I can hear you and answer your questions.

"During a current-life and past-life regression, I perceive the information in the same way. I sometimes observe the events as if I am watching a movie, while at other times, I become part of the movie, playing a role. I have a parallel awareness of being in a past life and also of being in this chair in this current life."

Chapter Two

Presence of God in the Universe

Throughout the history of mankind, people of different religions and cultures have had their own understanding of God. Some describe God as omnipotent (all-powerful), omniscient (all-seeing), omnicognizant (all-knowing), and omnipresent (present-in-everything). Some picture Him as a loving and nurturing being, while others portray Him as a paternalistic, angry, demanding, judging, and punishing being. They believe that if we sin, God will punish us and send us into the eternal fire of hell. My hypnotized patients describe God as they see, sense, feel, and understand Him. They say God is a loving, giving, caring, and nurturing being, one who does not judge, condemn, or punish anybody.

God knows that we live in duality, that we have a spirit within us that is a "piece" of God and contains all the knowledge. But we are usually blocked from accessing this knowledge while we live on Earth, so we can go through our trials and tests and grow spiritually. God knows that human beings cannot be completely protected from the dark influences while living on Earth. He understands that because of our human frailty, all of us from time to time are influenced by the dark beings and will make mistakes. It is all part of the overall plan for our spiritual growth.

God does not judge or punish anybody. It is we who do: in Heaven, while reviewing our lives, we judge ourselves after realizing the damage we have done to others during a lifetime by our wrong doings. We are our own harshest judge and jury, and it is we who plan to resolve our negative actions in future lives. We have to balance our negative actions by going through sufferings similar to those we have inflicted on others. It is the universal law that nobody can escape from their wrong deeds. However, it is not God who decides the punishment; *we* make that decision to correct our negative actions.

According to my hypnotized patients, there is a dimension somewhere in the universe where Satan and his demons exist, and this "place" is called hell. Some human spirits after the death of their physical bodies, because of their confusion, fear, or anger toward God, do not go to Heaven. Instead, they are tricked and trapped, and willingly or unwillingly, taken to hell by demons. Some earthbound spirits in my patients were trapped and consumed in a demon, while others were infested by demons and appeared dark and claimed to work for Satan. However, it is not God who sentenced them to hell but they who on their own either chose or allowed themselves to be manipulated by demons and to be taken to hell.

Consistently, my hypnotized patients claim that God does exist. They report that He always was and is, and that the universe started with God. He is the creator of everything and everybody in the universe. My patients describe God as a "Ball of Light," a "Pyramid of Light," or an "Ocean of love and Light." They say that God is pure love and Light and that everything in the universe is composed of God. Plants, animals, humans, inanimate objects are all tied together in one system, in a being called God.

According to my hypnotized patients, God is a big golden orb of energy. The center of God is very dense and the Light there is intensely bright and iridescent. As you move from the core to the periphery of God, my patients report the Light is still golden but more porous and not as dense or as intense. God is a creative energy force that grows, generates, and is constantly in motion. The core of God is potential (stored)

THE GLOBAL OR CIRCULAR MODEL OF GOD

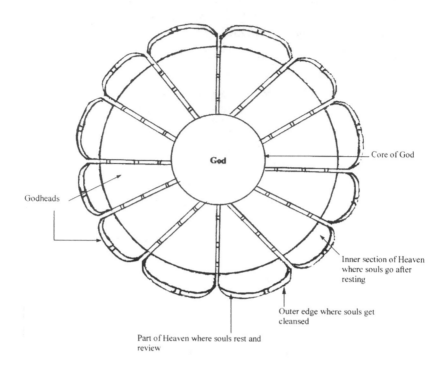

Core of God

Godheads

Inner section of Heaven where souls go after resting

Outer edge where souls get cleansed

Part of Heaven where souls rest and review

Figure 1

energy. As you move away from the core, the energy needs to be expressed and released.

Around the edge of the orb of God, there is a tremendous energy field created by the vibrations that come out of the core, where there are feelings of warmth, Light, joy, peace, security, serenity, and great power. Toward the periphery, the feelings are of being free, a restlessness, a sense of something that needs to happen, that needs to evolve to achieve equilibrium.

Some people under hypnosis describe God as a sphere of Light. Others describe God as divided into sections that appear as spokes of a wheel or pieces of a pie. (See figure 1.)

They describe each of these sections of God as a pyramid with God on the top. (See figure 2.) Patients claim these

PYRAMIDAL MODEL OF GOD

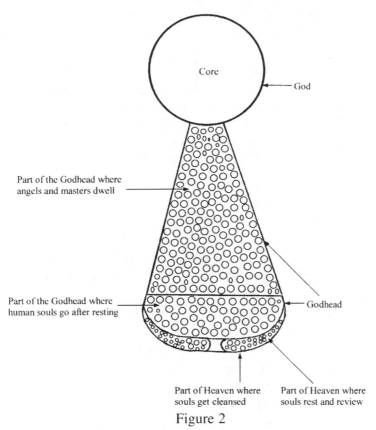

Part of the Godhead where
angels and masters dwell

Part of the Godhead where
human souls go after resting

Core

God

Godhead

Part of Heaven where
souls get cleansed

Part of Heaven where
souls rest and review

Figure 2

pyramidal-shaped energy sections around God are called a godhead. We all come from and are connected to one of these godheads. At the outer edge of the godhead, we re-enter, rest, and
review our life after we make our transition to Heaven following the
death of our physical bodies. We also spend our time between lives
learning, teaching, and studying at the periphery of our godhead.

God before Creation

Many of my patients have regressed back to *before* creation,
when there was nothing but the sphere of God and the surrounding black void. There were no universes and no separate

souls—only God. They describe themselves as being one with God, saying there was nothing else: they were The God. Under hypnosis, they sometimes feel shocked and surprised and, at times, embarrassed to report this realization, and they find it hard to express their feelings. As God, they felt pure love, contentment, and peace; there were no negative emotions. Often they describe having no thoughts, only feelings.

During a session, under hypnosis, I first ask the patients to look back in time, to look at God from the Akashic plane *before* the creation, and to describe what they see from the outside. Then I ask them to look closely at the "ball of God" as if they are looking with a telescope from outside and to describe what they see. Then I tell them to regress back in time to when they were in that ball of God and to tell me what they are aware of.

Hypnotized patients often describe God before creation as a creative energy force, as a huge ball of Light with multitudes of energy swirls or balls inside it. They feel one with God but still have an individual consciousness. It is as if God is one huge, integrated entity, composed of countless little energy swirls, each with a separate consciousness.

Patients give different descriptions of these individual energy swirls: as "shiny, white, iridescent crystal balls"; "marbles," "jewels," "pearls," "sparks," "stars," "gems," "diamonds," "seeds," or "amoeba." They have different shapes, sizes, and colors. Here are some of the descriptions of God before creation, as given by my hypnotized patients:

• "From the Akashic plane, I see that God before creation is a massive, brilliant, golden white ball of Light inside a vast bluish-black void. The ball is constantly moving and growing. It is like a lava lamp, which moves around, constantly forming different shapes. There are many separate and distinct individual consciousnesses all over the sphere of God. They look like swirls of fluid energy, like balloons filled with water, moving, but still retaining their shape.

"I am one of those swirls. I move around but stay within an area in God. I could move into any part of

God, but I am more comfortable in my area. I am a bigger than average swirl. If the smallest consciousness is pea size, I am orange size. I am bright white, with iridescent gold and blue. I have the consciousness of the whole God, but I also have my individual consciousness. I feel calm, content, love, and peace. I have no thoughts and no negative feelings. I am just floating around."

• "From the Akashic plane, God before creation looks like a gigantic, ever-moving, brilliant cloud of Light, a vast ocean of Light. It is a constantly churning, ever-changing, moving and expanding energy, pent up and wanting to release itself. All around God, there is nothing but a vast black void. Even though it seems like a random churning and expanding in this ball of Light, there is a knowing of what is happening and why, and the sense of a benevolent, loving intelligence. It is an awesome spirit force, a vast ocean with an infinite number of glowing swirls or facets, which are also God.

"When I look at God closely, It looks multifaceted, and every facet is a different aspect of God. Even the incredibly small facet is extremely intricate. I see an infinite number of facets of God, each of which is becoming bigger, expanding to engulf the dark void around it. All the facets I see are like different seeds in God that are going to grow into all the diverse things of creation later. It feels like everything is ready to burst. These facets, in all their diversity, are expressions of the all-creative intelligent force. These facets are like a kaleidoscope with ever-changing patterns and colors.

"As I regress back in my own little facet inside God before creation I feel like a baby in the womb, surrounded by love, and feeling peace and harmony. I am a medium-sized facet of God, like a bright jewel. There are infinite facets all around me of different sizes. I am one with God and have the whole consciousness of God, yet I am a separate facet of God with an individual consciousness. I can reflect from the viewpoint of the whole and I can also go into my tiny jewel, my individual consciousness, and think from my perspective.

"I feel peaceful, contented, and loving. There are no negative feelings or thoughts. As God continues to churn and expand, there are feelings of restlessness and anticipation that something is going to happen. I feel myself as God—the whole, all-knowing and all-powerful—but 'I' also feel lonely and have a need to share."

• "When I look back in time at God from the Akashic plane, I see God as an incredible ball of blinding, white Light. It is round and is spinning constantly. It flattens out, then becomes round again. There is a kind of brilliant fog around God, and a bluish-black empty void around this fog. There is nothing else: no planets or any other aspect of creation.

"As I look closely inside God from the Akashic plane, there are multitudes of jewels or stars inside the big ball of God. They are like different cells in the body of God, like sparkling balls of Light. But when you look closely at them, they contain specks of different colors. Each is a mini version of the big ball of God.

"When I regress back to God before the creation of individual souls, I am like an amoeba of Light. I have a separate consciousness and also the consciousness of God as a whole. I am white from the outside, but as I look inside myself, I appear as a sun with different colors of sunset, that is, gold, yellow, and orange.

"There are other bright amoebas of different sizes all over the ball of God. I am a medium-sized 'amoeba' and feel calm and content. I have no other feelings. I am aware of the one consciousness of God as a whole, and I am also aware of this individual, separate, and discreet consciousness of my tiny 'amoeba' form. I am part of God along with the other 'amoebas.' There is no individual consciousness assigned as God at this time. Together we all are God."

• "As I look at God from the Akashic plane before the decision to create was made, It appears as a brilliant ball of Light. There is void all around It. There are no universes or planets. As I look at the globe of God

26

more closely, It appears like a city of Light containing an infinite number of Lighted balls, or like a crystal ball containing multitudes of smaller crystal balls. It is like little baby Gods inside the big ball of God.

"I see a mansion with long hallways, tall ceilings, and many rooms. My feeling is that it is inside my ball. It is my dream house and anything I can imagine is here inside my sphere, which is inside the big globe of God. It is like there are many mansions inside the big mansion of God. As I go inside my smaller ball, I feel I am 'Home.' I feel complete and have a sense of greatness, wholeness, oneness, knowingness, contentment, peace, and beauty. There is no sense of time and space, and there are no limitations. I sense the whole consciousness of the big globe and the consciousness of my smaller ball. I have no other thoughts.

"The ball in the core of the globe of God continues to grow, split, and multiply into many balls; these go out of the ball at the core. Thus the ball of God is continuously expanding, increasing in size, with a multitude of balls appearing around the core. All the balls in God have a male and a female aspect. As I look at my ball, I see my male aspect has an emerald green color and the female side has a pinkish color. As I look at the ball at the core of God, which is the parent ball, it also has a male and female aspect. The male side is bluish and the female side is pink. Each of the balls also has multiple colors."

God at the Beginning:
the Divine Fetus in the Cosmic Womb

Over the years, different patients under hypnosis have described God before creation as a brilliant mass or globe of energy with multitudes of swirls or facets in It, with their individual consciousness and also the one consciousness of the whole, as God. I began to wonder if these swirls or facets were always there in that big ball of God or was It once a homogeneous sphere of Light, which at some point began to divide into individual balls, like a cell multiplying.

I posed this question to the angels present as helpers during different sessions. Initially, their response was vague, as if we were not ready to understand it. To my surprise, the angels claimed that even they do not have this knowledge, because like humans, they also experienced the "first forgetting" after the creation of their souls.

The angels claimed that the information they were giving us came from the patient's subconscious, which has *all* the memories from the beginning of creation. They said it is my purpose to retrieve this information from the subconscious mind of my patients and present it to the world. According to them, it is time for humans to receive this information because it is important for our spiritual evolution.

I continued to ask patients to see if the ball of God at some point was homogeneous, without any facets. Initially no information came, as if it was not the time for this particular answer. I continued to ask the question to different patients and eventually the answer began to emerge. Maybe it was my persistent desire for this knowledge, or maybe it was the truth of the phrase, "Ask and you shall receive," that produced the information. Since I persistently asked the question, we must be ready to receive this knowledge, because we are given only what we are ready to understand. The timing has to do with the vibrations of our planet. According to the heavenly beings, we humans have raised the vibrations of Earth through our prayers and humanitarian actions worldwide over the last several decades. As we continue to raise the vibrations, we become ready to receive new knowledge.

I asked my hypnotized patients to look back from the Akashic plane to the very beginning of time or the beginning of that ball of God, and to tell me what was there. To my surprise, they stated nothing was there, only a vast black void. I wondered what had happened to that ball of Light, the sphere of God?

I next asked the patients to look inside that black void and tell me if there was anything in it. They saw a spark of Light, the size of a pinhead, a pea, or other sizes, depending on where they were at this point in time. The following are some of the descriptions given by my hypnotized patients on this question:

- "As I look back from the Akashic plane, all I see is a black void. There is nothing else. As I search inside that black void, I see a circular beam, like from a little flashlight. The beam is the size of a dime, without any facets or consciousnesses. I do not know how it came into existence. It is moving very slowly, and as it grows slowly, it begins to divide. All of a sudden, small facets appear. It is like a baby developing and you begin to see the buds of different features, as the fetus starts to form. These facets are noticeable along the edges of the circular beam. As it moves and grows, it continues to divide, like a cell dividing into two, and two into four, and four into eight, and so on."

- "Moving back billions of years, I see only the black, empty void. There is no Light anywhere. As I look carefully inside that dark void, I see a streak of Light. It is just there. It does not connect with anything. It looks like a crack in that black void. It is a very tiny dot in the center of that empty space. It is as though something ran into the void and poked a hole in it. I do not see where it came from or what poked the hole in the void. Maybe this speck of Light poked the hole. The dot of Light is just floating around, but gradually it grows and divides into many parts. It is like a single-cell amoeba dividing into many cells. As it grows, it spins and continues to grow."

- "As I look back from the Akashic plane, all I see is a vast, bluish-black void. There is nothing else anywhere. As I look closely inside that black empty space, I see a small spark of Light like a little 'Tinkerbell.' Only one spark of Light, which was there all along, but it was not visible in that huge void. It is the size of a pea. It is a bright, glowing, white Light floating around passively. I do not see where it came from. Maybe it was always there. Now it is moving and growing slowly.

"It looks like a small, homogeneous white spark or glowing ball with rays of Light coming from it. There are no other swirls in it. It is like a sun. As it grows slowly, it begins to divide, again and again. As soon as these swirls split, they become little swirls in that ball of Light. I see little lines around these little swirls, like a cell membrane, but they are still one with the bigger ball."

• "I see a time when there was nothing but black empty space. But looking closely inside that void, I see a very tiny spark of Light. It is the size of a pinhead; it is very quiet and not moving much. It is a homogeneous shiny ball of Light. I do not know where it came from, how it came into existence, or how it was created. As this small spark grows, it divides vertically into two, and each spark becomes round. This process continues as the ball continues to move and grow and more swirls (or consciousnesses) are created. These swirls are interconnected."

Creation of the Original Spark of Light

The above information piqued my curiosity even more about from where and how this tiny spark came into existence. As I continued to ask patients about it, they began to recall how that original spark of Light was created. Under hypnosis, they said that in the beginning there was nothing else but the vast, black void, no creation or sparks. But even that empty space was a kind of matter and had different particles in it. These particles in the black void produced different sounds and forms like clouds, yet were still a part of the void. These were not the forms of Light, and sounds were not sufficient to create anything.

According to different hypnotized subjects, these sounds were created by the friction between different particles in space. Not all my hypnotized subjects could hear these sounds; only those who had the gift of clairaudience could hear them. They stated there was a friction between two particles that created a specific type of sound, and this created the special spark of Light. Some patients said these particles had male and female or plus and minus characteristics, so that when struck together, they created a unique spark of Light. Before the creation of the spark, God-consciousness was always there, and through Its intent the spark of Light was created and then God-consciousness entered into it.

Some of the descriptions given by my hypnotized subjects about how the original spark of Light was created are as follows:

• "I see a huge void all around, and as I look carefully, I can see one spark in that void and nothing else. It is a small spark, round, homogenous, soft, yet firm. It is deep and has intelligence in it.

"The black void is a kind of matter. Even in an empty void, there is matter or particles. The void sometimes would produce forms like clouds, but they are still part of the void and are not forms of Light. I do not see any real creation before that spark. I hear different sounds, but not all sounds are strong enough for the creation of this spark. Sometimes these sounds can echo for a very long time in space, because space is so vast. This particular sound (the one that creates the spark) is very different and was created from an accumulation of a lot of different sounds.

"As I look back to find where this spark came from, I hear a sound that is coming from the void. It is created by friction between two particles in space. One is a very dark blue, dense particle, and the other is purplish-blue. When they come close and rub together, it creates the sound and spark of Light. This sound is very beautiful, like 'Om,' but far better. 'Om' sounds boring and dull compared to what I am hearing. Vibrations spread in circles from the original spark, creating beautiful sounds.

"It took a long time for this spark to be ready and to grow. It has intelligence and everything else inside, because this sound is the accumulation of everything. This sound has all the sounds from which it came, so it is like an alphabet.

"At the beginning, the spark is a brightly lit, homogenous single cell. Everything is inside it. There is a lot of movement and color. The spark is a circle whose

CREATION OF THE ORIGINAL SPARK OF GOD

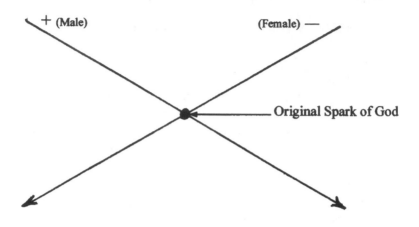

+ (Male)   (Female) —

Original Spark of God

Figure 3

edges are Light. It is white but, like mother-of-pearl, it has all the colors of the rainbow. It is constantly moving and, as the movements expand, the vibrations grow. After a certain growth, there is a division, but it is not separated into two parts. It is like a figure eight."

• "I see two particles or energy beams. They come from two different directions, and when they meet each other, a spark is created. These energy beams have plus and minus, or male and female, characteristics. The spark looks like a pinhead of pure bright energy. At this point, the spark is homogeneous and undifferentiated.

"As I tune into the feelings of that spark, it feels complete and acquires a critical mass. As it grows, I see it dividing vertically with definite intent to expand

VIBRATIONAL SOUND FROM THE ORIGINAL SPARK

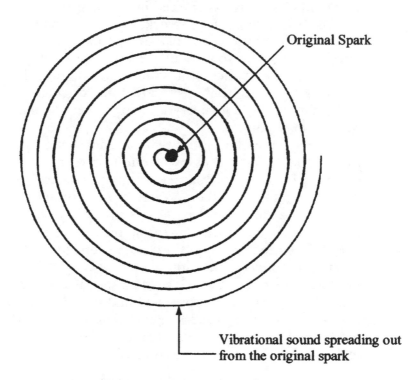

Original Spark

Vibrational sound spreading out from the original spark

Figure 4

itself. The two halves quickly turn into the form of balls. They become like male and female, then split vertically again and change instantly into four balls, and the same process continues.

"We all come from this original ball. I see myself in the original ball, splitting, and splitting again. My individual awareness begins at the third split. I split from the plus aspect of the original spark, and then from the plus a minus appears. When it splits again, then from the minus there is a plus. So, I am plus, minus, plus."

• "I see a 'male' and a 'female' particle coming from two different directions. As they strike together, they create a brilliant spark of Light (see figure 3), which has a 'male' and 'female' aspect. It seems like God consciousness was always there in that void and It *intended* to create that spark of Light. Then it seems that God consciousness entered into that spark.

"As those two particles struck, I heard a sound that is beyond description. It is like every tone that can be imagined. It is as if you can play every note at once on a piano, and yet they still sound harmonious. The sound is complete from a very low to a very high frequency, and it includes everything in between. It overwhelms my senses.

"I feel that each of those two particles that created that special spark had its own sound present in it all the time, but when the particles came in contact with each other, together they created a new sound that then created that special spark. It is as if you have two musicians playing at the same time on two violins, at two different notes, and a third note is created out of them as a more complete sound.

"With the creation of the spark, a special sound was created. Circles of sound spread around this spark. I see the vibrations creating increasing circles around the spark, producing beautiful sound.(See figure 4.) There is a feeling of warmth and beauty and completeness to all this."

• "I see an explosion. It is like two particles of matter coming together and creating a spark. As the spark is created, there is a beautiful sound. Each particle has its own vibrations and creates its own sound. When two particles collide, they create a different sound. The vibrations create a series of circles around the spark, and this produces beautiful sounds. This spark has positive and negative, or male and female, aspects.

"I feel that God consciousness was always present, and It intended to create this spark of Light. The whole of God consciousness entered into that spark of Light after it was created. Then after some growth, it divides into two, like a cell division. A vertical line divides it and the two halves immediately become round. Then they divide into four, and on and on. The division depends on the conditions outside. It is as if the whole cosmos is a womb."

34

Chapter Three

A Brief History of Creation

This chapter is a brief history of creation as described by my hypnotized patients, which will be explained in detail in the later chapters. It begins with God existing. According to my patients, God before creation was a ball of Light and had black void all around It. Inside God, there were little swirls or facets of energy. These little swirls were individual consciousnesses that went into the making of the whole of God, and all of them together were God. Initially, no one consciousness was assigned as "The God." At some point, these little consciousnesses came to the conclusion together that they should create. There were many reasons for this that they knew and understood. Most of them felt happy about the different reasons as to why they wanted to create.

Most parts or balls of God were in favor of the creation. Then in a tapering scale, there were those who agreed to it but did not really want to, those who were negative about the idea, until we get down to a black ball called Lucifer and his strongest followers, who were absolutely opposed to the idea. According to the hypnotized subjects, Lucifer took with him as many parts as he could. As these little balls passed through the wall or the outer edge of the ball of God, they became the "demons." They became the individual souls that were discreet, dark, and separate from the Light. They had gone through

35

their own "forgetting" and did not remember where they came from or why. They were not created as angels, as some people believe, and they did not take any part in the creation.

After they went outside the wall of God, Lucifer educated them, feeding them information or misinformation in his way. He told them he had created them, they were his property and the Light was their enemy. They should stay away from the Light because it would consume and kill them. He set up his whole scheme for fighting the Light—The God.

People under hypnosis stated that God did not begin to create until Lucifer and his followers left because He did not want them to influence His creation. After Lucifer and his demons left, God created masters and angels. He created them first so they could protect the universes and other beings from Lucifer and his demons. Then the universes and other dimensions were created. Dimensions ranging from those that are just energy areas to those that are almost entirely matter. The one we are in is the intermediary, part matter and part energy. Lucifer took his demons away to a dimension that had the lowest vibrations, far away from the globe of God, because they could not tolerate the higher vibrations near God.

After the initial creation of all the universes was finished, God created the things to go into the universes, such as inanimate objects, plants, animals, and ending with the creation of the individual souls of the intelligent beings (humans and other souls for other planets) that would do most of the developmental work in the universe. As they go through their individual development, they will be developing that portion of God.

So, the proper order of the creation was masters, angels, universes, inanimate objects, plants, animals, and the souls of intelligent beings.

Chapter Four

Why God Decided to Create

As mention before, sometimes while under hypnosis, my patients regressed back to the time when they were one with God and there was nothing else in existence but a vast black void. There was no creation, only that one ball of God containing multitudes of individual consciousnesses. Together, they were The God. At this time, they described feelings of peace, harmony, and contentment. There were no negative feelings.

I began to wonder: if everything was so harmonious and there were no negative feelings, why did God decide to create? I asked patients to move back to a time when God made the decision to create. Under hypnosis, my patients recalled many reasons why God decided to create.

Reasons for the Creation, in God's Mind

My patients, under hypnosis, recalled many reasons why God decided to create. They were as follows:

1. My hypnotized patients claimed that at some point as God, the individual consciousnesses were beginning to feel lonely and empty, as if something was missing, but they did

not know what. I asked them to go back in time to determine what had changed to create those feelings. What they recalled was that over millions of years, as the ball of God was growing and expanding, its vibrations became faster and its energy moved faster. As a result, pieces of God's energy began to splash out of the ball and then fell back into the ball of God again. However, as the ball of God began to spin even faster, the parts of God that were thrown out randomly were getting lost in the void without any intent or control.

As a result, God and all Its parts began to experience loneliness, emptiness, and sadness. Some consciousnesses began to feel anxiety and fear, because they did not want to disappear in the void. So, when God became aware of losing parts in the void, a decision to create was made by every part of God. Some patients say the idea originated in the core of the big ball of God and spread instantly to all parts of God telepathically, while other patients said they did not know where the idea originated. It seems that all parts of God *collectively* decided to create by properly and purposefully releasing the ever-growing energy so that it did not disperse chaotically.

Also, over the course of billions of years, the energy of God built up inside the globe and there came a point when God, as a whole, knew that in order for the energy to grow, something had to go. As a consequence, God decided to let some of the energy out with protection. This way, the energy of God, released with protective shields, would continue to grow and expand, so that in time, God could spread out through the whole void and cover it in such a way that pieces of God would not be lost in the empty space.

2. People under hypnosis recalled that as different pieces of God began to break off and were thrown off into the empty void, the process created fear and anxiety in different parts of God; these parts began to vibrate and grow at different rates. Before this, all the balls or pieces were of the same size, vibration, color, and brilliance. They were all white.

After a while, God realized that every consciousness in It was growing into a different size, color, and brilliance and was no longer the same. Some parts were better developed than others. They all had the same powers, but not to the same degree. So, through creation, God desired to create, so that every part could grow to be equal in size and power and could evolve to perfection and to have all the knowledge and awareness.

3. Some patients recalled that it was very still, calm, and tight in the core of God. You felt wrapped up tightly in the core; as you moved away from the core, you shed some of this wrapping and calmness. Away from the core of God, you felt a little bit freer. The wavelengths were narrow near the core and wide as you went toward the periphery. (See figure 5.) Since God was not the same all over, It chose to create to achieve perfection and equilibrium.

EXPANDING WAVELENGTHS IN GOD

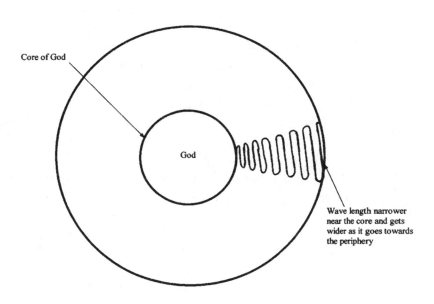

Figure 5

4. Other reasons for the creation surfaced in time after the decision to create was made. For one, when God as a whole began to lose pieces of Itself, It began to experience loneliness. The basic nature of God is love, which is ever expanding and growing. God wanted to experience Its most wonderful attribute of love through the creation. It wanted to create partners to communicate and help one another grow through love. Love cannot be contained and must be experienced in various ways.

5. Other reasons to create emerged later, after Lucifer and his rebellious beings left the globe of God. God wanted to send parts of Itself out to help bring back Lucifer and his followers, giving them another chance to return "Home." Without them God cannot be whole.

As we were searching for reasons for the creation, one hypnotized patient, who was at the Akashic records trying to look back to the time of creation, suddenly heard a faint echo, which said, "We are the communities of God and God is also perfecting Himself through us." Patients began to describe that these "communities of God" are different parts of God that were initially "splashed" out in the void by accident. They have continued to expand and grow independently, like God. Now they look somewhat like different planets around God, but they were not created by God. They still have connecting cords to God. According to the patients, there are multitudes of these communities (or dimensions) around God, and these are also growing continuously.

Following is some of the information given by my hypnotized patients regarding why God decided to create:

• "As God is constantly moving and churning, It is growing and the energy moves faster. It is like when a pregnant mother is fully expanded and ready to push the baby out. Similarly, as God is growing, expanding, and moving faster, swirls of energy spin off at times. Initially, when the vibrations are slower, energy balls splash out of God as 'drops' and fall back in again. However, as the vibrations intensify, 'pieces' of God are thrown off and disappear in the void. Thus God loses pieces of Itself and does not have any control over this. This is the first time I as God as a whole and I as an individual facet began to experience loneliness and sadness. So, God as a whole decides to create because the energy needs to be channeled purposefully, rather than allowing it to disperse all over without any control. Also, God wants to expand and cover the void so It does not lose parts of Itself in the void.

"Another reason to create is that as God began to experience loneliness as a result of the loss of Its parts into the void, It felt a need to express and share love. When I am in the awe of God, I feel contained and surrounded by love and peace. Love is ever-expanding. It cannot be contained or limited. It needs to be expressed in different ways. So God, as a whole, decides to create partners to expand and share the love.

"Another reason for the decision to create is that all the parts or facets of God are not the same. They are of different shapes and sizes and some are more brilliant than others. Each one has the same type of powers, but not to the same degree. So, God decides to create so that every facet of Itself can grow and evolve to the same size and power."

• "God is like a glowing golden, white ball, constantly moving, growing and dividing. As It grows, Its vibrations increase and It moves faster and faster. As a result, initially parts of God splash out and fall back into God, but as the vibrations and speed of God increase, more pieces of God are splashed out and get lost in the void. Some parts of God are anxious and scared. They do not want to get lost in the void and want to keep this from happening. As a result, God and all the little balls in It feel upset, lonely, and sad. There were no such feelings before. There is a desire to get the pieces back and God does not want to lose any more parts of Itself. I, as an individual consciousness in the big ball of God, am also feeling alone and scared of being separated from the whole.

"So a decision was made together by every part of God to create some kind of boundary and security so we don't lose parts of ourselves. I sensed that the idea to create started with the one big ball of God at the core and then spread all over the big globe of God instantly as a telepathic communication.

"There are different reasons for the decision to create. One is that we want to reproduce ourselves, to grow and evolve so that every individual ball of God is the same size and has the same power, knowledge, and awareness of love. Thus we want to create perfection and develop greater awareness. Another reason is that we want to create partnership so we can share love and knowledge and not feel lonely; we want to help each other grow to perfection.

"We also want to create so we can grow, expand, and fill the whole void, so we do not lose parts of ourselves in the void. It took a long time between when the decision to create was made and when creation began. When the decision to create was made in God, the sphere was about the size of a house, and by the time we began to create, God as a whole was almost as large as a small planet."

• "I see God as a big, cylindrical ball or mass of whirling golden, white energy. The pieces of energy sprout up into little peaks and small beads of energy shoot out a little from the top of the peak, then fall back into the ball of God again. This action is repeated all over the 'body' of God. As the vibrations and the energy of God grow, It moves with much greater intensity. As a result, 'pieces' of God splash out into the void. There in the void; these pieces of God continue to grow and spin off. Multitudes of these energy balls or 'pieces' are growing in the void around God.

"When there is a knowledge that parts of the big ball are splitting off, it causes feelings of loneliness, sadness, fear, and anxiety in all the parts of God. This jogs an idea in God as a whole: to create and release the energy in a protective way, so it does not get lost. We, as God, want to grow and fill the whole void, so we will not have to worry about losing ourselves in that empty space.

"Before, all the balls in God were of the same size. When some parts of God began to splash out in the void, this created fear and anxiety in various balls of God and they began to vibrate and grow at different rates. After a while, not all the parts of God were of the same size and power. They now all have power, but of different intensity. Through creation, God wants to provide an opportunity for every part to grow and have a chance to become equal with all the others, and perfect themselves.

"Another reason to create evolved after Lucifer and his followers left the globe of God. God wants to send parts of Himself out, which in time can persuade Lucifer and his followers to return 'Home.' God wants to give them a second chance. Without them God cannot be whole.

"As I look back at God from the Akashic Records, I can see that It has grown a lot and has covered up most of the surrounding void. I can also see that parts of God, which broke off and got lost a long time ago, are also growing and look like planets now. There are multitudes of these 'planets' growing independently. They were not technically created by God, but they still have connections to God because they came from God."

• "One of the reasons to create was to maintain structural integrity in the 'body' of God in terms of staying together. God is constantly moving and growing. As It spins ever faster, It loses pieces of Itself in the empty space around It. The only way to stay integrated is to separate purposely and orderly, thus reducing the mass of God and distributing it in other places. So the choice is to divide and be separate or create and disperse the parts in a protective manner and thereby remain integrated, and also reduce the mass of God.

"Another reason to create was that before the decision to create is made, God is a single entity composed of different swirls. Some swirls are larger and better developed, while others are smaller and lesser developed. God therefore decides to create to develop all parts equally."

• "Before the pieces of God began to fragment and splash out in the void, all the balls in the sphere of God were of the same size. But after some pieces broke off from the globe of God and got lost in the empty space, all the balls inside God began to vibrate and began to change their size. In a way, the vibration was part of the intent to create. Each of these balls experienced the awareness of free will, and experimented and grew at whatever rates they decided upon. Free will had its origin when the pieces of Light began to break away from God.

"The decision to create was made at different levels of evolvement of the globe of God. When sparks began to break off and fly into the void, the decision to create came with the notion of free will. Then came the decision to experience the vibrations, which in itself was a creation. Each ball was mostly white because experience itself had not begun, and they were like empty white pages.

"As all the balls in the bigger globe of God began to vibrate, they grew independently and attained different sizes, vibrations, and colors. As a result, they were not the same, although they all had similar attributes and powers, but not to the same degree. God as a whole decides to create so all the parts can go out, experience, and grow, so they can become equal.

"As I focus on my ball, I feel vibrations and commotion. As the sparks splash in the void, there are feelings of apprehension, joy, and fear. I feel a sense of adventure but also sadness, which is coming from the various parts of God leaving 'Home.'"

Chapter Five

Rebellion and Revolution: Lucifer and His Followers Oppose Creation

People under hypnosis recalled that as different parts of God began to break off and splash into the void, this created a lot of anxiety, fear, and other disturbances in different balls of God. They all began to vibrate and grow at different rates and to display different colors and brilliance, whereas before that they were all of the same size and color. Some people said that as all the parts of God began to vibrate and grow, there was a kind of malfunctioning in one ball, which, over time, became gray or black. Patients recognize this as Lucifer's ball. Others mentioned that a black energy like a virus or a tiny device from the void hit Lucifer's ball and cracked it, and it gradually became black. Then Lucifer began to influence other balls in God that were not in support of creation. After a while, these parts of God also began to change into gray and black balls. This happened in only a small part of the globe of God and not all over, according to my patients.

When the decision to create was reached in God, there was a variety of feelings in different parts of God. Some felt joyful and excited, but were scared and anxious because of the unknown. Others were hesitant, and still others did not understand what would happen, so they did not want to change. Some were completely against the creation.

A larger ball in God, which my hypnotized patients recognized as Lucifer, disagreed completely with the intent to create. He rebelled and wanted to separate rather than develop all the parts of God. He wanted to be the biggest and the best; he wanted to be God. He did not want others to grow and be like him. My patients described Lucifer as a shiny black ball before the decision to create was made. He was larger than most balls, but many other balls were much larger than his. As Lucifer began to rebel, his shine disappeared and he became very black and dull, like coal.

My hypnotized patients claimed that at that time, as part of God, Lucifer's idea of being God himself was not necessarily a bad or good idea. The only drawback was that Lucifer was not developed enough to do it. All the parts of God could see that Lucifer was not developed enough, but Lucifer could not. He wanted to be God, yet it seemed that a critical size was necessary for him to become God. Even by taking like-minded souls with him, this was not enough to make him God.

According to my hypnotized patients, Lucifer gathered all of the souls that were against the creation. He pulled the souls that were opposed to the idea of creation but that were willing to go along with it, toward him. Some were willing to go, some had to be pulled, some he talked into going, and some he tried to trick. He appealed to their vanity, to their need for power, telling them they could be God themselves or whatever else they wanted to hear. Like a political campaign, Lucifer promised many things to get them. All the parts of God felt sad when this happened. For God, it was acceptable if they wanted to exercise their free will and leave the Light, if they felt they had to.

As Lucifer went out through the edge or wall of the globe of God, he became a separate entity, a "black blob" unto himself. Other parts that went out with him also changed into gray and black blobs. Hypnotized patients recalled that Lucifer took about 10 percent of the Light, or parts of God, with him at the beginning, but later he tricked more parts into leaving. As they went out of the ball of God, these parts became individual entities. They were not created as angels as we believe here on Earth. They forgot their origins; they did not remember they were part of God; they did not remember anything before their leaving. It was as if they were created brand new. They became what we know as demons.

Lucifer also forgot his origins after he came out of the sphere of God, but not to the same extent as the demons. Lucifer remembered where he came from and that he was part of God. He knew why he was "out" and he knew these other souls (the demons) did not remember. Lucifer told them *he* had created them and they must obey him. He informed them that the Light is their enemy and is very dangerous to them, that it will destroy them completely and that they will go out of existence if they come in contact with it.

As Lucifer left God with his followers, he was surprised to find he would have to dwell in the physical worlds. He did not foresee this, but he tried to make the best of it. After the creation of the universes, Lucifer took his demons through the universes and dimensions, looking for the dimension with the slowest vibration, far away from the globe of God. He felt repelled by the faster frequencies. He did not like them and could not tolerate them. His rebellion and his leaving the body of God could be seen from our present-day perspective as an abortive attempt to become God.

Creation of the Ball of Lucifer

According to my hypnotized patients, initially all the balls in God were brilliant white and of equal size. After some of them were thrown off in the void, fear and anxiety were created and all the balls began to vibrate and expand. There was a malfunction or an accident involving one ball that gradually became black. This was the ball of Lucifer. Some of my patients claimed there were malfunctions in the vibrations, while others saw an energy or an object from the void cracking and entering the ball of Lucifer, making it black over time.

Following are some descriptions of what happened to the ball of Lucifer:

• "In the sphere of God, there are multitudes of balls. They all look alike and are of the same size, and they have 'male' and 'female' aspects. The core of God is the parent ball and also has 'male' and 'female' aspects. Every ball in the globe of God is brilliant white. As I look at the ball of Lucifer at this point, it is also a bright white ball, but as I move ahead in time, Lucifer's sphere looks like a piece of coal.

"As I look back to find out why it became black, I see something like a crack in that ball, like a crack in an egg. Something causes it to crack and the darkness comes in. Gradually, the whole ball became dark. I can even smell a bad smell, like a rotten egg. Later I see dark wires going to other balls from the ball of Lucifer. I see a few other balls that are cracked, and these also become black. Lucifer's ball sends the black tubes or wires to many other balls and influences them; this also changes them into gray or black. They move far away from the core of God. I see this happening in only a small section of the globe of God."

• "As I look at Lucifer's ball, originally it is white like all the other balls. There is some outside influence, like a dark projectile energy from outer space, thrust into this ball of Lucifer, like a speck of darkness. That dark energy initially intrudes into only Lucifer's ball. It causes a state of confusion in him. As I move back in time to see where that dark speck came from, I see a tiny dot of black energy like a virus or an object like a device, and does not seem to have any Light. This goes into Lucifer's ball, and over time, it becomes bigger and spreads throughout his ball. Then, like an infection, it begins to spread to other balls, which are vulnerable. I see this happening in only a small section of God and not all over the globe of God."

·

Different Feelings about the Decision to Create

As described above, the decision to create was made together by all the parts in the sphere of God. There was a broad spectrum of feelings experienced by different consciousnesses, ranging from excitement, joy, and feelings of adventure, to fear, anxiety, confusion, and resistance. Not only were they able to recall their own feelings, but they were also able to tune into the thoughts and feelings of the other balls. Some examples are as follows:

• "As the decision to create is made by God as a whole, I feel excited and joyful, but there are also feelings of restlessness and fear of the unknown. Some are hesitant to change while others want to stay the same and do not want to change.

"There is a large facet whose name is Lucifer. He is against the creation. He is larger than most facets, but there are others that are larger than Lucifer. He looks shiny black, like obsidian, but he does not sparkle. He is unsettled about the idea of creation. He does not want other parts of God to grow and become as large as he is. He wants to be the big shot. He wants to be God."

• "I feel excited and adventurous about the decision to create but also have some fear and resistance because of the unknown nature of this plan. Lucifer is a big black mass. He is thinking that he will have an opportunity to rule; he is not for the creation, because he is afraid that others will become as large and as powerful as he is. There are many others who are against the creation and others who are not sure."

• "I am feeling better about the plan to create. We are getting too big, and, as a result, we have to create, so we will not lose parts of ourselves. There is a feeling of adventure and excitement, but there is also anxiety and fear of being away from God.

"There are a variety of feelings in different parts of God. Some are for creation, others are not quite sure about it, and many others are totally against the creation. Parts with the same idea congregate in a group. We are reorganizing according to our thoughts and vibrations, and we move toward those who have similar thoughts and vibrations.

"There is one group that is not happy about the idea of creation, especially one large ball called Lucifer. He is very black and totally against the creation. Other balls around him look black and gray. Lucifer is bigger than most balls, but not as large as the balls that will be the masters. [For more on 'masters,' see chapter 13.] He is angry and he does not want other parts to grow and become like him. He wants to be God. He is scared of losing his power and control and is afraid of being pushed out. He feels deceived, unwanted, and threatened. He is arrogant and thinks he is better and more powerful than the other larger balls.

"Every group has different balls of various sizes. My group wants to have its own space and wants to create harmony with each other. We are white and shiny. We are happy about creation, but there is a slight fear about it.

"Each group has balls of different sizes. Groups that are positive and for the creation gather close to the core of the ball of God; others assemble away from the core. Lucifer and the beings in his group are at the periphery of the big sphere of God. They do not want to be too close to the core of God. They cannot stand it because their vibrations are lower.

"Lucifer is trying to convince God to change His mind. He is telling God, 'We should not create. It is great the way it is and just let it stay the same because we do not need this creation.' God is telling him, 'It will be okay. You have nothing to be afraid of. It will be interesting and good for everybody, even for you.' We all are trying to change Lucifer's mind, because he is part of us, and we want him and others to stay with us, but they refuse to cooperate."

Deceiving, Gathering, and Leaving
the Globe of God

People under hypnosis vividly recall what happened in
God when Lucifer and his followers rebelled against the decision to create. They describe how Lucifer tried to talk to them
and others and gathered other parts of God by tricking them,
and what happened to them as they left God by crossing over
the edge of the globe of God. Following are some examples:

• "Lucifer is spreading a damper, a heaviness, and a lack
of desire to create. There are many other parts that are
against the creation and that gather around Lucifer. They
appear gray and black. There are other facets that are hesitant and not sure about creation. Lucifer is using his energy to mobilize them. He is trying to convince them that it
is in their best interest not to create; he is sending his
thoughts, like radio waves, to anyone who will listen to
him. He does not communicate with me and many others because we are sending out positive vibrations.

"Lucifer gathers those who are against the creation
as well as those who are not sure. They leave in a disor-
derly fashion. They go out through the wall of the globe
of God and become individual souls scattered all over
the outside of the sphere of God. As they step out of the
wall of God and come into existence as individual souls,
they have forgotten everything. They forgot that they
came from God and that they are the part of God. They
forgot about their own Light. Lucifer tells them they can
be as good and powerful as God. They are separate now
and can be whatever they want to be. While waiting
outside the globe of God, Lucifer continues to deceive
the vulnerable facets and pull them out of God.

"When the universes and different dimensions are
created, Lucifer and his followers choose one of the
dimensions, which is slowest in vibrations and far
away from God. They cannot tolerate high vibrations
and God's brilliant Light.

"God and His parts are feeling sad because a part
of God chose to rebel and be unloving. The feeling is

51

that unless Lucifer and his followers freely choose to be with us, we cannot hold them. So free will was always there. As Lucifer and his followers departed, this left holes in the ball of God. So God created more energy to fill those holes so there will be no empty spaces. Those demons and Lucifer are still connected with God with silver cords, which also became black. But they do not see or remember them."

• "Lucifer sends out thoughts to every part of God through telepathy. He tells everybody that if we create, then they are going to be lonely and separate from God. It is good the way it is, and we should leave it that way. Lucifer is trying to turn me against the creation and wants me to talk to others in my group and attempt to change their minds, but I ignore him.

"Lucifer and his beings are not glowing anymore. They are dull and are of gray, red, and black colors. Lucifer tries to trick others into leaving by lying to them. He tells them God does not know what he is doing; that they will feel worse when they separate; that they will be lost in the void like the other parts that got lost. He is trying to influence everybody all over the globe of God; he is able to pull some of the parts toward him. He creates chaos and disharmony by doing this.

"God tells Lucifer that, if he does not want to join us, then he will have to leave the Light, because he is disrupting everything and creating chaos and disharmony in the globe of God.

"Lucifer is not sure what will happen when they go out of God. He does not want to get lost in the void. So he sends his followers out first to see what happens. He tells them, 'We have to leave because they do not want us. We are going to create our own space.' As they go through the wall of God, they become gray and black individual souls that are not created by God and do not participate in the creation. They forget everything: they forget they are part of God and the Light. They are still connected to God by a silver cord, but this is masked by Lucifer.

"After his followers leave, Lucifer remains inside the Light for a while to recruit more parts. If they get close enough, he grabs them. His energy field opens up and engulfs different balls. They then become dark, and he sends them out through the edge of God. At this point, he takes about one-fourth of the Light and continues to work on other parts of God to go with him.

"God feels sad but lets this happen. He gives everybody free will and lets them decide what they want to do. There are mixed feelings all over the sphere of God; there is both sadness and relief. I am glad they are leaving, because they have created confusion and disharmony. I do not want them to take any more parts of God with them."

• "Lucifer looks like a large black ball. He is larger than most balls, but there are other balls that are much larger than he is. He is against the idea of creation. He wants to be The God and does not want other parts of God to be as big as he is. He is gathering different parts of God around him that are also against the creation.

"He is trying to put black tubes in other balls to influence them. He is trying to put a black tube in my 'head.' I know it is not good, so I remove it. Many other balls do not know this and do not remove the black tubes. Lucifer is like an octopus with many, many tentacles, and with them he is reaching to different parts in various directions. As he puts these tubes into the different parts, they become black and their thinking changes. Then he pulls them toward him. These are the parts that are not sure about the creation.

"Lucifer and his followers go out of the wall of God, and as they cross over, they become black and gray blobs. They appear to be dazed. They forget everything about themselves, that they are part of God. They become individual beings as soon as they cross over the wall of God. They are not created by God. I see a spark of Light in them, but they cannot see it and do not know it is there. They still have connections with God, but Lucifer has covered them up with black stuff. Lucifer is telling them that Light does not belong with creation and Light will make them the opposite of what they are supposed to be. After the universes are created, he takes them to a dimension that is far away from God. It has the slowest vibrations and it becomes their home, what we now call 'hell.'

"As God creates, Lucifer puts 'black stuff' over the universes, galaxies, and planets, wherever he can. He does that by putting black tubes in them and infusing them with black energy. Some of the universes are totally protected, so he cannot affect them; their vibrations are very fast. He puts black tubes in our planet also and infuses negative energy into it. As a result, when we humans are put on Earth, we are influenced negatively by these dark energies."

• "I can see the ball of Lucifer. Originally he is a white ball with some gold. Then as he starts to vibrate, something goes wrong, like a malfunction, and he becomes dark. He begins to grow as a dense, dark ball. There are many balls that go through the same process. I see a localized action in only a small portion of the sphere of God, maybe in about one-tenth or one-fourth of the globe of God.

"The dark ball of Lucifer is becoming rebellious. He is talking to and gathering up other beings because he does not want them to grow as big and powerful as he is. He gathers around him all the others who are against creation. He then campaigns against the creation, focusing on the doubters. He communicates telepathically all over the sphere of God, sending out false promises to those who are not sure. Lucifer tells them that he already has the knowledge that they will be better off with him and that those who choose the creation will get lost in the void and will be separate and alone forever. Like political campaign promises, he tells whatever they need to hear to get them to follow him. He tries to talk to me, but I ignore him.

"He puts a magnet-type of device connected with a black tube on different balls and fills them with negative energy. They are pulled toward him as if they are being towed.

"After a while, Lucifer is told by God that if he does not want to cooperate, then he and his followers will have to go outside the globe of Light, because they are causing confusion and disruption. So he chooses to leave the ball of God with his followers. Lucifer and his followers use their negative energy to break away out of God by leaving through the outer edge of God. I feel upset that many parts of God are going with him. As they cross over the edge of the globe of God, they become demons. They forget everything about themselves and where they come from. They are not created by God as angels, as we on Earth believe."

Chapter Six

The Creation of Universes and All of Their Dimensions

My patients report under hypnosis that God waited to create until after Lucifer and his followers had left because He did not want them to affect the universes negatively. All the consciousnesses in God began to group together according to their vibrations and affinity. It was as if there was a churning throughout the ball of God and a regrouping of different parts. It was as if they erupted from every part of the ball of God and went in a specific direction and grouped together. Each group gave its intent to be the part of a certain creation; some expressed a desire to be created as a universe.

There was an intent that permeated the sphere of God, to be a part of an individual universe. The balls with matching frequencies went out together. They knew how they wanted to group and how they wanted to create a unique universe. All over the globe, there was a knowing in every consciousness about what part of the creation each was supposed to be involved in.

Before releasing the energy to create the universes, God, through Its intent, first created protective pathways, like tunnels, all over Its globe. Patients described them as similar to "spokes of a wheel," "pathways," "tunnels," "channels," or "rays" such as you see around the sun. Groups of energy swirls of similar vibrations were released through these channels out of the edge of the globe of God in a protective sac, so they would not be lost in the void. Some of these groups remained close to the ball of God, while others went further away. Sections of God in between tunnels automatically became god-heads and later were programmed for their special purposes.

Patients described the energy swirls in each group, after leaving the globe of God, as clumping together in a ball and beginning to expand and contract. As the energy bounced back and forth, the balls grew, just as the globe of God had done earlier. After a certain amount of growth, the energy in each ball broke up and regrouped according to its vibration and created multiple balls inside the bigger ball; this continued to expand and grow and created galaxies. The energy in each galaxy continued to bounce back and forth, allowing it to expand and grow. Then the energy in each galaxy broke up and regrouped again, then continued to expand and grow again, creating the planets, moons, and stars. Then through the intent of God, different planets in each galaxy were rearranged to create different astral systems, such as our solar system.

So globes inside globes were created, all overlapping each other. Multitudes of these universes were created all around the sphere of God. (See figure 6.) Over uncountable years, the universes changed from this spiritual form of energy expansion to the physical form familiar to us.

According to my hypnotized patients, after the creation of all the large components in the universes, such as galaxies, planets, and stars, the energies were used to enhance these components. God planned the details for each dimension. According to my patients, God did not control (or "micromanage") every aspect of creation, but there was an overall control. The placement, regeneration, growth, and cocreation were all part of God's overall plan before sending the energy into space. When He sent out the energy, even He did not have a definite idea as to how it would turn out. It was trial and error and that is why every universe is unique. This process continued all around the globe of God, creating multitudes of universes with their own galaxies and systems of planets, moons, and stars. Here are a few descriptions given by my hypnotized patients about how different universes and dimensions were created:

• "After Lucifer and his followers made an exit from the ball of God into the void, there is chaos inside God. Different facets in God are drawn toward others of similar vibration and affinity, and they regroup and reorganize all over the sphere of God. All of them give an intent to be part of a certain type of creation.

"Different groups of balls of different vibrations in the globe of God give their intent to be part of the universes. God first creates multiple pathways with protective coverings, so He can release the energy swirls with protection so the energy will not be lost in the void. Then He releases different groups of energy swirls through different tunnels all around the globe through His intent. As the energies are released out of the edge of God and form a ball, they are covered with a protective covering. They still have connecting cords with God.

"These balls continue to expand and contract and grow. The energy passes through the middle and hits the outside wall and bounces off, expands back through the core and then goes back to the outer wall. Every time this happens, a new vibration is created. For example, when the universe was tiny, it had a very fast frequency. As the globe expanded, the frequency rate became slower because the walls continuously moved further apart. Every time it expanded and contracted with different vibrations, a new dimension was created.

"There are multitudes of dimensions, each with different vibrations, overlapping one another. The top one has the slowest frequency rate, and as you go down the layers, the frequency rate increases gradually. Our planet is in the middle."

• "After God as a whole began to lose parts of Itself, we felt lonely and sad. So an urge to create emerged in God. After Lucifer and his demons left, God as a whole planned to release His energy to create universes, but

THE UNIVERSES ALL AROUND GOD

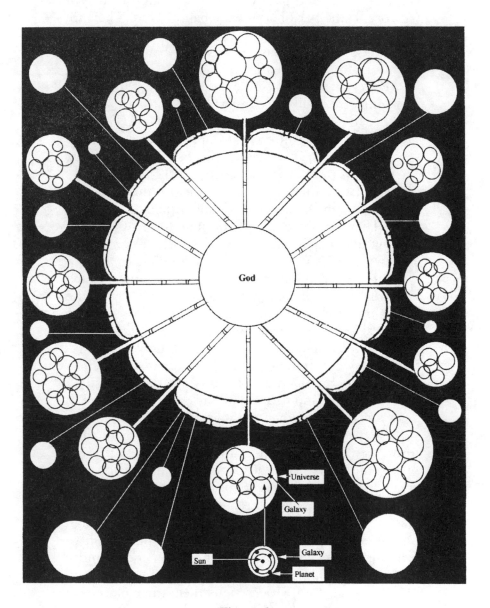

Figure 6

He did not want to lose energy in space. He wanted to disburse the energy in a controlled and protected way.

"So God created tunnels, or Light pathways, all over the globe to ensure protection, direction, and control while releasing the energy from the ball of God. These lighted pathways extend from the edge of the core to the periphery of the ball of God. They are like spokes in a wheel. These tunnels are of different vibrations, which release the energy balls of similar vibrations through them.

"Different parts of God express an intent to be part of a universe. Balls of similar vibrations are drawn together in groups all over the globe of God. Through the intent of God, different groups of energy balls are spun out through specific tunnels of similar vibrations. There is a protective cover over all the energies released from these tunnels. Some of these energy groups remain close to God and others go farther away. They form a ball and continue to grow by contracting and expanding, back and forth. As a result, energy increases in the globe of each universe.

"After a certain amount of growth, energy in each ball breaks up, then clumps together according to the vibrations, and then continues to grow as separate balls inside the big ball, which is a universe. These globes in the universe become what we now call galaxies. As they continue to expand, energy inside each of them breaks up again and clumps together according to its vibration, and forms new balls. These continue to grow and become what we call astral systems.

"As they grow, the energy breaks up again and forms new balls, which grow and become different planets and stars. After all of the large dimensions are created, weaker energies are used to enhance the planets. God then decides to create suns for different solar systems to help sustain life on their planets. Although a sun's energy comes from the galaxy, God wills it to be more intense and vibrant, then the sun creates more energy in itself. After all the galaxies, suns, moons, and planets are created, God assigns them their place. He programs them with their purpose."

• "God creates different tunnels all around Its sphere. Energy between two tunnels automatically becomes a godhead. Groups of energy swirls of similar vibrations are released within a protective sac through different tunnels in different directions, like waves of energy. These tunnels look like streamers on a maypole; at the end of each streamer there is a universe. (See figure 7.)

GOD AND THE UNIVERSES LOOKING LIKE A MAYPOLE

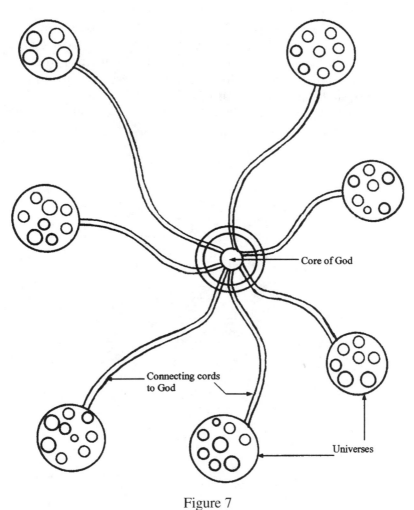

Figure 7

• "The groups of energy that are let out through tunnels form mini globes all around God and continue to expand and contract and grow. As they grow, the energy in them breaks up and gravitates toward others with similar vibrations, and these mini globes group together and form more mini globes inside the big globe of each universe. These mini globes become the galaxies, and these continue to expand and grow. They break up and regroup again according to their frequencies and form different planets, stars, suns, and moons, and these regroup again to form different solar systems in each galaxy.

"They continue to grow in layers, one on top of the next by growing and regrouping according to their intent. It is a burgeoning of energy—a growing, expanding, and a constant development into new forms. This is going on in each universe all around God, making each one unique."

Chapter Seven

Creation of Individual Souls

My hypnotized patients report that God waited for Lucifer and his demons to leave before He created universes, masters, and angels because He did not want them to be contaminated by the demons. He wanted to create masters and angels before the universes because Lucifer and his demons were out on their own and He wanted the universes to be protected from them. The order of creation was masters, angels, universes, plants, animals, and rational-thinking beings, that is, humans and other beings who will inhabit Earth and other planets.

After creation, each soul went through similar experiences in different degrees, including the "first forgetting," feelings of being separate, and receiving instructions from God.

The "First Forgetting"

According to my hypnotized patients, after its creation every soul went through the "first forgetting." When we were one with God before creation, we had all the knowledge, memories, and energies of God. After the creation and separation, we had only a small part of God's energy and, as a result, fewer memories and less knowledge.

God has all the memories because He is still connected with *all* the souls. Godheads forgot a little, masters forgot slightly more, and angels even more. The rational beings, that is, humans and other beings of different planets, forgot the most. It happened the instant the souls were created. After creation, the souls did not remember that they were part of God and that they had made the decision to create. They did not remember the overall plan.

Feelings of Being Separate

After the creation, all the souls (including masters and angels) had feelings of separation from God in various degrees. Some felt surprised, joyous, and elated, while others felt confused, anxious, sad, rejected, or as if they were being punished.

Receiving Instructions from God

According to my hypnotized patients, after the creation of each soul, God spoke to them individually, giving information and instructions about their purpose. Some human souls were told to form groups they would work with for spiritual evolution on their planet. All were instructed to "pray" (to stay in communication with God) and thereby have direct access to the power of God through their silver connecting cord.

Creation of Masters

Hypnotized people report that after Lucifer and his followers left the globe of God, masters were created first, because they were the ones who would organize the progression of the creation and be in charge of it. The angels were created next to act as helpers, protectors, "managers," and "foremen." They would organize, protect, and help. It is like creating a chain of command.

The larger balls, which were created as masters, grouped closely around the core of God. They had most of the awareness of God. They flanked around the core of God, facing outward. Each had its own region (godhead energy) and groups of helpers (the angels). Their purpose was to make sure that creation proceeded properly and in order as originally planned and not go off track.

Being near the core of God, masters have most of His awareness and knowledge. They understand what creation is about, and how it should happen. They are also the translators, the bridge between God and the rest of the creation. They are created to be the ultimate protectors against darkness, that is, against Lucifer and his followers. They are the most powerful in creation next to God and have the most powers and attributes of God. They are *like* God but not God. They were created to remain in Heaven but from time to time will incarnate on a planet to help the beings there. Like all the souls, masters have a silver cord connecting them to God.

The masters handle a reciprocal energy movement. The energy flow comes out of God through different masters to the universes, then it comes back through the masters to God. They are the link between God and the rest of creation. From time to time, every soul comes back to God through its silver cord, which is connected to and passes through one of the masters. Each master is in charge of a section in God, that is, a godhead.

My patients report that there were many large souls grouped together around the core of God. There were multitudes of such groups of master souls all over the globe of God, and they gave the intent to be created as masters. Each group of these master souls had a larger soul, which was like a group leader. God created masters by condensing their energies through His will and intent. He gave them forms and shapes and then programmed them for their purposes. After some time, they were released into one of the godheads. After a while, their energy permeated through the whole godhead section, after which that master became the godhead. Each godhead had the essences of many masters going through it. After their creation, masters forgot to some extent about how things were before their creation, but they forgot much less than other souls.

People under hypnosis claim we were all there in God, observing and participating as God created the masters, and that we were able to tune into their thoughts and feelings. Some descriptions given by my patients about how the masters were created follow here:

- "There are larger souls that have assembled near the edge of the core of God. There are multitudes of them. They all have given an intent to be masters. They are large, brilliant, and beautiful. I watch one of the masters being created and tune into his feelings. I see it as a ball being stretched out like a piece of taffy; it has that kind of stringy connection. God creates this master by condensing it into a ball and giving it a form, a human silhouette, but I do not see any special facial features or body form, just a brilliant, radiating general form.

  "After the creation, this master feels overwhelmed by the awe and wonder of it all. He feels enthusiastic, responsible, fearful, and separate. He has forgotten some of how things were before his creation.

  "After the master is created, God programs him for his purpose. God tells this master: 'You are to be my reflection in every way, so the rational beings (humans and others) will know the power and presence of love. You will be a clear channel for that. I give you the gifts of seeing into man's heart, of understanding, of demonstrating, and of teaching that God is love; I give you toughness and resilience, the ability to love everybody unconditionally and to understand them. I give you the gift of humor; the awareness of oneness to the level that no one seems to attain; compassion; and the ability to see the importance of the little things that are very important in life. It is a gift to recognize the unseen heroes and all the characteristics of what God really is.'

  "After the creation of godheads, this master soul floated to the top of his godhead, which was near the core of God. Each godhead energy has many such masters. Masters seem to be tucked into their godheads around the core of God. After a while, this master's essence permeates through the whole godhead. In this way the godhead energy and master's energy become one."

• "After Lucifer and his beings left, God created masters and angels first, so they could be ready to protect the universes and the beings who will inhabit them when they will be created later. God does not want them to be negatively influenced by Lucifer and his beings. Masters will be helpers of God. They will act as intermediaries between God and other rational beings. They will protect and oversee the spiritual development of the intelligent life in their respective area of the universe.

"As Lucifer and his beings rebel, there is much chaos in the globe of God, and different consciousnesses of similar vibrations and affinity begin to migrate toward one another and to form multitudes of groups all over the sphere of God. Balls of consciousnesses, which are largest, brightest, and of the fastest vibrations, gather in groups all around the core of God. They express their intent to be masters. All the consciousnesses are observing and giving their input as God creates the masters. We are all in God as part of God at that time.

"God creates the masters' forms. They will have the same form as the intelligent or rational beings (like humans and others) on their respective planets. This way, the humans and other beings can identify with them. Next to God, the masters will have the highest vibrations and greatest powers. The masters will be the spiritual agents for their respective sections of intelligent life. They will have a domain of their own and will have the responsibility for coordinating the disbursement and reception of the souls. In considering the population they will serve, they will be recognized as deities, and people can pray to them; those prayers will pass through the masters to God through their silver cords. In this way, the souls can journey back to God through their respective godheads and masters.

"Masters for our planet are created as ones who

have the same qualities as humans, so they can communicate with them and understand them. There are multitudes of masters created for different universes. Masters for our planet are created as half-human and half-spirit. They will remain mostly in Heaven, but occasionally they will incarnate as humans, such as in times of trouble, to help humans and to teach them the ways of God. They will be the link between humans and God and will help humans to become like God. They will help souls to learn, develop, and grow. The masters will protect their domain of the universe and the souls in it. They will have most of the attributes and powers of God, but they are not God.

"Everybody is watching as masters are being created. God pulls out their individual balls and condenses them into a ball and gives them a shape. Some masters feel disoriented and dizzy for a brief period. After their creation, they feel happy, joyous, excited, and positive, although they have some uncertainty.

"After their creation, God speaks to them individually and programs them for their purpose. I am able to tune into what God is telling one of the masters. 'You are my equal. Next to me, you and the other masters have the highest vibrations and powers. You have a special mission. From time to time, you will go to a part of the universe in the form of a human or other being. One of your responsibilities will be to show them that there is Light, that they are from the Light, and that they can come back to the Light. You will look like other inhabitants (human and others), but you will have special healing abilities and other powers. While you are on a planet, even though you will have special powers, you will suffer like other humans. When your mission is finished, you will return to the Light and remain mostly in Heaven. I give you the power to heal, communicate, to be an outstanding leader and a teacher. I give you compassion and power over darkness.'

"Multitudes of masters go into each godhead section. Most of the masters remain on top of the godhead. After a while, their energy permeates through the whole godhead. This way, they and the godhead become one and the same. God creates various connections between corresponding godheads as bridges over the tunnels, so they are in constant communication with one another."

Creation of Angels

My hypnotized patients recall that after Lucifer and his followers left the globe of God, He began to create. First, He created masters; then He created angels. Angels were created to be the protectors of the universes and the beings who will dwell in them. They are the "go-betweens" among humans, godheads, masters, and God. They guard the gates of Heaven and provide a buffer zone between the godheads and the universes out there. They were created to be the holy helpers of God.

Groups of balls all over the sphere of God gave their intent to be created as angels. God created different types of angels, then He programmed them for their purposes. God made angels in different shapes and forms: large, medium and "baby" angels; some were created as male, some as female, and some androgynous; they have two, four, six, or more wings, which were created for mobility. Some have no body, just heads and wings; some have less-defined shapes, while others have well-defined shapes. Angels for different universes are created differently, depending on their vibrations.

God created angels for different functions: to avenge, protect, or defend. Some were formed to be leaders such as archangels, who are like masters of the angels. Some were made for healing, ministering, guiding, teaching, or rescuing. Some were created as muses, assigned to humans who produce art, music, painting, sculpture, or other types of art. Some angels were made to stay around God, while "baby" angels were created to bring joy and happiness to those who are sick and in despair. Angels also have a silver connecting cord to God.

Angels remain in Heaven as spirit beings and do not incarnate on the planets. They were not created for that purpose. After their creation, God speaks to them and programs them for their purpose. My patients gave many accounts of the creation of angels, a few of which follow here:

• "Angels were created after Lucifer and his demons left the globe of God and after the creation of masters, but before the creation of universes. These beings will be the protectors of the universes and go-betweens for God and the creation. They have to be willing to serve forever.

"Parts of God, or different consciousnesses in God, want to become angels. They give their intent to be angels. We also give our input as they are being made. Archangels are created first. They are large and powerful angels. I can see the core of God creating one of the archangels. A large ball of Light was chosen. God wants him to be pure of heart. He will be a protector and a helper; he will watch out for Lucifer and his demons. He will protect the universes and assist in God's plan and purpose.

"God creates this archangel through His intent. I almost see hands molding the soul. I think 'hands' are symbolic. He creates a form by pulling, squeezing, molding, and giving the being its purpose. God gives him a form that is like a human with wings. Creation of angels is going on all around the globe of God. They will protect and help different universes and the rational beings (humans and others) who will be created later to live in those universes.

"God creates different categories of angels. Some are for protection, some for wisdom, some for love, some for communication, some for creativity, and some for guidance; there are large angels and 'baby' angels. Some are male, some are female, and others are androgynous; some have two wings, others have four wings or more. Baby angels are created for love and joy. After their creation, angels are sent to the outer edge of the globe of God to protect and watch over the universes that will be formed."

• "Angels are created because they will be needed to watch over and protect what God is going to create. God has many purposes in mind for them. They will be the protectors of the universes, God's helpers, messengers, communicators between God and other rational beings in the universes, guides to those life forms returning to Heaven, and a prototype for creating the humans. They will act as intermediaries between God, godheads, masters, and humans. They will also teach, preach, and heal. Superior and high-ranking angels are created first from the larger balls in God; these are called archangels, and after them, the rest of the angels are created.

"Angels for each universe are created differently, depending on the vibrations of those universes. God takes a ball that has given its intent to be an angel. Through God's thought and intent, the energy is condensed and spun until it reaches a certain vibration and intensity. After this energy ball is created, God wills it into a form. He thinks about specific features and these are created. He then speaks to the angels and programs them for specific purposes with His thoughts. After creation, angels are sent to the periphery of the globe of God through the godhead (from which place their original swirl of energy came) so they can protect and watch over the universes that are to be created."

• "God is planning to create angels as intermediaries to help and protect all the universes and the thinking beings (humans and others) on different planets. Because thinking beings (humans and other beings) on the planets will have free will, they will be prone to do things that are not necessarily right, healthy, or good for them. These angels will protect and help them to learn the lessons from the mistakes they will make. They will remain in Heaven and never incarnate on the planets.

"God picks different parts of energy balls that have given an intent to be angels. God creates angels as a model for the thinking beings (humans and others) who will inhabit the planets. The angels have to be light like air in order to remain in God.

"Some angels are created to remain near God as His companions, and as intermediaries between Him and the other angels and humans. These are the largest and the strongest of the angels. They are created to be the leaders of the angels and are known as the archangels. God also creates tiny angels, like babies with wings; they are to bring joy to those who will be sick, handicapped, or in despair.

"Some angels have no discernible bodies, yet they are winged and look like the heads of human beings. Others have fully developed bodies, but with no substance to them. They are just Light, an outline of Light, but their 'bodies' are basically the same as a human's. They were created first and the intelligent beings (humans) were patterned after them.

"After their creation, the angels are released into the peripheral area of the sphere of God, through a godhead, so they can watch over and protect the universes and the beings who will dwell in them."

Creation of Plants

My hypnotized patients report that after the creation of the universes, God enhanced them with plant life. God realized that the energy within the universes has to have something to rid them of the built-up gases. Otherwise they will explode. So God had to put something in that can use the energy that is created in the universes. God therefore created plants to balance out the energy.

Some plants are created for purely ornamental purposes as an artistic creation. They are created to be a cover or as trees to protect the land. Another purpose is topographical, to hold things in place. Plants make roots that prevent erosion. For example, if there is a hill without trees, it will wash away with rain. But if you have trees with their roots to take up moisture, they will hold the hill. Other plants are created as an energy source, that is, food for humans and animals or for use as shelter.

God created plants by focusing on separate balls that gave intent to be a plant. He condensed them into a form and gave them a purpose. They were sent down through a godhead on a planet. Following is an example given by a patient about why and how God created plants:

> • "After God created the universes, galaxies, and planets, He thought of enhancing them with the life force. He created plants that would be helpful to the beings, which will be created later, that is, animals and thinking beings (humans and others). Plants will be useful as an energy source as food and shelter and for cleaning the air. Plants will also hold and nourish the planets with trees, holding the ground through their roots.
>
> "God takes a swirl of energy, which has given intent to be a plant, and condenses it through intent, and then wills it into shape and gives it a purpose. He sends that energy through a godhead to Earth and other planets. The soul is still connected to God with a silver cord and returns to God from time to time through it."

Creation of Animals

My hypnotized patients state that after planets and plants were created, God saw a need for something to take up the energy the plants give off. It is as if, when one thing was created, it caused the need for something else. So God produced moving organisms with discrete souls. God also developed some variety.

He created birds, fishes, and other things that live on different planets. Then he brought forth four-legged animals. He also created two-legged animals with arms instead of four legs. He kept on perfecting. Animals also reincarnate again and again and grow spiritually like humans, but, as a rule, animals do not evolve into human beings. They are a different line of creation. They remain as animals.

Animals also become a source of energy (food for humans) and are here to serve and procreate. Some are predators to prey on other living things for population control. Others are here as part of the life cycle, with humans preying on animals, and animals preying on humans or other animals.

God made animals by taking certain energy balls that had given intent to be created as animals. He first condensed the energy by spinning it through his intent. Then he programmed them with their purposes. In time he sent them onto different planets. Their souls are still connected to God with a silver cord. The following description is given by my hypnotized patient about why and how animals were created:

- "God has physical characteristics in mind for animals. The vibration of a swirl that intends to be an animal is higher than the swirls that volunteer for the plants. God condenses the swirl energy, spins it, and molds it into a form. He gives it a purpose and in time, sends it to Earth through a godhead. These created souls also have a connecting silver cord to God.

    "Animals are created as predators on other animals and humans, thus helping balance nature. They also help humans as an energy source (food) and also serve them. They also take up the oxygen created by plants. God creates a variety of animals over time as the need evolves. Their souls also go through reincarnations and grow spiritually, but they do not evolve into humans."

Creation of Human Souls and Souls for Other Planets

My hypnotized patients say that, after the creation of masters, angels, universes, plants, and animals, God began to create the intelligent or rational beings, that is, humans and other beings to inhabit Earth and other planets. These beings would be responsible for most of the growth of God. Through incarnating again and again, they will learn and grow, and as they grow, God will grow. God wanted to create intelligent beings that would look different from animals. They were to have more soul knowledge and superior communication skills and more wisdom, and they were to be able to eventually walk on two feet. They would have a purpose, which would include the expression of free will, which is needed for spiritual growth. They would also procreate themselves.

In creating human beings and beings for other planets, God took different things into consideration, such as function, beauty, the capability to adapt and survive in the environment they would be in, and the ability to communicate. He developed their forms according to the different universes souls will inhabit. He gave them denser bodies so they can function on the planet to which they would be sent. God gave them power to think and make decisions.

God also created a silver connecting cord linking Him with all the souls just as He did with masters, angels, universes, animals, and planets. This is so He does not lose touch with them and so they can have constant communication with Him when they are on a planet. Through the silver connecting cords, souls can travel to Heaven from the planet they live on, both while they are alive and after death. The souls' connection with God is eternal, and they will never be separated from God.

Under hypnosis, my patients recalled that after the creation of their souls, they forgot almost everything about their existence before their creation. They forgot that they were one with God and what had happened before their creation. They call this "the first forgetting." Then after each subsequent incarnation, they report they forgot almost everything about their previous lifetimes. They call this "the second forgetting." After the creation, God spoke to every soul about their purpose and gifts. Then they were released to their respective godheads. Here are a few descriptions given by my patients about the creation of their souls and how they felt before and after the creation:

- "After the creation of the universes, minerals, plants and animals, God plans to create the intelligent beings, so God will not be lonely. They will be his partners. They will go down to different planets to learn and grow, and as they grow, God will grow.

"My group gives intent to be humans. Before my creation, I am nervous because I will be separate from God and do not know how it will be. So there is a fear of the unknown, but I am excited to be created. There is a sense of adventure. It will be a new experience.

"As God is creating me, I am anxious and scared. I feel squeezed, shaken, pulled, and tossed around. It is like being born. I want to stay here and don't want to leave. After my creation, I am alone and away from God. I am happy, scared, and anxious, feeling alone, and rejected, and I have separation anxiety.

"After God creates me, He speaks to me. He tells me He loves me and is proud of me for being brave. I will always have contact with Him. He wants me to grow and develop and enjoy life. He wants me to remember where I came from, that I will be safe and have power over Satan, and not to be afraid. I will return to Him. It makes me cry because He is sending me away.

"He tells me to seek out people who are like me. This will give me more purpose and direction. Together we will have more strength. Through prayer, I will always be with Him. He gives me the gifts of music and wisdom; a good heart; and the ability to communicate well, to get my point across, to teach, to care, and to pass on the word of His love and intent. This will ease the suffering of people. He tells me to teach people how to love each other.

"After a while, I am released into my godhead. I float to the top third layer in the godhead in a pyramidal model of God."

• "My group and I have given an intent to be created as human souls. I feel great joy and happiness. I am also anxious, uncertain about what I will feel and how I will survive. My husband in my current life is at my side and we are holding hands. I think we are twin flames, two separate souls created from one ball with a male and female, or plus and minus, aspect. We are from one ball, but of two different polarities.

"My husband is created first, then me. I cannot wait until God pays attention to me. I feel great joy and happiness. God gives me form and color. He paints me with beautiful colors. It is as though He is putting cosmetics on me and extra happiness in me, and I want to say God created me on a very happy day because He was excited.

"God tells me he wants me to be a creation of beauty. He wants me to share this beauty with others because beauty is good. It is happiness and joy; it is to be shared with others so they can become beautiful. Beauty is everywhere and I will only see beauty in everything. My purpose is to deflect all darkness, ugliness, and misery. God gives me knowledge about perfection and the sense of no limitations.

"He gives me the gift to make people happy and beautiful. He gives me gifts of healing, art, knowledge, wisdom, and the gift of being a warrior. He also gives me the understanding of balance, geometry, and astrology.

"After my creation, I forgot everything about my previous existence. My twin flame and I stood side by side, holding hands. We are from one ball of consciousness, created as two separate souls. Before we were created, I was on the left side, holding him with my right hand. After the creation, I am on the right side, holding him with my left hand. After our creation, we are released to a godhead. We go to the top second layer in that godhead."

• "Before my creation, I am excited and curious, but I am also afraid. I do not know what is going to happen, what it is going to feel like, what the surroundings will be like, how it will be when I am separate from God. What will I look like?

"God takes my ball of energy and puts it together by squeezing it. It looks like yellow Play-Doh. He sculpts me and gives me a form with His thoughts. Then He gives me life and programs me as to how I will be. After my creation, I feel anxious and scared, like a question mark. What is happening? Where am I? Why am I separate from Him? I feel like I am losing my memory. I forget a lot of things. I feel confused, sad, and rejected because I am not with God.

"God speaks to me after my creation. He tells me that I have forgotten how some things were before my creation, and that when I am sent to Earth, I will forget even more. He has created angels to help me and to protect me and others. He tells me He will give me families, so I will not be alone and so I will have someone to take care of me.

"God tells me about evil and that I will have power over it through prayer. When I die, He has a place for me to stay. He advises me to pray and He will help me. He tells me He loves me and that He is always with me. Then He sends me to a section of God, to a godhead. When He releases me, I float to the top third layer, if the top layer of the godhead is the first section and the bottom layer is the tenth."

• "As God is getting ready to create thinking or intelligent beings (humans and other beings for other planets), He has different criteria for creating them. We all participate in the planning because we are one with God. We each have our individual consciousness, but we also have *one* consciousness.

"God creates me and other thinking beings the same way He created masters and angels—by focusing on the energy. Only this time it has to be a denser focusing because we will be corporeal on a planet. When we are created in God, we have different shapes and forms, yet we are still energy. Being created for a planet will be different.

"Before my creation, I get ready for it. I give my intent to be a human. I am excited and have a sense of adventure. I am also anxious, restless, and scared because of the unknown. As He is creating me, I am excited and wonder what is going on. The activity around me is stimulating. Something big must be about to happen. I sense being shaken and shaken. It feels like being in an earthquake, yet it is exciting and confusing, frightening and also challenging. Then there is a burst and I am out here, separate.

"As I am separated from God, I feel alienated, sad, and cast out. I sense I lost something, and I feel confused and uncertain. I am scared, hurt, and rejected. I do not know why I could not stay there. I guess I have to leave for some reason. I do not like this, but I do not care. If this is the way it is supposed to be, that is what I will do. I seem to have forgotten everything about how things were before my creation."

• "As God begins to create me, I am spun around. It is disturbing and unsettling. I am anxious, scared, confused, concerned, and insecure. I feel like I am being pulled apart, like a plant that is being uprooted, that I am losing myself. I am wondering what is happening to me, what will become of me. I feel like an object being compressed, squeezed, and bounced all over as though I have lost all direction. I am confused, and all of a sudden I am cast out.

"Out here I feel alone, anxious, and concerned about what will happen to me next. I have a sense of discontentment. I am hurt and disappointed, because I have been separated from God and feel less peaceful and more vulnerable. I sense being empty, lonely, and rejected by God and angry and resentful toward Him. I forget how things were *before*. I only remember that I am from God and do not remember I was in God and the type of existence I had before.

"After my creation, God is telling me that I and others are going on a great mission. We are going to be sent to a place somewhere in a universe. We are the first ones of our kind to be sent there. We will have free will to make choices as to how we live. When we get there we are supposed to make this place habitable and to produce and multiply. God gives me gifts of resourcefulness, organizational skills, self-discipline, determination, and psychic powers.

"There are many circular or oblong balls of energy being created around me. I am a round ball. We are of different sizes. Most are smaller than I am. However, there are other balls that are larger. After a while, we are sent through an opening in a godhead. We all have a silver connecting cord to God. As we are released in the godhead, some stay up, some go down, and some stay more or less in the middle. It has nothing to do with the size of the souls, but how they *felt* after their creation. Many larger souls are going down because they are very unhappy and confused. I remain on the second or third layer from the top."

• "I have already migrated toward my group and given my intent to be created as a human soul who will inhabit Earth and maybe other planets in the future. Before my creation, I hear "Are you willing?" and I answer, "Yes, I am." The question is from God as a whole. I do not realize what I am going to be at this point. It is as if I agree to extend myself to do whatever it takes to do the will of God, and I will be shown what that will be. I do not know what it is ahead of time.

"I am excited but a little frightened because I do not know what is going to happen. I do not know what it will mean to become human. All I know is that it will allow me to grow. It is funny, as if I have to go out and grow in order to come back and be a part of God. To be part of God we need to continue to grow and have a better awareness.

"As God is creating me, I feel separate and aware of boundaries around me that I never felt before. He is giving me a shape. I feel as if I'm being molded into a form. Before, everything enveloped me, but now I feel a separate entity, and it is scary. I have to remind myself that it is part of my growth to experience and understand that separateness. I feel alone and uncertain. I am aware of being separate, something I never experienced before.

"After my creation, God speaks to me: 'Go forth and experience.' He tells me, 'Use all your experience to remind yourself who you are, so you do not forget that you are always a part of Me. These experiences will lead you to higher degrees of awareness and ultimately to oneness, which is achieved by experiencing separateness. That is why you must go out and do this. I give you silence. I give you solitude in your experiences. In your solitude, you will know I am with you so you will not forget who you are. Then I can speak to you and guide you from one experience to another. Reflect on who I am in all that you do because you are a part of Me. You are a part of the whole and will always be. But at times you will forget this. Let love always be your guide. Love will be your standard. Find others like you and form a group.'

"God gives me gifts of acceptance, intelligence, gentleness, spiritual awareness, compassion, strength, and curiosity for knowledge.

"After my creation, I have forgotten almost everything. I remember I am created by God, but I have forgotten I was part of God and how things were before. It is very hazy and dream-like.

"After all the souls in my group were created, we proceed to our godhead. As we enter the godhead, some float to the top layers, some float down to the middle layers, while others sink to the lower layers of the godhead, depending on how they felt after their creation. Those that were joyous and excited remain on the top layer, those that were less joyous go to the middle level, and those that were scared and unhappy sink to the bottom layers. I float to the top second layer."

• "When some parts of God were thrown off in the void, this created anxiety and fear all over the globe of God. All the balls in God began vibrating, expanding, and growing. I see myself going upward to a different plane with my group. I assimilate the Light. Then I move to another plane with the same group, but we all do not move at the same speed. Some take longer and others do it faster. I am moving faster, so I move ahead with the faster ones and we go to another plane, with another vibration and quality, and we assimilate those qualities. It is a process, and it keeps going on. I see seven different planes I go through, and I assimilate those seven qualities.

"After Lucifer and his demons leave, God begins to create. God has already created masters, angels, and the planets, and He is ready to create souls that will inhabit the planets. I give my intent to be created as a soul that will inhabit the planets later. My ball has male and female aspects in it. I am of the female part.

"As God is getting ready to create me, I am afraid of what is going to happen and whether I will be able to fulfill my purpose. I am also excited. God with His intent creates two separate souls from my ball. I feel I am being torn away and we become two separate souls. It is not a nice feeling. I go to the right and the other part goes to the left. There is a connecting cord between us. After my creation, I feel happy and believe I am going to have a nice experience.

"After my creation, God speaks to me. He says He is creating me to bring beauty and harmony to the world. He gives me strength and tells me that He loves me and He will always be with me. There are about one hundred souls created with me. Then we are sent back to our godhead. I go to the upper middle level."

• "I am in God as one with God. I am in the top layers of the middle section. I give my intent to be created as the one who will go to a planet. My ball has male and female characteristics. As God is getting ready to create me, I am anxious, but excited about the unknown. My ball is pulled out from where I was and starts to change shape and split into two globes. These are the male and female parts and they become two separate souls. I am the male aspect of my ball. As He created me, God wrote down a symbol on a page of the Akashic Records.

"After my creation, I feel sad and depressed about being separated from God and not having any sense of my purpose. But at the same time, I am looking forward to what is going to come. I feel strange and incomplete to be separated from the female part of myself. I am wondering how long it will be until we will be brought back together again inside God. We have a connecting cord between us.

"God speaks to me after my creation to comfort me. He tells me that I will have to suffer a lot. In my suffering, I will bring other souls closer to the Light. People will not believe what I will try to tell them. He tells me He loves me and someday I will rejoin Him. He gives me the gifts of endurance, perception, warmth, caring about others, gentleness, sensitivity, patience, and a constant connection with Him.

"Multitudes of souls are created with me. I recognize my present brother in the group of souls created with me. After our creation, we are sent back to our own godhead. As I go back to my godhead, I float down to the middle section and remain there.

"Masters are on the upper levels of the godhead. Some of the very high human beings are also in the upper level. I am in the middle level."

Human Souls Whose Energy Permeates the Whole Godhead

Occasionally, some people report while under hypnosis that after the creation of their soul, they went to a certain part of the godhead, and after a while, their energy permeated through the whole godhead the way masters did, but they were created as human souls. There are very few humans souls that go through the whole godhead. They say that this has to do with their purpose. When their essence permeates the whole godhead, they become one with the masters and the godhead and thus receive all the attributes and strengths of the masters and the godhead.

• "As Lucifer began to rebel, balls of similar affinity began to group together. I am going upward because there are some balls there I want to join. They have some attributes that attract me. It is not a random attraction; there is a pattern here.

"As I look at my ball, there is an awareness of polarity, a male and female aspect in my ball, although it appears homogeneous. Part of my ball has a bluish color, with patches of green, and the other part has a light shade of pink. The quality of the crystalline structure is different in the 'female' aspect, which is finer than in the 'male' aspect of the ball. As I look at the core of God, it also has this polarity. It is the parent ball. There is a sense of boundary between the male and the female aspect, but it is still one ball.

"I have mixed feelings about being created. I feel excited and adventurous yet apprehensive. I am squeezed out of my ball and the male and female halves are separated and created as two separate souls. There is a boundary between the male and female polarity of my ball. God applies pressure on my sphere, and the male and female sides are separated and created as two separate souls. I am the male, or plus, side of my ball.

"There is a feeling of connectedness, almost like sharing, bonding, or holding hands. There is a connecting cord between me and my other part. After my creation, I do not remember much. I know that I came from God, but I forget that I was one with God.

"God tells me that I am going to be a guide for the other souls. I am supposed to remember who I am and to remind others if they forget who they are. He is putting something in me. I feel overwhelmed with what I am supposed to be doing. It is too big a job. I have a feeling of 'How am I going to do it?' It is almost panic.

"As I am released into my godhead after my creation, I remain on the top second layer. After a while, my essence permeates the whole godhead. My energy is purple. The original godhead was gold, but when my purple energy went through the godhead, it became purple.

"I seemed to be aware of myself as a separate soul and also as the whole godhead, a simultaneous awareness. Only about 1 percent of the human souls permeate an entire godhead. My twin flame—the female aspect of my ball—does not go through the whole godhead."

• "I give my intent to be created as a human. God pulls out my ball and squeezes and condenses it and gives me a form. As He is doing it, I feel shaky, tossed around and being shaken. Then I am thrust out. I feel confused for a few seconds. I realize that I am separate out here but still connected to God with a silver cord. I am upset about being pushed out, but soon feel positive, excited, and adventurous. I sense a heavy responsibility.

"After my creation, God speaks to me. He is telling me that I am a pathfinder, a trailblazer. Much is given to me and much is expected from me; He asks me to use my gifts well. I should honor and acknowledge that God is my source, as I will have great challenges and I will be given the strength to meet all these challenges. I should never lose sight of my connection to God. What I will do will have an important effect on other souls and the planet.

"God is telling me I will be a pioneer in the age of consciousness, as we realize that we are all consciousnesses and have a wonderful, infinite mind we can use for our well-being and healing. I will open up the world to consciousness and our connection to God. I will be the one leading souls back 'Home' to the Light, to God. I need to find people who think the way I think and have a similar purpose, and join a group so we can work together to bring change in the world. God tells me He loves me.

"He gives me the gifts of intelligence and curiosity, the desire to serve, deep spiritual awareness, the ability to communicate with people, courage with a capital "C," the ability to see patterns; develop new ideas, concepts, and theories; and to see connections. He also gives me compassion for people, very strong principles, and the integrity to do the right thing.

"After a while, I am released into a godhead. I float up into the top second layer, and after a while my energy permeates through the whole godhead, and I become one with my godhead and the masters in it. This way I can draw strength and power from them when I am on Earth and fulfill my purpose."

Chapter Eight

Formation of Groups in Heaven

According to my hypnotized subjects, God created souls in groups. As souls were created, they came into existence in long strings. As the souls were released into their respective godheads, there were differences between them, depending on how they *felt* about their creation. Some of them came out, drifted, and floated to the upper layers, while others went down a certain distance and stopped, and some went further down. Some of them seemed to sink to the bottom layers. As a result, there was a stratification of souls.

Under hypnosis, people recall that as the individual souls were created, they experienced a variety of feelings. Some felt fear, confusion, rejection, separation anxiety, and a belief that something had gone wrong. They felt they had done something bad and were being punished, but did not know why. They did not remember how things were before their creation and did not understand the creation process. They saw it as a negative, scary, upsetting, and traumatic event. These especially troubled souls got so self-involved that they contracted and folded in on themselves, as if tucking in all their parts so that nothing was sticking out. If the godhead is divided into three layers, then these souls settled at the bottom layer.

Other souls did not remember what happened but did not go through the agony as discussed above. They seemed to be more positive and felt elation, even exaltation, as if saying "I am separate, I am free, and I am ready to begin the work." Of course, at this instant the soul did not know what it was talking about. It had the feeling but not the exact knowledge, because it had just undergone its "first forgetting." It did not remember that it is part of God, nor did it remember it made the decision to create with the rest of God, nor did it remember there was a plan. All it remembered was that it suddenly emerged into separate existence. These joyful souls remained on the top, or inner, layer of the godhead near the core of God. They were expressive and outgoing, and they spread the Light everywhere.

The middle layer souls were happy, but not joyful. They were a little dazed and confused. They spread some Light, but they were not sure what was happening. As we go down the layers, the souls were more inward, more confused, less giving of their Light, until at the bottom layers, all the Light of the souls was turned inward. They were folded in on themselves, self-conscious, and concerned with their survival. They had a misunderstanding of what had happened, along the lines of "I have done something wrong. I am being punished. I have to be really careful. I cannot express myself. I cannot be outgoing. I cannot spread my Light outside."

The surprising thing was that when souls were created, even God did not know which would sink and which would rise. He had an idea how it would go, but He was not sure. So, as He created them, He watched what happened. Where the souls went did not depend on their size but on their feelings. Some of the larger souls sank down to the bottom because they were scared and confused, while some of the smaller souls floated to the top layers of the godhead because they felt joyful, happy, and excited after their creation.

So, when the souls were released after their creation to the godheads, they stratified themselves into layers, depending on how they felt about their creation. There are many, many layers of souls in the Light. But for practical purposes, we can say there are three main layers in a godhead, and each layer can be subdivided into literally hundreds of layers.

According to my hypnotized patients, after the creation of souls, God talked to souls at every level, but He did not say the same thing to each level. For the bottom group, He gave a straightforward message, leaving little chance for confusion. "Pray, study, and try to develop spiritually." His message for the groups higher in the layering increasingly became more complex and more subtle.

For the top group, God's message was, in effect: "Remember to pray. You have access to My power through prayer, through your silver connecting cord to Me. You can channel the Light through yourself and use it in your life. The dark beings, the demons, will have a difficult time trapping or confusing anyone who is filled with the Light. You have the ability to go beyond that which is normal by using the powers of the Light. While living on a planet, you can develop these powers through understanding and diligent practice. Love, compassion, sensitivity to the needs of others, fulfilling the needs of yourself and of others; these gifts you can take with you as you incarnate. They can also be acquired in any individual life if you do not bring them as gifts. In fact, much stronger spiritual development results if you develop them during a lifetime." God also mentioned the possibility of souls developing into God-like beings. "If you live your human life well, you could develop into a God-like being," He said.

After the creation of souls, God told those in the top layers to form groups. He told the next three or four layers, "Soon you will develop and join a group," to prepare them for the idea of developing and joining a group. By the time they were fit to be working in a group, the original levels would go up even more. Even though these souls on the top layers had gone up and were ahead of them, the others had developed enough to join a group. The souls below the top group layers could still do good, constructive work just as those on the top layers. They would not be as sophisticated or knowledgeable, but they would be capable of cooperating and doing effective work.

You see this with young students. In elementary school you have fifth and sixth grade students capable of doing quality work. You know they are bright and articulate, but at home, as far as their parents are concerned, they are just little children. The difference is in the expectation: teachers expect one thing, parents another.

The beginning group members on the top level, who in God's eyes were just "children," were still capable of doing real work. As they grew and developed, their childish characteristics dropped off and they became more developed. Like God, they can do a higher-quality of work. Over a period of time, the fourth, fifth, or sixth layers had moved up, but at the same time the original top group members had developed more and moved even further up.

According to my hypnotized patients, God did not assign individual souls to a particular group, nor did He specify a group's purpose. He simply told them they were to form a group for spiritual development. He outlined the plan for the group's development, for how the groups would work in the Light together, and how the souls within a group would cooperate on a planet. He told the souls to set up the main objectives, to pick out the steps, and to work within the group to achieve those goals.

When a soul determined what it was most interested in or needed to do, it broadcast a signal, and other souls that were reaching the same conclusion were receptive to that broadcast. They got together and went about creating a group, attracting others to the same location. They could be from different godheads. All they had to be was an individually created soul.

Some of the groups that exist are: psychological, scientific, healing, religious, cultural, nutritional, educational, political, artistic, and humanistic. Different groups have different approaches to the spiritual development of human souls. Many groups work in each field, in Heaven and on Earth, all with the same basic interests—that of cultivating a complete and thoroughly developed soul. Here is a description given by one person about the instructions from God on forming a soul group:

- "After the creation of my soul, I feel anxiety and confusion, but overall, I am excited, happy, joyful, and adventurous. God tells me, 'Pray and develop spiritually.

You can draw the power of Light through your connecting cord, and you can overcome any obstacles and cross any barriers. You are going to have special duties, jobs, and assignments. You will form a group without barriers, ignoring any differences, both here in the Light and in the universe. This group will be your functional mechanism and your particular assignment.

"After a while, I go to my godhead and float up to the top third layer. I feel affinity toward certain souls and we get together. First we are six, then seven, and then soon there are eight of us. This is my original group. Some of these souls are here in my current life. The group has grown a lot, and by now we have about two thousand members. The purpose of our group is to help foster the spiritual development of mankind."

Chapter Nine

Planning in Heaven, for a Life on Earth

According to my hypnotized patients, we incarnate on a planet to learn, grow, and evolve, so that we ultimately can perfect ourselves and become one with God. We develop our purpose in the Light (Heaven) as the basis of our incarnation process. The purposes of those souls in the lower layers of the godhead are usually concrete and direct and may involve only personal goals. They may have two or three purposes, which are comparatively small in scale: usually, they are to learn to be compassionate and to avoid violence.

The purposes for the more advanced souls are more complex. They usually have personal and group goals. Their personal purpose may be learning to be more loving toward family members and more compassionate to the poor and those who are suffering. For the souls that belong to a larger group, the objectives encompass higher purposes. The more developed the soul is, the more abstract, generalized, and lofty are its purposes. Advanced souls in a group will have group objectives, and these are usually concerned with effectiveness in transferring knowledge and information between Heaven and Earth as part of an effort to speed up the developmental process for humans.

In Heaven, we try to understand what we need to do to develop. We try to carry back to Earth (or into the universe) the analysis we have done in Heaven. In this manner, spiritual understanding among souls in the universe can be increased, and this can speed up the development process.

For souls belonging to a group, plans are made among the group members to set up ways of helping one another. In contrast, souls that are not part of a group face the prospect of going to Earth alone and going through the developmental process without much help from others. Their development will likely be more haphazard than that of the group members, who will develop faster and more purposefully.

As explained before, not everybody is in a group in Heaven. Eventually, all souls will develop to the point at which they realize they need to join a group. For example, let us say that on Earth there are charitable organizations that use volunteers, but not everyone sees the need to volunteer. It is the same way in Heaven: not everyone feels the need to join a group. Some prefer to remain separate and do not understand how important it is to join a group to support their developmental process.

In Heaven, group members meet in small groups to discuss their individual and group goals. They consider how they can meet both sets of goals in the same life. Some people in a group have similar personal goals, while others have very different ones.

In a small group, perhaps of five, souls discuss their individual goals and how their life can be molded to meet these individual goals as well as the group goals. But say one soul in this group has personal objectives that do not mesh well with the objectives of the other four. This soul can go to another group in which its objectives might mesh better. It is a process of building small subgroups based on an affinity of goals. After the main goal has been set, you start to talk with individual group members until you find someone whose development process and yours mesh well. Then you add other small-group members until you have one or two dozen people, whose group interaction on Earth will be beneficial to all. Even though there might be one thousand to twelve hundred souls in the main group, in a particular life you might work with five to thirty-five group members because, their specific developmental goals mesh with yours. They will compose your main working group while on the planet during your incarnation.

In terms of planning a life on a planet, first the determination of individual goals must be made. This is done in Heaven by talking with advanced souls and with souls on your level, and even with souls below your level, as you try to determine what things you need to work on and how you should go about it. When this determination is made, the next step is to define the group purpose. This is decided at major group meetings held every lifetime or perhaps every couple of lifetimes. A series of subgroup meetings are also held to discuss purposes.

In the small groups, souls decide many things, such as what the coming life on Earth should be like. These details include who will be born where and into what culture, what events will take place, how we will end up together, how we will interact, what we will try to achieve, and how we can fulfill our individual and group goals. Group members can incarnate in different states or different countries and still work together. In some cases they can incarnate on different planets and still work together when conditions are favorable for communicating from one planet to another.

Unfortunately, even when we plan for good results, it does not always work out that way. Sometimes plans go wrong, because everybody has free will, which means, once incarnated, they can change their plans; and there often is demonic interference. So not everything planned in Heaven turns out well on the planet.

The important point is that we plan *everything* before incarnation, according to my patients. We choose our parents, spouses, children, and other key people in our life. We choose our profession and plan the key events in our life. Not only do we plan happy and productive events and situations, but we also plan unhappy and trying times, even tragedies, so we can grow spiritually and evolve. We choose a spectrum of gifts and skills, such as spirituality, intelligence, determination, compassion, strength, perseverance, intuition, creativity, and musical and other artistic abilities as well as psychic ability.

Some gifts we bring from Heaven and are born with them, others we develop on Earth. We make that choice in Heaven. Some of the gifts that can be developed on Earth are psychic gifts, perceptions, and writing and speaking skills. For example, we can develop speaking ability with practice, but we cannot develop feeling at ease in front of a crowd; that is a gift. Resolving karmic problems can help improve this problem, but we still need the natural ability to be at ease in front of a large group. A gift such as high intelligence has to be inborn. When there is a limitation about what can be brought, a person can cleverly bring those gifts that cannot be developed and improved while on Earth.

Under hypnosis, people described Heaven in two ways: as a sphere or a pyramid. (See figures 1 and 2 on pages 46, 47.) In the spherical model, the whole of Heaven is round, divided into multitudes of small pyramidal sections all around the core of God. Each pyramidal section or godhead is responsible for watching over several universes. In the spherical model, God is in the core of the globe and godheads (pyramidal sections) are all around God, from the edge of the core to the periphery of God. In the pyramidal model, God is seen at the top of that pyramidal section (godhead). In the spherical model, souls go to the outer edge of the globe of Light after death to get cleansed, review their life, and rest; then they go to the inner section of the Light (Heaven). In the pyramidal model, people enter Heaven at the lower level, after death, and then go to the upper level of the Light. It depends on how narrow or wide their perception is.

Souls that are less developed are not restricted to any area in the Light. They can go anywhere. But generally they choose to stay toward the outer layer of the sphere, or, in a pyramidal model, toward the bottom layer of the pyramid. The most advanced souls tend to cluster around their godhead. No soul is restricted from going anywhere, but they have natural preferences, depending on their vibrations. Less-developed souls have slower vibrations, so they tend to remain at the outer or lower part of the godhead where the vibrations are slower, while highly evolved souls have faster vibrations and tend to remain at the inner or higher level of the Light in a godhead. The souls closest to the godhead and those in the middle teach souls below them, helping them to advance. Souls closest to the godhead may be working with the souls in the middle layer today and working with the souls in the bottom layer tomorrow and learning from souls that are on still higher levels.

Once the general plans are made, souls move to a "departure area," which is like an observation lounge on the outer or lower level of Heaven. There souls tune into life in the universe and choose exactly where they will go, how they will put their life plan into effect, and with which people. The final stage of planning and selecting is done at the departure area. Once we have picked a place on a planet (it is not always Earth), we select the culture, continent, nation, people, and parents to provide the characteristics we need. My patients say that we plan the month, day, and time of birth, according to astrological signs.

Once the planning is done, souls are ready to incarnate. Not all souls in a soul group leave at the same time. They leave in the order in which they need to be born. The one that is going to be oldest in a given time period on Earth departs first, incarnates, and goes through the growing-up process. If they need to be younger than their peers, then they leave Heaven a few years later. We also plan when and how we are going to die. We choose to die with a disease that is karmic. Sometimes a soul will enter a body that is destined to die before birth. For example, souls that formerly were concentration camp guards who killed many people, including babies, may plan a stillbirth, miscarriage, or abortion as a way to balance out their past negative actions, according to my patients.

Sample descriptions of planning for a current life, as given by my hypnotized patients, follow here:

• "During the review of my life in Heaven, just before the current life, my counselors, some of whom I think are masters, help me. They ask me if I really want to go through it. I have a choice to work on one problem in one life or to work on all the problems in one life. I tell them I want to do as much as possible. They say that first I need to study. After I accomplish this, then I will have another counseling session to see if my soul is ready for the intended life. The counselors, who are masters, want me to visit their domain, so I visit each of them. Each teaches me and gives me gifts and knowledge that uniquely theirs to help me with my life mission on Earth.

"I am involved in a lot of preparation for this lifetime. I watch over my mom and dad, making sure that they will meet each other and get married. I chose them as parents before, a few embodiments ago. I have some karmic problems to work out with them. I also chose them for genetic purposes, to provide me with certain artistic qualities in this life, that is, intuition and the ability to hear from my mother; musical talents, especially vocal, from my father, so I can do prayers and decrees. These had to be developed so I could manifest the word of God through my voice.

"I planned my multiple marriages as learning experiences to enable me to understand humankind. They were partly my karma, that is, the result of problems from past lives, but I chose them to learn faster. Some of the people involved have my missing soul parts, so by resolving the issues from past lives, I can get those parts of myself I lost in those past lives back from them to heal. My marriages were short, but it was my choice. I had the choice to stay married to these people for a long time to work out karmic problems or to be married for a short time. I chose the short-term marriages.

"I did some planning for the sake of other people. In one marriage I had to experience a severe trauma to bring me closer to God faster; it was an inner awakening, connecting me to God. My current marriage is part of the plan too, as both of us are closer to God. We are like two pillars supporting each other in the house of God. I also chose to have and raise my son. Through my suffering I will learn to be very compassionate.

"I sense this can be my last embodiment. The

counselors are telling me that it is not going to be easy, especially being with my parents. I have to be very brave. They are showing me everything the evil forces will do. If you think Satan and demons have devices, be assured that beings of Light have better devices. My counselors tell me I will have skills to draw the Light to me without having possession of the Light, because I am going to be born in a country where nobody will believe in God. I will be born with zero knowledge of prayers and God.

"I have chosen to be a woman in Russia. I chose that country to balance some karmic problems. I chose the time of my birth down to the second. Everybody chooses their time of birth. It has to do with the lining up of the planets. The planets form certain configurations that will affect the physical forms of our body, bones, skull, and physical appearance, all of which will affect the outcome of our life. It is a very scientific setup.

"It is as if 'meridians' of the planets are connected to 'meridians' of our body. This has something to do with our blueprints, and it involves mathematical calculations. The connections between the patterns of the soul and its nervous system are related to configurations in the planetary system.

"I have chosen the time for my birth to be between 6:00 A.M. and 9:00 A.M., and no later than 9:00 A.M., because my Moon is supposed to be in line with the constellation Libra. This is very important for me. Libra is an astrological sign of beauty, and I have a longing for beauty so I can express it in my physical life. My birth date also has a meaning in numerology.

"The counselors tell me I will be especially guarded and protected and I will have some kind of device like a Light box around me. The counselors say that a lot of missions I will start will be aborted. The missions are for my practice and learning, but my main mission is to bring Light to Earth.

"I will use my body for blessing, and when I touch a lot of people through my profession, people will get blessings and heal. I will have healing hands. I will also challenge the darkness with the power of God, and I will bring love, because not many people know what love is.

"I planned to do something that has to do with a constitution, with the laws of mankind. Some of the laws were made for barbaric ages and they should be changed for the golden age to come. What was good before cannot be good now because the generations are different today. For example, during the American Revolution, it was okay to be armed. It was perfect for that time because people without guns could not defend themselves. Now it is not necessary for people to have arms, because guns are not for peace, but for destruction. Now kids and others can get hold of them to kill themselves or others. People still claim their right to have guns because this has been so for hundreds of years.

"The law about abortion is another example. People say it is a human right, but there is much more that people need to know. From Heaven's point of view, abortion is never right, because if conception occurred, it was planned in Heaven. There is no conception by accident. It could not manifest without plans or divine intercession. If it be without plan, then the pregnancy will be terminated naturally through a miscarriage or a stillbirth. If we have the knowledge that conception is planned, this means everything is prepared and taken care of. Then it will be easier to cope.

"At the same time, it has to be a mother's free will. Nobody has a right to judge or punish her, because free will for every soul is the law of God. We have to educate people about what is right and wrong from the heavenly perspective, but we cannot force them to make a choice. It has to be their free will. However, nobody can escape from their negative actions. These have to be corrected in future lives, not as a punishment by God or heavenly beings, but through a person's own choice to balance their negative actions. We have to stay away from judging and hurting those who are involved in abortion, because they will have to face their own negative actions in Heaven and they will be their own harshest judge.

"For the laws to change, people have to come to a higher awareness. Light beings respect human rights because they treat humans as divine beings. People need this heavenly knowledge as to why keeping guns today is different than it was two hundred years ago; they need to know why abortion takes away human rights and free will. It is really the dark forces that are snatching free will. It is not a person exerting her free will, but dark beings in her who are influencing her to go through abortion.

"I have planned to pray and do decrees. There are various types of prayers to use at different times. They can be soft, loud, or quiet, and other times you have to cry from the bottom of your soul to reach God. All of these prayers work, but it depends on how much you put into them. Soft prayers sometimes can open up your heart. Your love, devotion, humble forgiveness, and your willingness to serve God—these can all contribute to the effectiveness of prayers. You can talk to God forever if you are comfortable with the idea.

"It is similar to when you have to get to a certain destination by driving a car. If you drive at twenty miles per hour, you will probably see a lot of scenery, but it will take a long time to get there. If you go faster, then you have to be focused, alert, and concentrate on reaching your destination. Similarly, if your prayer is 'slow,' it might reach God slowly. If you pray often, you get better results. If you pray for a longer time, you can also get better results. If your mind is concentrated on God, this also acts like a prayer. If you repeat prayers, they will reach a higher level. Mantras help to penetrate and break the density between Earth and Heaven.

"After I have prepared for my next life, I go to a grand palace of Light. There they are preparing my body for protection. This 'palace' is like a laboratory of Light. My body is checked to determine how well I will resist the darkness when I am born in Russia. There is a lot of darkness there because people do not believe in God and do not pray.

"First, the heavenly beings examine all the aspects of my being for strengths and weaknesses, and they check me for my vulnerabilities. They write down all the information. When they find the weak and vulnerable parts in my being, they shield those areas. This process takes a couple of months. They recharge certain parts of me and put the protective shields over me. These are made of Light, but are hard like a walnut shell.

"I study books about God and other topics; then I go through some courses. I see a place like a study hall with a long table at which a lot of people are studying with me. I think these are the people who will incarnate in the same country. We all have similar goals and purposes for that country. We are a big group of hundreds of people. I also work with thousands of souls in my group and other groups. I teach others who are at a lower level than I. I teach them about what I am going to do and what they have to do. I am in a leadership position with this group.

"I am also planning goals with my group. We are planning to bring changes in our country, such as overturning the Communist Party. This will be done on many levels. The main plan we are working on is not political; it is to bring spirituality and the word of God to Russia. If everybody will Light up with spirituality, it will change everything, including the politics. We plan to meet with different group members on Earth (or in Heaven when we go to sleep) and work toward these goals.

"I planned to come to you for my healing and spiritual awakening. You and I made plans to unlock something as a next step. I see we will work together to help people. With our abilities combined, we can do a lot of good work. Important work is waiting for us and we have to get ready. We have to prepare for this, because in three years in this lifetime, we will have a deadline. We will have a chance to do something important and all our work will be paid off. I have chosen the gifts of healing, love, patience, and integration."

• "I am in Heaven, planning my current life. I see souls that are going to be my father and mother. They are already married and are sleeping on Earth, but their souls are here. We are focusing on India, where I am going to be born; afterwards I will emigrate to America. I see a meeting take place in which the time and place of my birth are determined. My characteristics are decided on for that life. I am aware of my personal astrology. The placement of my Moon is important. The best combination of the alignments of my Moon and Sun have been decided to bring out certain traits in my personality.

"The birth month has also been decided. The placement of the Sun has to deal with the balance in this life. Balance and discernment are supposed to be my main characteristics. My birth will be in the month of October, which is Libra and deals with balance. The date has been decided, almost as a mathematical equation. The next thing determined is the placement of the Moon; this will give more characteristics. Now it narrows down to the number of possible days during which my birth can occur. During the next couple years, the position of the outer planets will change. That will set the characteristics of the entire generation and people. But exactly what will take place will be determined by the planetary influences.

"I see the planning that occurs when parents are involved. On Earth, they have a sense of when conception is supposed to happen. At some level, they know what is going to take place, and that is the time they come together in the physical act of sex so conception can take place. Even cycles of fertility are taken into account. The angels that do these calculations are specialists. My parents are instructed as to the quality of the child they are going to have and what they need to bring through the child (me). This type of planning and instructing goes on for all parents, but not all parents have the advantage of making it happen. Some of them are in the denser levels, so they do not get this information clearly. This causes problems, because they do not have clear knowledge of the purpose of the child being conceived.

"Parents are given knowledge about when to conceive. But there is an uncertainty here, because it depends on the free will of the parents and how much they are aware of the plans. When we come to Earth in conception and then as we go through the pregnancy, there are other possibilities for the determination of the day and the time of birth. The angels affect the mother's womb and try to cause things to happen at certain times. I sense that in some pregnancies, the plan is not always followed and the fetus gets aborted. Because of the influences of dark forces, not everything happens the way it is supposed to. I get the sense of conception of those who have planned for certain purpose, and of those that are karmic, but also planned. I see events dealing with chance meetings, like rapes, where karma is involved.

"I am inside a chamber in Heaven and do not have a form. I look like a ball of Light. My next life is going to be important. I see that having an awareness of making changes on the planet and the use of prayers will be important. There are others who are guiding me in making my plans. These are the angels, other higher beings, and my higher self, all of whom are aware of my next step and what needs to be done.

"I plan major events for my coming life. The work I will do is connected with science. Major events are planned, but how I accomplish them is up to me. After a certain age, I will be introduced to spirituality.

"My first marriage is planned. This marriage is not for karmic reasons, but to fulfill duty. My second marriage is to resolve karma and is not supposed to be as bad. It depends on the choice of the other person and how she decides to deal with it.

"My choice of career is consistent with my life plan. One of the lessons I am supposed to learn is humility and simplicity. Teaching and writing books are part of the plan. The type of the books I am supposed to write is up to me. The placement of Mercury in my birth chart is used to influence that. There will be two phases to my career. In the second phase, I am to work on spiritual things. This involves some type of education and the writing of books.

"There were to be some children but this did not

happen. The plan got derailed. I will go through some agony about not having children. This problem was created by some of my earlier lives, being a warrior who caused the destruction of villages, and from lives in which I did not look after my children.

"I am in a room in Heaven. I wear a gold and white robe and am writing or transcribing something. Real work needs to be done in Heaven, and I help with this work. There is a task assigned and I am good at something that looks like mathematics. I am helping by writing about that.

"I see master beings and some archangels. There are many souls from my group here. We are planning group goals, like participating in prayers and decrees. We have an inner link in which we form a mandala in which you have all these points and each point is a soul; when you join them together with a line, you get a geometrical shape.

"Our geometric shapes seem to be circles and triangles. The circles suggest we affect the whole planet; the triangles represent the direction of the energy of the planet. Each person has a particular purpose and we provide assistance to one another. For example, if I were to 'fall' and be influenced by the dark side, it would affect some of the other people linked to me. They would have to be stronger and pull me up. Being together in a group is like being on a ship: we sail or sink together.

"Here in Heaven I go through schools to learn. I am learning to write. There are classes on reading and speaking. There is also a class on keeping your heart open, on how to communicate with a group of people, and on how to get through to people without being threatening to them. I seem to be taking a class on the history of the planet; this involves its civilizations and what the planet has been through. There is also a class in taking care of younger souls that have not evolved. All these classes are conducted by masters and angels.

"I also teach here, instructing in subjects such as math, science, and astronomy, although I do not know anything about astronomy in this life. I have the feeling that in some of my lifetimes, I was a well-known mathematician. I also go down to the lower levels to teach. All of this seems to be taking place almost continuously. Even now, as I am here on Earth, part of me is somewhere else teaching others, even on other planets.

"I get a sense of receiving a gift or blessings from the godheads Vishnu and Shiva. I get a rose from a Divine Mother figure in the godhead of Vishnu. The rose is supposed to be a reminder of where I came from, so when I get lonely, I can receive that special sense of love from God and not feel dejected or discouraged.

"I get a sword from one of the archangels. The sword is charged with energy to help me cut through density and to see clearly. I also get a circle of Light, like a Vishnu sudarshan chakra, that is to be invoked for the clearing away of demons. About three years ago in this life, I started invoking that, but then I stopped.

"I choose gifts of writing; the ability to talk to a group of people; telepathic communication; and the ability to talk and broadcast ideas to different people. I also chose the gift of clairvoyance, but it is not to be operational all the time. I will have the choice to block it. I will have the gifts of clear seeing, healing, wisdom, love, peace, harmony, perseverance, and determination.

"I have planned to live a long life, living until perhaps age eighty-eight, and to die in such a way that it will balance my karma. My meeting with you and doing this work is part of my plan. We met in Heaven three years ago in spirit and confirmed the plans. You and I have important work to do in the future.

"This can be my last life depending on how I do, but there is no guarantee. This is a very important time for everybody to be born on this planet. There will be a lot of Light on Earth, but there will also be a lot of darkness."

• "I am at the Akashic Records. I see my life blueprints I prepared for the current life while I was in Heaven before coming to Earth. They look like interconnecting lines that indicate where I will go and people I will contact. I see some of the physical weaknesses and strengths I will have in this life. I plan to have mental and physical problems; I will suffer with them so I can resolve karmic problems from past lives. I plan to have vision problems so I can appreciate the Light even more. I planned to come to you for treatment, so I could heal as well as learn, and then to talk to other people about it. I plan to learn about the dark beings and how they create symptoms; this will enable me to appreciate the Light even more. I plan to try to act more in accord with Light in my life to be an example for others. I chose the doctor who delivered me, because I knew he would use forceps during my birthing, a process that would weaken my brain and make it possible for more physical problems to come into my life. I also chose my other psychiatrist.

"I chose my mother, because we have been together in many lives and because I would need her for support during my sickness. I picked my father so I could resolve my karmic problems with him. I planned to be born in America, because my parents will be there.

"I chose the day, date, and time of my birth. I chose to come as a Gemini, because I felt alone in many lives, and having a twin [as an astrological sign, Gemini is represented as twins] will make me feel comfortable; I am also drawn to my twin's perception, insight, and intelligence. It is important for me to seek out the companionship of other people. I planned to be born when Jupiter is close to Earth, because it is a planet of strength. It will give me inner strength to deal with my problems. I decided to be born in the middle of the day as a sign of the fact that as I would be dealing with so much karma and problems from past lives, it would all come to me as if it were a central part of everything thrown at me in my life.

"I selected the day of my birth, because Robert Kennedy would be assassinated on that day. He and I were brothers in a past life. As he was forced out of life on that day, it was appropriate for me to go into life on the same day.

"I planned to go into science and become a physicist. I will try to shed Light on the nature of the physical universe and help humanity reach new levels of civilization. I will research and discover new sources of energy. I also planned to be a teacher in science.

"I planned to take care of reptiles like iguanas, because I have been involved with reptiles in many, many lifetimes. I worked closely with them during human evolution. They were considered sacred, and I have close spiritual ties with them. In this life they have given me more energy and the desire to keep fighting for life. I decided to grow plants when I have my own home because plants are an expression of life and beauty and bring in positive energy.

"It is part of my plan to seek marriage and have children, but it is not definite if this will happen or not. I planned this with the soul that may be my wife, but we might get sidetracked if life gets too difficult. I planned to have four children. Three of them are old souls that will benefit from having me as a father, learning from the suffering I have gone through and the insights I have gained.

"I planned to come to you for treatment. I see many of us meeting in Heaven and planning. There are some higher beings with us who will be your guides. We are discussing the difficulties of meeting like this on Earth. We met again in Heaven after your book was published [*Remarkable Healings*, 1997] to plan how we are to get together. You will heal my mental and physical conditions. I see myself healing completely. Part of my story will be published in different articles. My mom and I may write a book about my problems and my healing. I see myself on television because of my discoveries.

"I am part of a group in Heaven that tries to develop Light in themselves and live in such a way as to show the Light to others. I also have group goals. I will live somewhat in the Light so other people may follow. They will see my kindness and goodness. I will not keep what I have gone through in the past a secret, and people will be inspired by that.

"Different shields are put on different parts of my being for protection. I have a small white shield behind my shoulders. I also have a protective shield over my liver to protect it from different medications I will have to take. This looks like a white pyramid with an energy source. There are also shields over my ears to protect me from words spoken by the dark beings.

"Another shield is placed around my thyroid gland in my neck. It is a diamond shield that protects me from dark beings trying to drain off my energy. There is a shield around my heart to protect me from having too many dark thoughts. A shield around my brain will reduce the effect of some of the head injuries I will have in my life.

"I am planning this to be my last life depending on how I do. But I have also planned a future life just in case I do not succeed in this one. I am planning to die when I am in my eighties. I have chosen to die from the collapse of my arteries, because it seems appropriate after having had so much heartache in my life."

• "I am standing near a beautiful building, which looks like a university library. It is made of crystalline Light. I am in the center of the library, in a room that goes in four directions, like a cross. I see myself sitting at a drafting board preparing my life blueprints like an architect. I see a flow chart: it starts out at the left side and moves to the right. As I get to the right side, the things I am responsible for or have to do increase.

"The chart begins when I am born. Then I grow up and become me. I have increasingly greater tests and responsibilities as I go to the right side of the blueprint. I see different schools I will go to and my various projects. I have achieved most of them in this life as I planned. There are some places where I did things differently, but I think 80 percent of it turned out as I planned. The blueprint is like a paper scroll and the ink is purple. The plans are written down, but if I look at it, I can see pictures in the blueprint.

"During the early days in my present life, I see a lot of plans concerning music. Playing musical instruments and understanding musical language are big foci for me until the age of fifteen. I planned to have music open my heart and connect me with God. When I sing and play music, it puts me into a state of consciousness that takes my mind to a higher spiritual level.

"Pursuing athletics was also part of my plan, because it is a way to connect with the higher spiritual level. Through running and exercising, I see Light filling my body, and I feel I can almost fly. I remember now that during one race in this life I was far behind. I prayed for the Light from Heaven to come into my body, and it felt like Light came into my body and pushed my body forward faster than I could have otherwise achieved. I passed everybody and won the race. Now I realize that, even as a child, without knowing it consciously, I knew how prayers worked. As I look back from Heaven, I can see as I was running and praying, a golden Light came from Heaven into my body and pushed me faster and faster. It looks like my higher self joined and helped me. Physical exercise opens up different channels and energy centers in our bodies, just as music does.

"When you plan a life, you choose different things to enable yourself to become more of who you are. Sometimes you have to work on things you need to improve. I see that all the things I planned follow a simple system: to open the heart and all the channels and energy centers and to realize my divine self in the physical body. I planned to accomplish this by pushing beyond what I was capable of at that time. In other words, I planned to expand myself.

"I also planned to be in a marching band to learn how to be a part of a bigger group and to be in harmony with it. Marching in a single direction while playing an instrument would enable me to learn work discipline with a group. I also planned to do painting, drawing, and sculpting, and I have done all these. A lot of things I planned would help build my self-confidence and self-worth. I see in my blueprints that I planned general objectives and goals for each year, and that there were certain specific tasks designed to help me achieve those goals.

"I chose my mother for many reasons. I had a past-life connection with her and some unresolved issues. I needed to be with her again so we could resolve things. So far we have resolved many issues. I chose her also because of my grandfather (her father), who taught me many skills; he was also a very spiritual person. He lived on a farm, which was very important to me because I needed to feel the freedom that comes with wide-open spaces.

"I chose my father because of his mechanical expertise. I needed exposure to that; also, I wanted to help resolve our problems from other lives, and he needed me in his life to help him to open up spiritually. I feel very strongly that I chose my mom and dad more than they chose me, because I needed to be in certain places at certain times to do certain things. I planned my first marriage and the divorce, because I chose to give my wife a chance to resolve different problems from the past.

"My second marriage was also planned. It is so powerful and emotional that it takes over my physical body and makes it hard for me to talk about. I see my second marriage as a grand design on paper. I see a circle and rays of Light coming out of it, and my wife and I are inside this circle as pillars of Light. As I look at my blueprint after my second marriage, I see it lit with beautiful, white Light. It is like the dawning of a new age for us. We will work on resolving all our problems from the beginning of the time. We have to resolve all our past-life issues together. We have already worked on this many times and will continue to work on them.

"We have planned to do hypnotherapy. That is where we are at this point. Three more things under hypnotherapy will come into the picture later on. The goals that are achieved are written in purple, but hypnotherapy is written in gold, meaning it is like an illumination or awakening.

"Architecture is also indicated. It has to do with building consciousness on a higher level. I see the plans for this like a book or a very detailed seminar. It will be related to gradual systematic enlightenment steps for people, so they can be enlightened on all levels of their being in a short time. I see that at every step there will be 'exams' and that the person cannot go to the next level of understanding until he gets 100 percent on that exam.

"I see a design for health-care practitioners and people doing hypnotherapy. I see a series of hypnotherapy sessions designed as lessons, but in a new way that nobody is doing now. It is something taught to hypnotherapy practitioners to use in their private practice. I see myself teaching this new approach in a large classroom.

"The next plan I see has to do with physical exercise as it corresponds to spiritual exercise, such as stretching or yoga. It is a series of exercises that can be put on video or taught in a classroom. The exercises combine physical movements and spiritual visualizations to increase the amount of Light that can flow into the body. They can increase the energy flow to the body to push away darkness by a combination of willpower and physical postures or movements. With exercise and breathing performed at a certain rate, people can get access to another dimension or level of their beings.

"I see columns on my blueprints. They do not necessarily represent specific years, but stages of growth. It is as though I designed a specific series of growth steps. The next column is in ruby and has six lines. The first line has to do with the heart and love. I get the overpowering sense of divine love. It has to do with focusing on a ruby Light within the heart, with how to make it more powerful within one's being, and with how to radiate this into the world for constructive uses and with how to send it to other people.

"The second line has to do with friendship. The general picture I receive has to do with how to develop friendship with people. This line has a specific guideline, spelled out in a book, including all the types of instructions such as etiquette and procedures for developing friendships. I feel like everything I am describing here can be put in a form of a book or video. These are graduated steps, marked in different colors and themes, and they do not necessarily conform to an exact time line.

"The third line is in ruby blue and has to do with the techniques of communicating and working with Heaven. It has different guidelines for communicating with the guides, angels, and God. In the previous line, the information was more Earth-related; this one is higher up.

"The fourth line has to do with nutrition, charging liquid, foods, and nutrients with spiritual Light. I see guidelines for infusing greater amounts of Light into foods and how this will raise the vibrations of the body.

"The fifth line has to do with music and the importance of sound and vibrations in the physical world. I see instructions for producing and playing back the vibrations of the etheric world, putting them in different rooms of a house for different purposes. For example, I see a house with music speakers in each corner of the floor and ceiling. This is a new music theory, using the effect of sound in a new way within a room.

"The sixth line has to do with jewelry. Certain types of jewelry can be spiritual devices worn on the body, like radio receivers that can amplify the energy of people. I see different types of crystals used in bracelets. There is also something like a headband that goes around the third eye (brow chakra). It allows you to focus in another dimension.

"The next thing is so much higher than what I have described so far, I'm not certain if my human mind can comprehend it. This line is not a color. It is white or crystal. There is no physical way of describing the next line. I feel that when I am working on this line, I will not have my physical body. It may mean ascending to and working from another dimension in the Light. It is overwhelming. It is going to be my last life if I do it right.

"I chose to have gifts of speaking, communication, healing, music, drawing, painting, physical power, athletic ability, writing, psychic insights, and the knowledge of how to produce movies. People can receive knowledge just by watching movies.

"I have planned the day, date, and time of my birth. There were two different dates on which I could be born. Each has a slightly different astrology that can bring out different things in me. I see one date looking dark. If I was born on that date, dark beings would have more influence on me. The other date is brightly lit. It is the actual date on which I was born. Figuring the birth date is like a mathematical equation. It is as if there is a giant computer that can figure out all the different influences of the different magnetic poles of the different planets. I do not understand it.

"I see an astrology chart; when I was planning my life, I had an understanding of this chart from the guides. These guides are the heavenly specialists in astrology. They explained to me the significance of all the different possibilities of being born on a particular day, date, and time.

"I sense that I planned everything, down to the minute and second of my birth. A being stands next to me and explains it. We are looking at my chart on a table. The being has a gold pointer and indicates different details, symbols, and instructions. He is making sure I understand them. He is like an architect, constructing a building. He understands the sequence of what happens so that the building—'my life'—comes together.

"I have also planned group goals. The ultimate overall group goal has to do with divine love. These group goals are very similar to the different books I plan to write, as I described before."

• "I am in a glowing white room. There are two wise beings dressed in white robes. They have long white hair and beards. Everything is glowing here. I see a time line pictograph. It is a time line with pictures of different ages; there are spaces between the pictures, so you have an overview of the plan but not every detail of it. As I look at the pictures, information comes to my mind.

"It appears that I planned to be born without a father for the purpose of achieving a karmic balance. I abandoned him in another life, so in this life he will abandon me. I chose my mother to resolve karmic issues. I planned to marry my husband for karmic balancing and also for support during my spiritual pursuits.

I chose to have my daughter. It was a mutual agreement: we chose each other because we have been together before. I feel we have a soul connection. We have to work out karma together, and later I will help her with her life purpose. I planned to be a loner to develop inner strength and self-reliance.

"I also planned to come to you for healing and inner spiritual awakening. I see that you and I are meeting in Heaven, planning to do a lot of work. We are going to do our own work, but our paths will cross a lot. We also met in Heaven before I called you for this appointment. It was a wake-up call, and I had an inner drive to come to you. I feel we have worked together in past lives and may work together again. I will write two books about the knowledge I am receiving through these sessions and the knowledge that will come to me later; I also will teach. I see myself traveling a lot in the future.

"I plan to develop new healing techniques. As I heal and my awareness expands further, I am going to be able to receive different healing techniques from Heaven, using color, vibration, and sound. I am going to pioneer these new techniques and will open up a healing foundation. I did similar healings in Atlantis, and the knowledge will come to me in this life, later, when the time is right.

"I have chosen to be a Virgo because of its attributes, that is, the analytical mind, preciseness, and organizational abilities. With vibrational healings, you have to be precise. I have chosen the day, date, and the time of my birth because of some specific placement of the planets and their influences. There are beings in Heaven who are experts in astrology. You tell them what you want to achieve and they tell you in what planetary placement you will have the best chance to achieve your goals. Selecting the day and time of birth is a fine tuning. I planned to live a long life and die at ninety. I will not look physically old or sick, but I will have matured a lot. I see myself lying down, leaving my body voluntarily when my work is done, rather than dying of sickness or old age. It may be because of me praying for the violet flame.

"I have chosen several gifts for this life, such as love, compassion, perfectionism, empathy, organizational skills, and preciseness. I have chosen to open up all my psychic gifts later in life. I feel like they are there, but are turned off right now and will open up later. I have also chosen the gift of hands-on healing and will develop this later. I will develop the gifts of writing, speaking, and healing later.

"I plan group goals with my group, too. I am in a group meeting. There are about thirty people in it. I feel you are there too, Dr. Modi. We are planning to bring more techniques, more information, and more Light to the world. We will take spiritual knowledge and healing to the next level. We will bring true and undistorted knowledge to the Earth. Our group has people everywhere in different parts of the world. We chose it to be that way, so if one person cannot succeed in one place, somebody else will succeed elsewhere.

"I am in an auditorium with hundreds of people. I sense a familiarity with a lot of people, but I do not recognize them. A master being is speaking. It feels like a pep rally, a speech of encouragement. I think his name is Saint Germaine, an ascended master.[1] He is saying: 'Humanity's consciousness is expanding. This is our opportunity to bring more Light and new ways of healing to Earth. This is the time for the great leap in humanity. The more Light we can bring in, the greater our potential. We must be steadfast in our conviction and bring forth this new Light—the "violet flame"—and new ways of healing and transformation to all of the creation like never before.'

"I am in a laboratory, where guides put different protection shields on parts of my body. Lying down on

---

[1.] The name "Saint Germaine" is commonly used to denote a spiritual personage understood to be an ascended master, of which there are many. That means one who formerly was a human being but who has evolved to a spiritual state beyond that. Saint Germaine is believed to have incarnated, voluntarily, a number of times in human history, most recently in France in the late eighteenth century under his present name. Increasingly, many psychics claim to be in contact with Saint Germaine, who, they say, works constantly on humanity's behalf to further its spiritual awakening. He plays an important role in the dispensation of the "violet flame."

a table, I feel I am in an operating room. There are Light beings who are wearing white robes and who look like surgeons. They test my body with a wand for weak areas and put special protective shields on those areas.

"They are putting a pink shield around my heart, because I tend to be oversensitive. They put a blue shield over my reproductive areas; they put a green shield on the back of my head and around my sinuses and throat. They put two small blue shields under my feet for protection. I also see a yellow shield on my eyes and also on each hand, and there is a golden radiant shield all around me. It is like I am in a cocoon. It's funny, but I feel like I am a walking shield.

"As I am getting ready to go down in the body on Earth, I see a group of people here with me, including my daughter. I see the ascended masters Kuthumi and Saint Germaine. I think I have a soul connection with them because I see a connecting cord going from me to them. They are telling me, 'Be careful down there. It is a rough world. We wish you love.' You are here too. Your soul must be traveling here from Earth. You are saying, 'I will see you later. We have a lot of work to do.' I also hear Jesus saying, 'Go in love, my child.' My guide, Eleanor, is also here.

"They are telling me that, although I have made all these detailed plans, I will forget them when I go into the body; but not to worry, because I will be reminded at different times. Different events will trigger the memories. They are saying to me to go in love and they will see me when I return."

Chapter Ten

Making the Transition from Heaven to Earth

According to my hypnotized patients, after planning the next life in detail, the soul is ready to make its transition or descent from Heaven to Earth. People give different representations of the process of descending. Some mention stepping out of Heaven and floating down, reaching the planet and then entering the mother's womb and the fetus. Other people say they feel like they have wings like angels as they start from the Light, and that they spiral down through a great pathway until they land on Earth. Then the wings disappear and they enter the fetus.

Another way people claim to descend is by stepping into a tunnel, which is their connecting silver cord, sliding through it, and popping into the body. Some mention the connecting cord is already there and they simply slide down through it. Others report that as they float downward, their cord comes into existence behind them.

When souls come down through their connecting cord, the cord protects them. Other times a beam of Light accompanies their descent, providing the protection. Some choose to move quickly and unexpectedly, so the demons do not know when they are coming. Less-developed souls are more worried and fearful about demonic influences, so they often come in through the cord to avoid these influences. Some of the more evolved souls are brighter and less scared (or maybe overconfident) and choose to float down outside the silver cord, which follows them. Some souls are followed by demons, while others get attached or entrapped by them as they come down. The souls can also pick up human spirits while they are descending. Demonic influences can interfere with a soul's plan and can keep it from carrying out its goals. It may even lead to being killed or dying ahead of the time planned.

Most people recall feeling anxious, scared, and resigned about leaving Heaven to incarnate on Earth. They know they have to, but they do not want to. Very few souls feel happy or joyful about leaving Heaven; when they do, their thoughts are mostly about the prospect of doing good work and making a difference on the planet.

According to the heavenly beings, many things can go wrong while souls come down, but entering the wrong body is not one of them. They claim it does not happen. The following are a few of the reports given by my hypnotized patients about how they made their transition from Heaven to Earth and into their bodies:

- "I am getting ready to come down. The details about the time and day of conception and birth are already worked out. Conception is about to take place. The tube of Light, or connecting cord through which to descend, is being established. I am looking at my final goals and blueprints. My parents are in the background. I get some last-minute advice and blessings from different beings, including some masters. There are people all around me. I recognize some of them from my group. These are souls who are also getting ready to incarnate. I see people from my group who are already born at this time. We all have the purpose of helping one another.

  "I get special garments for my soul, a cape of emerald green with some blue and purple mixed in. It is supposed to protect my soul. A bubble of white Light surrounds it. The cape is a specialized protection, while the Light bubble is a generalized protection. As I am ready to come down, I feel, 'Oh, here we go again.' I feel resigned.

"I come down through the tube, which is circular and smooth inside. It is made of Light and is translucent. I slide down and end up in the womb. My whole soul goes inside the womb."

• "I have planned and prepared for my life. I am now at the outer edge of the Light and am getting ready to go down to Earth to enter the womb. There are three Light beings with me. They put their hands on my shoulders and bow their heads in prayer. I sense the presence of Jesus and also the souls of the children I may have, hoping they will be able to meet me. My mother and her father are also here. They came up from the Earth during their sleep to make me feel loved. I have a general shield all over my soul (this was removed when I was six years old and permitted me to have an illness that weakened my body and made me more vulnerable to disease).

"My mom is already pregnant. I have already sent a 'piece' of my soul to the fetus shortly after the conception. I am feeling anxious, hopeful, and nervous. I condense myself into a small star and travel down to Earth through the connecting cord and enter directly into the womb."

• "I know conception has already occurred between my mom and dad. I have a bubble around me. (My mom told me I was born with a 'veil' around me.) It is like a space suit made of clear Light. I have this so when I go to Earth, I will not be attacked by demons. I am going down through my silver cord. It is like going on a motorcycle, but there is no motorcycle. I thought I would be scared, but I am not. I feel almost matter-of-fact about it, business-like, thinking, 'Okay, I am going down and I have to be focused.' I am serious."

• "I am at the outer edge of Heaven, preparing to go down to Earth and into the womb. I have planned everything in detail for my coming life. Many other people I know on Earth are here. I see Archangel Michael. He gives me a special protective blue shield that wraps all around me. I see my godhead master Buddha, and also Jesus, Mother Mary, and Saint Germaine. They are wishing me good luck. They are saying, 'We will be with you and will give you the courage you will need. Do not forget to call on us. We will help you. Go with all our blessings.'

"My mother is five months pregnant. I had already sent a 'piece' of my soul to the fetus. I see a connecting silver cord going from me to the fetus. As I am getting ready to go down, I feel anxious. I do not want to go to another life, but I have to. I am resigned. I am going to do my best but I am not too excited.

"I go down to the Earth through my connecting cord and enter the fetus directly. I am kind of pushed down into the womb. It is warm and dark here."

• "I am ready to go down to Earth now. I feel there are other people around me, such as my grandfather. He must be visiting here from Earth, because he is living on Earth in a body. I want to get out of here because I have done all the planning, and now it is time to go. My mom is pregnant. The baby is ready to come out of the womb as I am thinking of going down. It was not necessary for me to go down before the baby is about to come out. I see a 'piece' of my soul already there in the fetus. It was sent at the time of conception and is very protected. I feel, 'Let's get this over with.' I feel a sense of power around me. I can do this and achieve my mission and, with the help of Heaven, I will succeed. There is no fear or anxiety about going to the Earth. I feel victorious.

"I see a golden Light around me, like a protective suit of armor. It covers my body, but the strongest protection is around my chest. I sense a blue protective shield around my soul. The golden Light shield has two purposes. It amplifies particular frequencies and, with its reflective power, it can deflect darkness. I fly down, and a connecting cord is created behind me as I go. There are four angels around me. I remember seeing these angels (later in my life) when I was a baby. They played with me and flew all around me."

• "I have made my plans and now I am ready to come down. I am excited and exhilarated. I cannot wait. I feel some fear and anxiety, but not too much. I feel I am ready to dive in. It is like a water slide in a play area, with tubes into the water and kids sliding through them. That is how I go through my connecting cord, which is already created. I go directly into the egg right after conception. It is a weird feeling, hard to describe. I can even feel the egg dividing."

Chapter Eleven

Memories of Prenatal Life and Birth

Hypnotized patients often recall memories of their prenatal life and birth. From conception on, the fetus experiences and records *all* the feelings and thoughts of the mother as its own, including depression, anxiety, anger, guilt, rejection, and physical pain. According to my patients, the fetus also hears the words spoken by the father, doctor, and other people around the mother. However, as it has not developed a separate identity, it has little ability to differentiate the experiences and feelings of its mother from its own. The information it receives is accepted by the fetus as its own without discrimination.

The reason the fetus can recall the events even before the development of the body and brain is because the memories are recorded in the soul (subconscious mind), which may be partly or completely present in the fetus. These experiences in the womb and during birth become embedded in the infant's memory and continue to affect the person after birth, during childhood, and into adult life. Many physical, emotional, and mental problems can be traced to traumas in the womb and during birth. Experiences in the womb and during birth can stimulate similar memories from one or more past lives. They can also trigger the memories and feelings of a person's "first birth," when they were created by God.

According to my hypnotized patients, not all souls go into

the fetus at the same time. Very few souls enter at the time of conception. As the fetus develops, the soul may come in at almost any time. Some might come in during the first, second, or third months, but the most popular month for entering the fetus is the fifth month. The incarnation time can be plotted as a hyperbolic curve: very low at conception; then, as you move forward through time, some enter the fetus at about the first month; a few more come in at the second month; then the curve starts to rise dramatically between the fourth and sixth month and, finally, tapers off again until there are only a few souls waiting until birth to enter the fetus. Some even wait until a few hours *after* birth to enter the body. In all cases, a small "piece" of the soul is sent on ahead to the fetus at the time of conception, and the rest of the soul enters later.

Here is how some of my hypnotized patients described the soul entering the fetus in the womb, and the experiences of prenatal life and birth:

* "I come into the womb right after the conception. Now I feel fear. I can feel the heartbeat of my mother. She has darkness in her lungs and shoulders. She is aware of being pregnant and is happy about it. My father seems to be happy too. It is funny how we hear people say they do not know whether conception occurred or not. As I sense now, it seems they *know,* just maybe not at the conscious level.

  "I am about three months old in the womb. My mom seems to be eating a lot of dairy products, but they do not agree with me. Some parts of my soul are missing, especially from my digestive area, which is responsible for my intolerance to milk. A lot of changes take place in my body, and I am aware of many bodily noises coming from my mom's body. I sense my features forming.

  "I hear an argument between my father and mother. My father is very arrogant and my mother is subdued. I do not like my father fighting with my mother. I am communicating with him telepathically, telling him it is wrong, and I resolve to change him later.

  "My soul sometimes goes out and then comes back

to the womb again. I even travel to other star systems and come back. But not all of my soul goes out; a small part remains in the fetus. It seems I go to planet Venus a lot. Some souls are not able to go out as easily because they are afraid and not well protected. I have a plan to work with beings on Venus in this lifetime.

"Now, I am eight months old. I feel suffocation around my throat from a lack of oxygen. I also have problems with my blood. I am panting for breath. I sense my mom is having these problems, which are transferred to me. Things are cleared up after a while, but I lose some soul fragments because of that experience. I see a bubble of Light form around me.

"I am ready to be born. I feel squeezing, pressure, and pulsation on my neck and my whole body. I am scared. In some ways, I do not want to leave from here because I am comfortable. But I know it is time to leave. It is a new adventure, like going to different planets. That is exactly what it is; I *am* coming to the planet Earth from Heaven.

"My head comes out first and then the rest of the body. There was no problem. I start to cry as I come out. I see some angels as I am being born. I also see a lot of protection in the room. I think my mother and father prayed for protection. As a result, it is provided. A nurse holds me and takes me to my mother. I am glad it is over. It feels strange because I am coming out to a different world. There is a sense of loneliness and vulnerability to different things, and the knowledge that I can die. There is a fear of death. I feel a shiver go up my spine. I still have about 60 percent of my memories of Heaven, but I have forgotten the rest, and over time all of it seems to disappear gradually. By age five almost all of it is gone.

"At six months of age, I seem to float up to the ceiling a lot. I seem to be fascinated with this. I go out of the body often. I am also aware of traveling to Heaven and other planets and of coming back."

• "I go directly into the womb when the fetus is three months old. I see the Light in it. A 'piece' of me was sent on before the rest of me went in. Inside the womb it feels nice, comfortable, warm, and good.

"At six months of age in the womb, I feel more aware of myself and get used to the place. I can move around now, which previously I could not. I am aware of the bubble of Light around me, and I feel very protected. The bubble shuts out all the outside noises and protects me from my mom's and other outside influences. I can hear my mom's heartbeat. My mom and dad are excited about me.

"When I am eight months, my mom is eating a lot. She is happy because she can eat all kinds of foods now. I get a lot of nourishment from these foods. Sometimes I feel my mom is sad and this affects me. By this time, my body is formed and now my skin is forming.

"By the time of birth, I feel crowded. It is time for me to go and I feel a pull, as if I have to get out. The force is so strong, like somebody wants to blow me out of the womb. I see a dark tunnel through which I have to go. I feel I am too big for the birth canal.

"I decide which part should I bring out first, my feet or head. My head comes out first. I seem to be standing beside my body and looking at it. I guess I must be out of my body. I see a lot of angels watching me being born. I feel a man's hand on my head. I feel a cord is around my neck or the doctor is pulling on my neck and I feel pain in my neck. When he grabs me, he squeezes my neck. Actually, being born is not as bad as I thought. It may have to do with my bubble, which is like a wrap around me. My mom wanted a boy, so she was a little disappointed. After my birth, I still have most of the memories of Heaven."

• "My soul enters the fetus when it is two months old, but earlier I had sent a 'piece' of my soul to the fetus. It was just after conception. When I come into the fetus, I do not feel as good as I felt in Heaven. I appear to be small. To some extent I am aware of my mom's thoughts and feelings.

"At three months of age I am slightly more developed and can move my fingers to some degree. I am more aware of my mother's thoughts and feelings and can also hear other people who are outside. I am aware of a lot of emotional pain my father brought to my mother as I was in the womb. It caused me to resent my father. I go out of the body off and on. My mother is very excited about having a baby, but my dad is disappointed because he did not want to be a father.

"At six months I begin to feel uncomfortable, especially in my legs. I feel a bit confused. This triggers vague memories of past lives, of pyramids and falling down in a pit. At eight months, I feel restless and cramped and want to get out.

"Now I am nine months old in the womb. I am very nervous. I am about to be born and I am looking forward to coming out and moving freely. I am scared of how bright the lights will be. I feel as though my head is contorted by the uterine contractions. I feel my head gradually moving down the canal with the contractions. I also feel that my mother is not in any kind of pain because she is given an anesthesia, but it confuses me.

"Some metal object is touching me. I feel it pressing at the back of my head and it hurts. It feels like it is pressing my head forever. Then I am pushed out. Everything looks blurry and I start to cry. I am thinking, 'I hope it gets more comfortable soon.' The lights are too bright and I am cold. They clean me up and put me in my mother's arms.

"The doctor is worried about something. I am put into a cart and taken toward an incubator. I notice that my arm is numb, but it comes back to normal soon and I start to move my hand. The man pushing the cart looks surprised. He looks at me, examines my arm and takes me back to my mom.

"I do not remember much about Heaven and the plans I made for this life except that it is going to be difficult and I have to seek the Light. I remember that there are people who will guide me and give me strength and that my mother will take good care of me.

"Two days later I am terrified because they are going to cut part of me. I am crying, shaking and red.

As they cut me, it feels they are cutting out part of my body. They are performing a circumcision. I do not know why they are doing it and why they are torturing me. It brings back memories of torture from other lives. I see the Light surrounding the area where they cut me. I lost many soul parts during the process of birthing because of the fear, anxiety, and trauma, and I lost some more parts as a result of the circumcision. They are all brought back and integrated with me now because you [Dr. Modi] asked the angels to help me."

• "I believe the angels who came with me to Earth are birth angels who assist in the birth process. They are assisting my doctor and my mother. I see them putting their hands on my mother and doing certain manipulations and adjustments. I do not feel any connection with the birthing process. It is as if I am standing on the side, watching. I enter the baby when it comes out of the womb. I go in and take a deep breath. It is my first breath.

"Being in the body is like an electric shock. Part of me says, 'Wait a minute. Just a few minutes ago I had this beautiful, powerful Light body and now I am squeezed into this little baby. What is going on here?' Everybody around is very happy about me. The doctor is saying I am a healthy boy. My mom is happy. I feel hunger but I don't know why, what it means, or what I am supposed to do about it.

"I do not remember a lot about Heaven. This is like being on a different planet. After I am fed, I relax and sleep and connect with God and the angels. I do not remember my purpose or why I am here. When I close my eyes and relax I see angels playing with me. I do not like being in this hospital. It does not feel comfortable. All my energies are messed up. My father is looking at me from the window. He has a smile on his face.

"Now they are putting me down on this stupid board. They are going to cut something; it is a circumcision. I am screaming and thinking, 'What are you going to do to me? Who do you think you are?' I feel a very sharp pain. It is a major shock to my system.

I scream my head off because I want to stop the pain, but I do not know what to do. My mother is not defending me. She is not protecting me. I am very angry at her. All this was so unnecessary.

"I feel that during circumcision, a large part of my soul fragmented and got lost from my penis because of the trauma and that it was replaced by a dark being. It is still here with me. When you asked the angels to remove the demons and bring back my missing soul parts, I felt a spiral of energy coming through the base of my spine all the way to the top of my head as the soul parts were reintegrated with me. There are still some soul parts missing; they do not want to come back because they do not trust me, saying 'Leave me alone. I do not even want to talk about it. I do not trust you.'

"From Heaven, I see that the dark ones vampirize the lower chakras of the little babies during circumcision, because they cannot defend themselves. It's like sucking the Light out of their bodies. This radical procedure is such a shock to their being that their immune system gets disturbed. I have a high fever after the procedure; later the trauma of circumcision gave me problems with a loss of sexual identity, because I felt a part of me was missing and that I was not a complete man. I felt like my protection was gone."

Chapter Twelve

First Incarnation on a Planet

People under hypnosis report that many thousands of years after the creation some of the planets became ready to inhabit. Some of my patients recall incarnating on Venus, Neptune, Uranus, and other planets in our solar system and also in other solar systems before incarnating on Earth because Earth was not ready to inhabit for a long time. Larger souls from the upper and middle levels in the Light, who were more developed, were sent to inhabit the planets first.

The purposes of incarnation on different planets included procreating and populating the planet, exploring and learning how to use things on the planet, discovering food, building shelters, and learning to communicate and live on the planet. Some of the planets, like Venus, Neptune, and Uranus, were closer to the sphere of the Light (God) and had faster vibrations. As a result, there was no dark influence at all on those planets and they were much easier to inhabit and populate. Unfortunately, our planet Earth is a denser planet, farther away from the sphere of God, and as a result, has influences from Lucifer and his demons. Consequently, humans were and are easily influenced by the dark forces, making it hard to live on Earth in a pure form.

Multitudes of souls were sent to inhabit different planets. For the first incarnation, all the souls were infused into adolescent bodies, which were already created by the heavenly beings on the respective planets. Then these souls were encouraged to procreate. After their first incarnation on the various planets, all the souls went through the "second forgetting" to different degrees. On Venus and other planets, which are closer to the Light (God) and have no dark influence, souls experienced the minimum of "second forgetting" after incarnation.

On Earth, the first group of souls that were infused into an adolescent body did not undergo a complete forgetting, but as they were influenced by the dark beings, all the next generations had to have a complete "second forgetting" after their incarnation. So they came to Earth not knowing why they were here and what they were doing.

According to my hypnotized patients, the mechanism of forgetting is like putting a filter on a camera lens or like using an aperture that opens and closes, allowing more or less light into the camera. At the point when the soul joins the fetus, the "aperture" closes and shuts off prior memories. It is as if one door is closed and another door is opened. There are different filters for different types of memories.

During each life, we have certain goals we are supposed to achieve and certain lessons we are to learn. We choose to do the "second forgetting" because it is painful and confusing to remember everything from every lifetime, back to the beginning of time, while also trying to deal with the current life. If we had all the knowledge from before, there could be no learning or growth. So forgetting is a part of the growth process.

First Incarnation on Planet Venus

As reported by my patients under hypnosis, Venus was one of the first planets ready to inhabit. Many of the souls who reincarnate on Earth report having incarnated on Venus first. The vibrations of Venus are very high because it is closer to

God than most of the other planets. As a result, there is no dark influence there. Lucifer and his demons could not tolerate the higher vibrations there and could not go close to it. So it was not difficult to inhabit, populate, and establish a civilization on Venus.

The larger, well-developed souls from upper and middle levels of the godheads were selected first to go to Venus. They gave an intent to incarnate as the first ones on the planet. The planet was prepared by the heavenly beings so it could be inhabited. According to my hypnotized patients, many souls from all the godheads of our universe were prepared to go to Venus. All the different souls, angels, masters, godheads, and God Himself were involved in planning the strategies for the first incarnation and the evolution of souls on that planet.

When it was time to incarnate on Venus, souls moved from inside their godheads to the outer edge of the globe of God and the godheads. Their physical bodies were created on Venus by the heavenly beings and placed in strategic places throughout the planet. Then the souls descended through their connecting silver cords to their adolescent bodies and were infused into them. After incarnating on Venus, these souls did some "second forgetting," but much less than we do when we incarnate on Earth.

The bodies on Venus were very light and not dense like Earth bodies. The Venusians had telepathic communication and did not have any negative feelings or behaviors such as arrogance, pride, anger, hate, or jealousy. There was only love, because there were no dark influences. Many of these Venusian souls, after many thousands of years of incarnating on Venus, chose to come to Earth to help and eventually got stuck here because of the dark influences.

Here are memories of different people of their first incarnation on Venus:

- "I see a connecting cord going from me to Venus. When I look for planets on which I had my first incarnation, Venus lights up more than Earth. I get the sense that Earth is not ready right now. The souls on my level and the groups above my level in the Vishnu god-head are planning to go to Venus together. The souls from other godheads are also planning to go to the same planet. All of the different godheads of our uni-verse are talking to one another to plan the strategy.

"There is a strategy at work, and the master souls have more awareness of it, while others only know of their segment of the plan. Our group represents the consciousness of love, while other groups of souls rep-resent other attributes of God, such as wisdom, illumi-nation, science, and all His other qualities, which they are supposed to bring to the planet. Souls will have free will on the planet, but we are supposed to exercise this free will in a positive way.

"My group is planning to help build the founda-tion for other beings to come. We will build cities of light and the entire civilization, and we will lay the foundation for the next generation on Venus. There is a great deal of planning about the way we will live and evolve. We will have free will, yet there is a lot of cen-tral planning from Heaven. There is a lot of excite-ment, because it is the first time we are working on these details. There is a lot of room for improvisation and creativity.

"There is a plan to procreate ourselves and for other souls to come here. My twin ray will be my com-panion. There is an awareness that those who were created from the male and female aspects of one ball of Light will begin together on the planet as a couple. There are no laws such as we humans have, but there is a law of which souls are instinctively aware, namely, that this is a cohesive unit, what we call husband and wife. There is an inner sense of spiritual morality, not the earthly morality.

"I do not have any awareness of darkness on Venus. I am aware of a tube forming from where I am in the godhead and connecting to Venus where I am going. At the other end of the tube, there is a body waiting for me to enter. I feel excited about going down to the planet. I have a sense of adventure, but also apprehension and fear about the unknown and a concern about not being able to fulfill my goals. I wonder what it is going to be like. I feel a pressure on my chest as if I am being squeezed, reminiscent of when I was first created from God.

"The bodies are created by angels. As the souls go down, their vibrations become slower, because they are going to a planet which has slower vibrations than Heaven. It is like a shaft of Light: you enter from one side, and when you go to the other side, you are encased in a body. The bodies on Venus are not dense like Earth bodies. My form is created as an adolescent male. It is tall, maybe six feet. It looks almost like a human form, a completely proportioned body—perfect, with no flaws. It looks almost angelic too, but it has no wings. Our bodies have a golden glow and we wear clothes.

"Venus looks pink and gold and there is no dark influence present. Before I start to descend, there is a blessing from God, masters, and other beings. I hear, 'Go forward, my son.' There are thousands of us going down to that planet from my godhead and other godheads.

"I go down through a tube and as I come toward the end, I seem to slow down. I step in and occupy the body. I enter directly into the heart and then my soul extends throughout the body. I feel encased, and I sense a loss of freedom and the presence of limitation, because there is now a boundary to my form. I have to work within this form.

"I also sense that I have an awareness of my connection to God, but a certain portion of memory is fading. I sense I have a mission to accomplish and I have the memory of the plan, but I do not remember how it was in Heaven.

"I learn to use my body. I feel my body through my mind and I also feel the emotions. I experiment with how to use my body. I do not have to know how the body works. All I have to do is issue a command and it gets translated into action. The body has its own intelligence, but it is a different kind than on Earth.

"I am walking down a path. The planet has been prepared. After a few days, we meet at a gathering place.

We all came into the body around the same time. There is telepathic communication among us. We are forming groups. We are addressed by leaders assigned to the group. We are organizing what needs to be done. We are constructing buildings and gradually build a city in a short time. The architecture here looks similar to that on Earth, but it is more graceful. The plant life is different, and the landscape is beautiful, with lots of rivers, ponds, and lakes. People can walk on water because the body is light, but we can swim if we want to. By our will, we can make the body lighter by filling it with Light.

"We have an ability to absorb energy directly. We have an intimate contact with angels, elementals, and masters. We use these contacts in our day-to-day activity. They guide us in building. We can create food directly with thoughts. We rest when needed, but we can go on for a long time without resting.

"My twin flame and I, who were created from one ball of Light as two separate souls, are together as a couple. There are many couples, but some souls are alone. Everybody is busy working. We have different jobs. My job is the construction of the buildings, while my partner's is to develop art and music. We wear clothes of different colors, such as gold, pink, or turquoise. I am wearing a cape of green and gold, similar to what angels wear. My partner wears a flowing gown.

"After a while, we decide to create children. We do this out of energy, as there is no sex here as on Earth. There is love between couples, but the body is not made like those on Earth. There are male and female 'organs,' but there is no desire for sexual intimacy. It is more of a sharing and a reunion. It is physical but not sexual as we know it on Earth, where the sperm joins the egg. That is not needed here.

"Both man and woman stand together and they have contact with their godself through their silver cords. In that contact they create a physical form outside themselves. After that, the soul that is supposed to incarnate enters the new physical body. It is similar to how we arrived on Venus: the soul is infused into a body.

"Here on Venus the gestation period is directed by

the thoughts and emotions of the couple. There is an inner knowledge about which form is to be created; this has already been decided in Heaven. You just tap into this awareness through your connecting cord. I look back to when there was planning in Heaven between the man, woman, and newly incarnating soul. We visit Heaven frequently, yet in some ways, Heaven is right here. There is no sexual attraction to other partners or jealousy or any other negative feeling. There is no darkness. We have three children and just one partner. There is a great deal of love between us and our children.

"People are maturing and their bodies become stronger. There is no disease or sickness, and we live for a long time. As souls, we know when our purpose is done and then we decide to leave the body on our own. There is no negative sense of death, only a sense that our life work is finished and it is time to leave. I live for about nine hundred years. Some people stay longer because their mission takes longer, while some stay for a shorter period because their mission takes less time. We go through death and leave the body, which is taken to a special area to be converted into energy. I sit down, contact my godself, and exit the body by cutting my tie to it. I do this consciously and with intent. I go to Heaven through my connecting cord and review my life.

"I feel sad because that was a good planet. Why did I have to leave Venus and come to Earth? Maybe that is why I feel I do not belong on Earth. As I look back through time, I see I left Venus at some point and came to Earth, but my children remained on Venus; I feel my family ties are there. People who are from Venus but who are on Earth experience a lot of sadness.

"I lived many lives on Venus (about five hundred lives). A decision was made to help people on Earth. I see a band of souls that comes to help out on Earth, but these souls had problems because of the dark beings. I do not think I have reincarnated again on Venus since incarnating on Earth. A group of Venusians volunteered to go to Earth a long time ago, before the time of Atlantis. There was a sense of it being a rescue mission, and there was also an awareness of risk."

• "I am in Heaven on the upper level of my godhead. I see myself in a big cathedral or castle. It is my house and I stay here for a long time. I am happy here. I know what is going on with everyone else. There are no feelings of time. I feel that God is telling me it is time for me to move on, because many other souls have already incarnated on Venus. I do not know why, but I do not want to go to any other place, yet I have to. I move to the outer or lower part of the godhead and I feel, 'What is going on? What did I do?' My twin flame had already gone down to Venus a long time ago.

"When I am ready to go to the planet, I sense more of an individualized existence there, compared to when we were whole and connected to God, godhead, and all the other souls. We were all together in the godhead, and the godhead had a connecting cord to God. Now, because I am getting individualized and separated from the other souls, my cord is becoming separate from others in the godhead and is much smaller than before.

"Preparing to go down to the planet, I study where I am supposed to incarnate, how the planet was created, what it is made of, and what type of vegetation it has. It is a garden-like planet. It is a female planet, a very creative planet with the highest expression of love. It is known as Venus. There are a lot of classrooms and study halls here in Heaven where I am. I will be working with herb and flower essences and bringing manifestations of God through different types of expression. I had a lot of preparation, and my soul is at peace and ready. I know what is going to happen. I do not feel fear. I see that you [Dr. Modi] have already incarnated on Venus.

"My body is waiting for me on Venus. It is like a suit of armor or a mannequin and my soul will be infused into that. Some Light beings, who are engineers or specialists, create the body on the planet before I go down.

"There are a lot of instructors in Heaven who are

telling me what to do, how I will feel when I am in the body, and how it will be to work with the body, because many have gone down and experienced it. They are teaching me everything about how to use the body. You have to push to move the body. I know about almost everything theoretically before I go to the planet. We are very well prepared.

"I go to the planet through my connecting cord. I enter the body through my heart. It feels strange, like I am in a heavy armor, and it is hard to move. There are many limitations. I move my hands and feet first, then I move my neck so I can look around. I forgot some of the memories of Heaven, but I remember all the instructions. We still have our connections with the angels and work with them regularly while on this planet.

"I have a female body. Everybody looks a little different. I feel very awkward and not very coordinated. Other people who have been here for a longer time move more gracefully. They look like humans, only taller. Everybody looks beautiful.

"A woman greets me. I feel love and warmth, and for a while I go around and get to know my surroundings and learn how to live in this body. My name is Ona. I communicate with others telepathically. We spend a lot of time praying to God; nobody starts anything until they pray. I do not walk. All I have to do is think where I want to be and I am there. It is telepathic transportation.

"There are many buildings for learning and places for worship, as well as places for fun. There is a whole city here. Here there is no cold or hot weather, so houses are open. Colors are very beautiful and there is a lot of Light everywhere. It is a very colorful planet. My home has a lot of golden Light in it.

"I wear very light clothes. We can change our attire just by thinking. We do not sleep as humans sleep, but we rest by lying down. It is more like meditation. After a while, I meet somebody and we live together. We consider having a child. It is a refined process. We plan the baby's body, including the characteristics of the hair and eyes. Angels create the body of the baby, and it looks like a two- or three-year-old. My partner and I stand in front of each other and beams of Light come from our hearts. It is as if we are praying, calling the soul to come in from Heaven into the little body of the baby.

"I realize we live for a long time, for several hundred years. Then I feel it is my time to go. I have lived a full life; I have had sixteen children and have made many discoveries. I decide to leave my body. I see everybody and ask for their forgiveness. I lie down in peace. I do not feel old, but not young either. I am wiser. There is a man with a white robe performing a ritual, praying for my soul and burning my body. I go straight to Heaven through my silver cord, and there are angels there to help me.

"I go to Venus perhaps six times; then I go to other planets. Earth was not ready yet. I went to Earth later because I wanted to help out, but I got stuck there because of the demonic influences."

First Incarnation on Planet Earth

People under hypnosis claim that after many thousands of years, after souls had incarnated on Venus, Earth became ready to inhabit. Souls from all the godheads of our universe comprising the top upper and middle levels of the Light expressed the intent to be the first humans to incarnate on Earth. There was a great deal of planning among the souls, angels, masters, godheads, and God. After the planning, the souls moved from inside the godhead to its outer edge. They were given instructions to stay away from certain restricted areas on Earth. Those places may look beautiful and inviting, they were told, but they belong to Lucifer and his followers, according to my hypnotized patients.

As on Venus, adolescent human bodies were created on Earth beforehand by the heavenly beings and placed in strategic places throughout the planet to generate human life. Unlike on Venus, here the bodies were dense so they could survive on Earth, which is a denser planet. The original couples may correspond to the biblical "Adam and Eve." They were the first humans to incarnate on Earth and were placed there to create more humans like themselves. After this, souls descended to the Earth through their connecting cords and were infused into their bodies.

After their incarnation, they all underwent the "second forgetting." They forgot that they came from God; they forgot about Heaven and why they were here. They had a vague idea of what it was they were supposed to do, so they did not undergo a complete "second forgetting." Succeeding generations, however, did experience a complete "second forgetting" after their incarnation because of demonic influences.

The following excerpt indicates the typical memories accessed by my hypnotized patients of their first Earth incarnation. I present this in a question-and-answer format to enable the reader to appreciate the dialog process by which we obtain this information during a hypnotherapy session.

Dr. Modi: Who decides that you will be one of the first ones to go down and become human?

Patient: I contribute to the decision.

Dr. Modi: What are the criteria?

Patient: Intent, because I have an inner knowing that I want to be on this mission.

Dr. Modi: Who else takes part in the decision?

Patient: All of those higher beings on the top upper and middle level who decide to go down.

Dr. Modi: What were the goals for the first ones?

Patient: Experimentation and exploration, to create more inhabitants for this place, and to find out if it is feasible for humans to stay in this place and manage their lives.

Dr. Modi: How are you preparing for this?

Patient: Heavenly beings help us with the planning, and we plan among ourselves.

Dr. Modi: What are you planning?

Patient: We understand who we will be with during this first lifetime. We plan what type of system we need to sustain ourselves. We decide on a strategy to protect ourselves and manage our welfare. We plan to increase our numbers and to make alterations in this place so we can live comfortably. We will need to organize and have specialists to handle the workload. Within this organizational process, we will have to learn how to communicate and get along to make this a successful venture.

Dr. Modi: Do you have an awareness of dark beings?

Patient: We have the knowledge that Lucifer can bring negative things to us. We have an understanding that Lucifer intends to make our lives dark and negative, and we plan strategies to prevent these circumstances. Everyone in the top levels is involved with planning. We all have given our intent and we are scheduled to go down.

Dr. Modi: As you are planning to go down, is your body already created?

Patient: Yes. A form of it is created on Earth. It looks like a teenager.

Dr. Modi: Who is creating the body?

Patient: God and angels, through their intent.

Dr. Modi: Do you know which is your body?

Patient: Yes. We are given this knowledge. We do our planning in the godhead and then move to the periphery when the time comes to go down.

Dr. Modi: How are you feeling?

Patient: Anxious, challenged, excited, but with a sense of adventure!

Dr. Modi: Do you know where you are going?

Patient: Yes! Planet Earth! Our entire group is going to Earth. However, there are groups that are going to other planets from the same godhead.

Dr. Modi: Is God talking to you before you go down in the body?

Patient: Yes. He warns us about not going into the garden.

Dr. Modi: How are you infused into your body?

Patient: From Heaven, we go down through a tunnel (our connecting cord).

Dr. Modi: What part of the body do you enter through?

Patient: The head.

Dr. Modi: Describe your thoughts and feelings as you become aware of your body.

Patient: Anxiety, insecurity. Doubt as to how I might be able to use my body.

Dr. Modi: What knowledge from the Light are you aware of?

Patient: I'm aware that I'm from God, but I don't remember much else. I am aware that I have a purpose and that I need to start working toward my goals.

Dr. Modi: Do you know your purpose?

Patient: Yes. I know that I'll be one of the leaders of this group.

Dr. Modi: Do you remember the Light?

Patient: Not well. I have forgotten the way I was before I left Heaven. I have forgotten much of my communication and understanding I had in Heaven.

Dr. Modi: As you are infused into the body, how do you feel?

Patient: I'm wondering how the various parts of my body work and what I can do with these parts, such as my hands and feet. I learn by trial and error and by accident. I learn how to use my feet, because my body almost fell to the ground and I had to use my feet to keep from falling. I realize I moved, so I start to understand I can move my feet to move myself. I used my hands when I was climbing and discovered my hands could be used for holding onto things or for pulling things toward me or for pushing things away. When I first came to the water, I tried to walk on it, but sank. Water came into my mouth and I almost drowned. I realized that I had had a bad experience, but it taught me to use my mouth to selectively take in water (only as nourishment) and food, and to swallow.

Dr. Modi: What do you see?

Patient: Plants, trees, rock, animals both large and small. I see the sky, and I see others who look like me. I find these others by discovery. At this time we wear no clothes.

Dr. Modi: Who do you meet first?

Patient: One who looks like me. We communicate by body movements, pointing, and hand gestures.

Dr. Modi: What do you do next?

Patient: I walk around and find more who look like me and some who appear different. These different ones are smaller and parts of their bodies are different from mine.

Dr. Modi: What happens next?

Patient: We learn to take items from trees and use them as food. We are now in a group.

Dr. Modi: Where do you sleep?

Patient: Under trees and overhanging rocks. We put leaves and grass underneath us for comfort. For a long time, we learn how to exist. We learn how important it is to stay in a group and protect ourselves from dangerous animals. We learn that we need to make our living areas on higher grounds so that we are protected from rising water. We learn how to get along in a responsible manner. Initially, we don't have different feelings toward people with similar bodies or different bodies. After a time, when we have learned basic existence skills, we realize we have feelings that draw us to those whose bodies are different from ours. We seem to know who to go to, and we do this without any competition from others.

Dr. Modi: What is your name?

Patient: Ogg.

Dr. Modi: Describe the one you are with.

Patient: Smaller than I am. I'm four feet or less. This other one may be three or more feet tall. Their features are generally the same as mine, maybe a little softer. Our features are apelike, with deep-set eyes, sloped forehead, big ear lobes, bowed arms, bowed legs, hair all over the body (not quite as coarse as an animal), and we are walking hunched over. The hair is necessary for protection. A male's hair is not as coarse as an animal's, but it covers most of his body. The female has larger mammary glands than the male and is less aggressive.

Dr. Modi: What color is your skin?

Patient: Brown or copper.

Dr. Modi: What part of the world are you in?

Patient: What we now know as Asia.

Dr. Modi: What do you do next?

Patient: The couples pair up so that they can begin to discover how to reproduce and to multiply.

Dr. Modi: How do couples pair up?

Patient: There is an inner knowing to come together. However, we do not continue as a pair. We go from one to another to another, and there is no idea of sex at this time. We do not have negative feelings toward anybody. There is no anger, hate, or jealousy. Overall, we feel free, joyous, happy, and content. We are positive and everyone lives together in peace and harmony.

Dr. Modi: When does this change?

Patient: When some members of our group enter a certain garden.

Dr. Modi: Where is it?

Patient: It is in the general area in which we live.

Dr. Modi: What do you know about the garden?

Patient: The fruits in the garden are supposedly better and more tasty than the fruits in our garden, but there is a feeling that we are not supposed to enter this garden.

Dr. Modi: How do you know that?

Patient: Through an inner feeling.

Dr. Modi: How is the garden different from where you live?

Patient: We believe that the fruits are more lush, the grass is greener, the water more blue, and the place seems to be more inviting and appealing. This garden doesn't really look better; it is just a belief that it is.

Dr. Modi: Is there a name for the garden?

Patient: I'm not aware of it.

Dr. Modi: What's next?

Patient: Some from our tribe decide to enter the garden.

Dr. Modi: Are you one of them?

Patient: No.

Dr. Modi: Who goes in the garden?

Patient: Both sexes of some other members of the tribe.

Dr. Modi: What do they do?

Patient: They explore and taste many of the fruits, and as a result, they turn a little darker.

Dr. Modi: How do they turn darker? And why?

Patient: Because this area is Lucifer's domain. We know this is a forbidden place, forbidden because upon entering it, negative energies come upon us.

Dr. Modi: What is this negative energy?

Patient: We do not remember Lucifer and his demons, but we are aware that perhaps our lives will not be as harmonious as before.

Dr. Modi: As they eat the fruits, what happens to their bodies?

Patient: They become darker. Later on, we experience negative feelings that we did not feel before, such as jealousy, fighting, anger, hate, aggressive traits, uncooperativeness.

Dr. Modi: Do you get that way too?

Patient: We all take on some of the traits to some degree as the dark beings come and influence us.

Dr. Modi: What happens then?

Patient: As time passes, there are more and more divisions in the communities because we are no longer in harmony.

Dr. Modi: How many people are there?

Patient: Thousands—they were all created for this area.

Dr. Modi: What happens next?

Patient: There are skirmishes, fighting, even wars between the communities. It is not as pleasant as it was before. There is an understanding of an attraction between male and female. We understand that we like each other better than any other adults who are there. That is when the reproduction process starts.

Dr. Modi: To whom are you attracted?

Patient: To someone who looks different from me.

Dr. Modi: Do you stay with one person?

Patient: No. I'm with different people and I have children with them. The process escalates as more and more people enter the population, and there is more and more darkness.

Dr. Modi: How have things changed?

Patient: The land has changed. There are more established communities now. There are more people now within these communities.

Dr. Modi: How many kids do you have by now?

Patient: Thirteen, with different people.

Dr. Modi: Do you have a place where you dwell?

Patient: Yes, underneath an overhanging rock. I have leaves and grass to sit and sleep on. I keep a sharp stick to push into fish, and I can use the stick for protection against animals.

Dr. Modi: What happens next?

Patient: I am here for several hundred years. I get tired and ask to be called back.

Dr. Modi: How do you ask to leave your body?

Patient: I do not have a specific sickness, although there is sickness in the world by this time. I'm just tired and weak. I don't die. I just leave my body.

Dr. Modi: What are your thoughts as you leave?

Patient: I'm very tired and feel I can't keep up anymore. I don't want to be here anymore. I want to leave and return to the place from which I came. I remember this place vaguely.

Dr. Modi: Do you know how to leave the body?

Patient: I have a certain knowledge that the spark within me can leave this physical presence and enter the connecting cord and gravitate up to the Light. I know that my soul can go up, but I can't see any of this.

Dr. Modi: What are your last thoughts about that life?

Patient: I feel it is a shame that things happened the way they did. It is too bad that we didn't keep the peace, harmony, and contentment that we had when we first came to Earth.

Dr. Modi: How do you leave the body?

Patient: My spirit enters a tunnel, which leads up to the Light. I am not sick. I lie down and think of this. I will myself to go out of the body.

Dr. Modi: How does your spirit come out?

Patient: It leaves through my chest. I go toward the Light. Angels are there to escort me up.

Dr. Modi: What happens then?

Patient: I go into the exterior part of Heaven, where I can rest and repair myself.

Dr. Modi: What happens next?

Patient: I review the life I've had.

Dr. Modi: Who is helping you?

Patient: Some guides who specialize in this. I understand that the lives of the inhabitants on Earth were changed dramatically and, at this point, there are many who have slower vibrations. The lives of the inhabitants will not be the same for a long, long time.

Dr. Modi: How were they before the fruit was eaten?

Patient: Peaceful and in harmony. The place was very bright. The vibrations were high.

Dr. Modi: Look at the garden after the fruit was eaten.

Patient: The vibrations are slower and it looks darker.

Dr. Modi: Why are those places tempting to people?

Patient: Because people were deceived into thinking that this place might be inviting and interesting to them.

Dr. Modi: How were they deceived?

Patient: By Lucifer and his agents who look like dark blobs. When people were exploring that area, some accidentally set foot in Lucifer's garden, but some walked in out of curiosity. Once they entered, they became influenced by whispering in their ears. They were told, "This is what you want to do. This is more fun than anything you've ever done before. This is exciting and enjoyable." People believed this was something they wanted to do and they had a desire to explore the garden and eat the fruit.

Dr. Modi: Are there snakes in the garden?

Patient: Yes. After people eat the fruits, they are bitten by the snakes.

Dr. Modi: What is the fruit and what happens when they eat it?

Patient: It is just fruit and both men and women eat it. As they eat, they become darker, that is, they are not as free, and they have negative thoughts and feelings that they did not have before.

Dr. Modi: Is anyone bitten by a snake?

Patient: People walk along, and the snake comes out of the grass and strikes them on the leg. The people experience a great deal of pain and agony. On the spiritual level, the snake is a demon, and when it bites, the darkness enters their bodies and their Light is taken out; it is sucked out of them. After the influence from the garden, thoughts of physical sex enter into us, and also negative thoughts and feelings. We are never the same again. We are controlled by the demons, life after life.

Dr. Modi: What do you see next?

Patient: After this experience, I see disharmony, fragmentation of groups into separate communities, and more negativity.

Dr. Modi: What problems come from that life into this life?

Patient: Not being able to get along with others and having negative feelings and attitudes.

Dr. Modi: Do you need to ask for anyone's forgiveness?

Patient: Yes, of many inhabitants I was with because I took on dark feelings toward them.

Dr. Modi: Do you need to forgive anyone?

Patient: I need to forgive those who were against me.

Chapter Thirteen

Living a Life on Planet Earth

As described in earlier chapters, my patients under hypnosis report that the main reasons for creation were to enable all parts of God to evolve and grow, so they could all be equal in size and power. As individual souls and universes grow, God as a whole will grow, and eventually the Light will fill the whole void and the parts of God will not have to worry about getting lost in the void as they did before.

Therefore, God created universes and individual souls with these reasons in mind, according to my patients. After the planets became ready to inhabit, souls began their spiritual journey, going through the revolving door of life and death, learning, growing, and evolving. They used planets as schools for learning, to perfect themselves, to "graduate," and ultimately to go back to their real "Home" and to reunite with God.

The reports of my hypnotized patients indicate that during each lifetime, we create different "plays" with different people, on the "stage" of different parts of the Earth, or on different planets. We play different roles in different lives: male, female, king, queen, priest, monk, teacher, preacher, rescuer, torturer, killer, victim, beggar, leader, follower and so forth. We die in the womb at birth; we die young or old. We die of sickness, murder, suicide, accident, old age, or by being miscarried or aborted. We live good, bad, peaceful, or traumatic lives. If we play our role of good or bad person successfully, we "graduate" and go to the next grade and plan another play and a different role. We have to play all the roles and experience every aspect of human life to grow and perfect ourselves.

My hypnotized patients state that we incarnate into a physical body not blindly or randomly, but with a plan and purpose. We choose our parents, spouses, children, and other key people in our lives. We also choose our profession, talents, skills, and gifts. We plan not only good and productive lives, but also traumatic ones, either to balance our negative actions from the past lives or to learn lessons from them and grow spiritually.

The same soul incarnates again and again in different bodies, like putting on different costumes that are discarded at the time of death. With each death, the body dies, while the soul continues, retaining all its memories from this life and all the other lifetimes and the time in between lives, from the beginning of time. According to my hypnotized patients, everything we have ever done, said, heard, sensed, touched, smelled, felt, and experienced in our current life and all our lives from the beginning of the time is recorded in our soul, which is our subconscious mind. Nothing is ever erased. We can access any of these memories anytime we want to and need to, as has been shown throughout this book.

Past-Life Causes of Symptoms

Living on a planet such as Earth has its liabilities. Over a series of lifetimes, problems, traumas, and issues that are left unresolved accumulate in the soul and await eventual resolution. They can often appear in the present life disguised in the form of physical, emotional, mental, and spiritual symptoms. Without this expanded view of reality and life provided by the reports of my hypnotized patients, it would be easy for the typical physician or psychiatrist to not understand the deep roots of the problems they see before them in their consulting rooms. My research indicates that all our emotional, mental, physical, spiritual, and relationship problems in the current life have their roots in one or more past lives. Among the different reasons for our symptoms and problems in current life as reported by my patients are different causes of death, different types of suffering while dying, and circumstances of life, which I will discuss next.

Causes of Death

Symptoms are caused by the different means by which people died. Death can result from carelessness, mismanagement, or gross neglect; an act of nature (earthquake, tornado, hurricane, thunderstorm); murder because of lust, jealousy, or the desire for money; or suicide because of guilt, anger, self-pity, or self-hatred. Problems are also caused by the different types of deaths experienced in past lives, such as from falling off a cliff (causing fear of heights); hanging, a broken neck, the head being crushed or decapitated (causing head, neck and eye pain, throat or thyroid problems, or numbness); death from different diseases, being frozen, old age, being miscarried or aborted and so forth, leading to different physical, emotional, mental, and relationship problems.

Suffering while Dying

Present symptoms can be caused by the type of feelings suffered during the dying process: suffering from thirst, hunger (weight problems); feeling hot or cold (intolerance to heat and cold); difficulty in breathing (asthma) and so forth.

In all of these cases, symptoms are produced by *unresolved* physical, emotional, and mental residues, and from one's last thoughts, promises, or decisions while dying. These are brought back with the soul in the current body, and manifest as physical, emotional, mental, or relationship problems.

These are all described in detail in my first book *Remarkable Healings.*

Circumstances of Life

Here there are two different types of circumstances in a life which can cause problems: (1) physical circumstances, and (2) spiritual circumstances.

Physical Circumstances: These are different circumstances in which you live in. These include where you live and under what conditions; who your family is; who your associates are; which people are part of your soul group and which are not; interactions between groups; religion and ethnic background; and health status. They all affect us positively or negatively.

Spiritual Circumstances: These include karmic influences, balance, spiritual development, and complex interplay between these three.

Karmic Influences: Karma is a Sanskrit word meaning actions or deeds. We develop karma as a result of our actions. Negative actions from past lives require corrections in future lives. Whatever we have done to others in past lives, we have to balance them by suffering with the similar problems in current or future lives. For example, a cruel master in a past life can try to resolve the effects of this behavior by suffering under a cruel master in a future life.

Balance: Similar to karma, but in balance, problem occurs in the present life and is corrected in the same life only; otherwise the amount of karma we would have to carry over to another life would be overwhelming. For example, a cruel master who gives generously to a charity or a church is *balancing* his negative actions in the same life. You do something wrong, feel guilty about it, and balance it by doing something good in the *same* life. Balance is about restoring a negative action in the same life before it becomes karma, requiring redressing in a future life.

Spiritual Development: During a lifetime, we can develop spiritually in many ways. We can develop faster by going to Heaven during sleep to learn and plan. We can also develop spiritually by studying scriptures and spiritual books, by singing devotional songs, and by going through different types of experiences that cause us to grow spiritually, such as spiritual retreats or meetings.

Prayers and prayerful acts, which are good works offered to God as worship, can cause us to develop spiritually. A good act is performed simply to benefit a person we are helping, while a prayerful act will have the same effect, but it is offered to God as an act of worship, and it will have a far-reaching effect. Meditation can help us enter the spiritual realm and can bring our humanity under control and move us closer to spiritual reality and God, and thus helps us to grow spiritually.

Complex Interplay between Karma, Balance, and Spiritual Development: There is a constant interaction which goes on among our actions, balancing, and how we develop spiritually. For example, if you do something evil in one life, you can do something good in the next life to correct it. These good acts force spiritual development. Similarly, more spiritual development forces more balancing. (See figure 8.)

HUMAN DEVELOPMENT

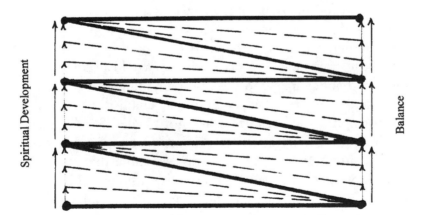

Interplay between Spiritual Development and Balance

Figure 8

Mechanism of Symptom Formation

According to my hypnotized patients, at the end of each life our physical body dies, but the soul continues to survive, retaining all its memories, experiences, unresolved feelings, and decisions. Everything is permanently recorded in our soul; nothing is forgotten or erased. When the soul incarnates in another body, it brings with it all the old "baggage" of unresolved emotional, mental, and physical issues; all its last thoughts, decisions, promises; all its relationship problems. All of this leads to different symptoms and problems in the current body.

During each lifetime, we plan to take care of some of these unresolved problems and issues from our past lives. We repress most of our earlier memories, whether normal or traumatic, storing them in our subconscious mind, except for the ones we are planning to resolve in this life. If we remembered everything that has ever happened to us, from this life and all the other lifetimes, from the beginning of the time, without the benefit of repression, our conscious mind would be cluttered and overwhelmed by these unnecessary and often painful memories. We would not be able to focus and function properly in our day-to-day living. We can become overburdened and even dysfunctional from too many painful memories as well as emotional, mental, and physical symptoms. In these cases we would either freeze up and become catatonic, so we would not have to deal with those traumatic memories; or we would become a full-blown psychotic, unable to deal with anything.

So our mind creates a protective mechanism of repressing and storing the memories that are not needed for day to day functioning. As long as this mechanism of repression works well, we function in a healthy way. Anytime this repression becomes weakened because of any circumstances, like a sudden shock to the psyche, chronic stress, use of hallucinogenic drugs, or premature opening of Kundalini, the memories can emerge from the subconscious to the conscious mind, bringing their physical, emotional, and mental problems, and causing different symptoms. What specifically develops depends on what types of memories are surfacing.

We have to heal all our emotional, mental, and physical residues and other issues and problems coming from all our past lives from the beginning of the time. Otherwise we cannot be free of these life-and-death cycles and go back to the Light permanently. But we cannot resolve all of them in one lifetime either.

According to my patients, we plan to resolve a few past-life problems in each lifetime. Sometimes we succeed and sometimes we do not. If we do not succeed in one life, then we try again and again in succeeding lifetimes, until we succeed and are free of past-life problems. Then we look at other problems to resolve; this goes on and on, so you can see why it is necessary to keep coming back into incarnation again and again.

During each lifetime, our soul fragments into many pieces as a result of different types of traumas. These soul parts are held by Satan and his demons and stored in hell, but they are still connected to our soul with a connecting cord. These soul parts contain memories of physical, emotional, and mental traumas of the lifetimes in which the fragmentation occurred. These missing soul parts create "holes" in the soul and help cause the weakness in the soul and body.

When we incarnate in another body, the demons "squeeze" those soul parts to restimulate the memories of the past lives traumas; these memories travel through the connecting cords to our soul and are experienced in our current body. In treatment, we resolve past-life traumas by recalling, reliving, understanding, and resolving them and by bringing all the missing soul parts back. This fills in the holes in the soul and heals it, which, in turn, heals the mind and body. So, to heal the mind and body, we need to heal the soul.

By going through these trials and tragedies, we grow spiritually. If we live a life in which we do not do anything good for anybody or for ourselves, even though we do not hurt anybody, we do not make any spiritual gains. We do not just stay in the same place, do not just mark time, but we go backward spiritually. Each life has to be a building block, a forward-moving process, according to my patients' reports.

Our past lives influence every aspect of our current life.

Our likes; dislikes; fascinations; gifts; talents; choice of profession, parents, spouses, children, and friends; dreams; positive and negative relationships; and physical, mental, emotional, and personality problems—all have their roots in our past lives. The mistakes made in our past lives follow us like a shadow and affect us in our current life.

If we think of the soul as on a spiritual journey, each life becomes a station along the way at which certain tasks are to be performed and certain lessons are to be learned. When for some reason we fail to do that, we carry that task or lesson over to the next life. In this way, our "baggage" gets heavier. At some point, it becomes necessary to stop and resolve the old problems and issues and learn the old lessons to reduce our load so we can move again toward our goal. Each life has to be lived in a good, loving, and productive manner, and as perfectly as possible, so we can continue to grow, learn our lessons, and perfect ourselves. Then, one day we can graduate and go back to our "Home" to God, our rightful place. That is our ultimate goal, which we can achieve through the process of repeated incarnations.

Chapter Fourteen

Death: Process of Leaving the Life

According to my hypnotized patients, before and during death the soul goes through a self-evaluation process. It reviews what it has been told in this life about what is going to happen after physical death as well as what it can recall from its own past deaths. It tries to figure out what will happen: Will it go out of existence? Will it survive? Will there be an after-life? The soul reviews its life, and in some cases it makes decisions and promises about different issues and people in its life. The soul continues to process this now-ending life even after it comes out of the body, deciding what to do and where to go.

My hypnotized patients consistently report that, as the soul comes out of the body, there is no loss of consciousness or of continuity of consciousness. The soul experiences an immediate freedom from any pain and discomfort it was experiencing before death. It feels as alive as it felt before the death of its physical body. It retains all of its memories and attitudes and its personality as before.

As the body is dying, the soul tries to loosen itself from the body gradually before it eventually leaves the body. There are three possible scenarios for how the body dies and the spirit comes out: (1) the body dies and the spirit leaves soon after, (2) the soul leaves before the body dies, and (3) the body dies but the soul remains in the body for some time.

The Body Dies and the Spirit Leaves Soon After

In this scenario, the body dies slowly and the soul prepares to leave by loosening its connection to the physical body. The body dies first and the soul leaves fairly soon after. Here is how some of my hypnotized patients have reported it:

- "I am dying at the age of sixty-eight of kidney failure as the result of heavy metal poisoning. I am afraid of dying, because I do not know what is going to happen. My consciousness is slowly fading out. My soul has pulled itself up and is concentrated in my head. My body is scarcely breathing and is choking on its own secretions. Pretty soon my body dies and my soul comes out of it.

  "I am surprised. I do not feel dead. I am free of the symptoms I felt before death. I go from room to room in the house. Nobody sees or hears me. I go to the garden but cannot touch the flowers or anything else. I feel confused. I look around and I see a big Light, but it is not the sun. A man comes to me. He is my father who died a long time ago. He looks young and healthy and is inside the Light. He takes me inside the Light."

- "I am dying at the age of twenty-eight. I beat up a woman in the bar, so another man shot me in the chest. I lived a horrible life. I stole and robbed banks and even killed a man. Later, I began to drink and did awful things. I am dying feeling worthless. I was almost relieved to die. I lie face down and my spirit comes out through the back of my body, head from head, legs from legs. I see my body lying in a pool of blood. I am surprised because I do not feel dead. I thought after death I will be relieved, but I still feel awful about my life. People throw my body in a river. I stay there for hours as if time is standing still. I do not know what is supposed to happen.

  "After several hours, I see a brilliant Light coming from above, but darkness comes up from below, too. Dark beings are telling me, 'Do not go to the Light.

What you did was bad. We can use you. If you go to the Light, it will burn you. We can help you. We have many others who are like you.' I am torn between the Light and dark. I see dark hands coming toward me. The dark hands look thin and bony, almost as if you could break them off. I can make out the dark beings' eyes. The dark beings are batlike and have pointy ears; they are ugly.

"Something in me tells me not to go with the dark ones. I decide to go to the Light. I see a Light being with a kind face. He is saying, 'It had to be your decision. You had to choose where to go.' He did not talk to me before as the dark ones did who were manipulating me to go with them. As I go into the Light, I am glowing and I feel better."

• "I am a maiden working for a pharaoh in Egypt. I am going to be burned to death for my belief that the pharaoh is not a god. I have to tell the truth. I will not tell a lie. I am brave and I can do it. I know I will go home to God. I am not afraid of death. They are tying me to a pole. I can see that I am surrounded by angels, and they are protecting me. They are saying, 'You will come and be with us in a short while.' I feel joyful as I see them.

"Now they are lighting the fire. My feet are burning. Smoke is filling my chest. I cannot breathe; the smoke is smothering me. I cannot scream. I take the angels' hands and pass out. I see my Light body coming out from the side of my physical body. There are two angels taking my hands; we float up a large funnel in which there are other angels. Way up on the top there is a bright, powerful, golden-white emanation of Light. It must be God."

• "Many lifetimes ago I was a dungeon guard. I was very cruel. I did not let the prisoners ever see the sunlight and kept them in total darkness all the time for years. In my late forties I became very depressed when I gradually realized what I had done to those prisoners. I felt guilty and did not want to live anymore. I went to the mountains. I found a black pit and jumped in. I felt that since I had caused those people to live in darkness, I deserved to be in that dark place, too. I would suffer with what I caused other people to suffer. I did not know how long it would take for God to show mercy on me. I thought after my death I would not go to Heaven or hell, but just stay in between.

"As I jump into the pit, a jagged rock goes through my shoulder and through the rest of my body and I die. My spirit comes out soon after my body dies. I do not feel dead. My spirit stays in the dark pit for a few weeks because I am too ashamed to go out because of my evil deeds. Then I see a Light coming down and I start to go in that direction. I am surprised to see in the Light some of the people who suffered because of me. They do not appear angry. They have come to take me to Heaven. I am reluctant to go toward them, but they are loving and help me along. They encourage me even when I want to stop going up with them."

• "I am dying of old age. I know I am going to go to Heaven because that is where everybody is supposed to go after death. My spirit gradually unhooks itself from the body and comes out from my forehead. I shoot up like a star, like a stretching point of Light, and I become part of the Light which is Heaven."

The Soul Leaves before the Body Dies

Sometimes the soul leaves long before the body dies, as in cases of unconsciousness or coma. In these instances, the main portion of the soul has already gone, but a small part, which animates the body, remains. However, in these cases, for all practical purposes the body is dead. Following are some examples:

• "I am dying of pneumonia. I am very hot and have difficulty breathing. My chest hurts and I feel weak, tired, and helpless. I fade down into unconsciousness.

During this time, most of my spirit comes out from my chest; however, a small part of my soul, filled with darkness, remains in my body. After about four hours, my spirit communicates with that soul part, drawing it like a magnet until it comes out of the body and rejoins my soul. At this point, my spirit severs its connecting cord with the body and thereafter the physical body dies."

• "I am dying of lung cancer at the age of sixty-two. My spirit is ready to leave because there is nothing in this life to live for. I have a lot of pain in my body. I go into a coma. Most of my spirit comes out and hovers over the body. My spirit feels tired but alive. It looks like a whitish ghost.

"My body is in a coma, and although most of my spirit is out, the tail end of it is still stuck in the body. It looks gray and keeps the body in a coma for a couple of days. My spirit wants to leave, but it cannot do so because part of it is still stuck in the body. After a couple of days, my spirit cuts the connection with that soul part in the body and leaves, and then the body dies."

• "I am a seventeen-year-old girl. My boyfriend was drinking and he raped me. I was enraged and hit him with a bottle, and as a result, he died. His father was a prominent man. I am tried for murder and it is decided that I should be hung. Nobody listens to me. It is unfair. I do not deserve it. How could they do it? I am afraid of dying because it is the end. They are getting ready to hang me. Townspeople are watching. They keep screaming I am a murderer and I do not deserve to live. My family is crying.

"They put a black cloth over my head. They are putting the rope around my neck and are going to drop the chute. I am scared. I do not know why this is happening. It is like a bad dream, but it is not a dream. A priest comes for the prayer. Then they pull the chute. Just before the rope constricts around my neck, my spirit jumps out of my body and comes straight out before my body dies. Then I watch my body dying.

"I do not feel dead. I do not know where I am supposed to go. I see townspeople laughing. I want to reach out and touch my family, but my hand passes through them. I tell them that I am all right and right here, but nobody hears or sees me. I wander around the town. I do not walk; I glide. I see a halo of Light around me. Then the sky opens up and there is a brilliant Light shining, brighter than the sun. A man at the top of that Light motions me to come to the Light, and I go to it."

• "I am a twenty-five-year-old German soldier who was captured by the Polish soldiers and kept as a prisoner. There are many prisoners here. We are kept in a box, like caged animals. There are bombs dropping everywhere and guns firing constantly. German soldiers are attacking us. I know that soon I am going to be hit and this will take my life. I hear planes flying over and bombs exploding. I hear men screaming, being blown up. I sense I am going to be next. I feel the ground shaking. I feel extremely anxious. I do not know what happens after death, and I am very scared of dying. The ground is shaking and mud and dirt are flying. My spirit comes out of the body just before I am hit by a bomb. I am out of my body, which is blown to pieces right after my soul comes out.

"I look at my dead body and feel sad about what happened to it. I am also relieved it is over. I see other spirits around whose bodies were also blown away. I stay around my body for a few days to make sure my parents are notified. I see German soldiers coming into the area. They are helping those who are wounded. "I see a soldier compiling a list of the men who were killed. My name is on the list and I know my parents will be notified. Then I see a bright Light coming down toward me and I get pulled into the Light, which I think is Heaven."

The Body Dies, but the Soul Remains
in the Body for Some Time

In cases of unexpected, sudden, or violent death, the body
dies immediately, because the chemical and biological process-
es no longer work. But the soul may remain in the body,
because it has not gone through a preparatory process. It goes
through different loosening steps following the realization
that its body is dead. It gradually loosens its grip on the body
and eventually leaves the body. According to my hypnotized
patients, the soul may remain in the body anywhere from a
half hour to four to five hours after the death. In cases of violent death, the soul is probably still there after a half-hour and
during that time, if it is possible to reestablish the conditions
of life, the body could go back to living. Here are some examples as reported by my patients under hypnosis:

- "I died of a snake bite. It was a completely unexpected and violent death. My soul was unprepared for
it. As I look back, I can see the soul is shocked to be
inside the dead body, which it cannot move anymore.
There is confusion and bewilderment. There is a loss
of motor power and the soul cannot move the body at
all. The soul is feeling frustrated and angry. After a
while, it slowly relaxes, realizing the body is dead. The
soul gradually gets reoriented, trying to understand
what is happening.
"It takes about a half-hour for the soul to relax and
to let go of its confusion, anger, and frustration. It is
still in the body an hour later. Then it begins to concentrate on pulling itself together into the head,
pulling out of the arms, legs, and trunk. One hour and
twenty minutes following the death of the physical
body the soul pops forward out of the face, and as it
comes out. It feels as though it is still a full-sized, living, breathing, walking human being. It comes out
very curious, wondering if it will continue to exist,
wondering if it will be terminated or pop out of existence. It looks around and sees that the physical world

is still there, but that it is not the only world. There is also the spiritual world. It sees the dark beings, which the soul interprets as demons, and it gets away from them. Then it sees the Light beings and recognizes some of its relatives among them surrounded by the Light, and it chooses to go with them to Heaven."

Sometimes, my patients report there are catatonic trances or near-death experiences, after which the soul returns to the body and the body becomes alive again:

- "I was a psychic, so my parents sent me to a temple to study. From the age of sixteen, I went from town to town to talk about the nature of God and about right and wrong. In one city, people did not like me and I was stabbed and killed. I was shocked because I was not supposed to die at this time. I died thinking, 'Lord, what went wrong? Did you make a mistake or did I screw it up? Did I not understand what I am supposed to do?'

  "I felt lightheaded and fell down. My spirit came out of the body and went to the Light (Heaven). There, Light beings tell me that I am not done with my life yet. I have to go back to the body and continue the work. This strikes me as a little odd. I know my body is dead. Everything is confusing and backward from what I thought it should be.

  "I go back to Earth in my body, which my friends put into a cave. They seal the entrance. When I wake up in the body, it feels funny. When my friends see me, some get scared and run away. When I recover, I can perform miracles, cure diseases, and heal people."

Sometimes, the soul, or part of it, is still in the body after death, and it experiences being buried or burnt during cremation. Following is an example:

- "I was a slave in Egypt. I was buried alive in a box because I spoke out against the mistreatment of another slave. Being buried alive in a box caused me to go berserk. My soul fragments into many pieces and they go in different directions. I feel like I am in limbo. Dark beings are squeezing, pulling, and tugging, trying to hold my soul. Some parts of my soul get away and others are trapped. After a couple of hours, my soul pulls itself out of the body and it comes out of my heart like a wisp of vapor. My dead body looks grotesque, and I am trying to figure out how to be whole again. I see a bright Light with angels in it. I decide to go up to Heaven even though many of my soul parts are still in the body. I think they are grabbed and taken by the demons to hell.

Chapter Fifteen

Making the Transition
from Earth to Heaven (Light)

After the death of the physical body, most souls realize they need to go back to Heaven and that if they look up, the Light will be there along with the helpers. In the normal process, the soul goes to Heaven after the death of the physical body. My hypnotized patients describe different things that can go wrong with souls after death. There is often competition for these disembodied souls. Demons try to get hold of them and try to talk them out of going to Heaven. If souls try to engage in conversation with the demons, there is a greater chance of their being captured and lured away. It is better for souls not to engage in conversation with the demons, my hypnotized patients state.

Things that can go wrong with disembodied souls include:

1. Souls who are angry with God because of what happened in their lives can reject God and willingly go to hell to work with Satan.

2. In some cases, souls are not aware their physical body is dead. They try to talk to people, but nobody sees or hears them. They go to the funeral home and get confused when they see their body in the

casket. Because of their grief, they may end up entering the body of someone whose energy field is open. Usually, this is a loved one or a friend.

3. Souls that have a strong demonic influence already in them are often talked out of going to the Light by demons who are afraid of the Light and who cannot go close to it. As a result, they keep the souls from going to Heaven and these souls may end up entering another human body, or they may haunt a place or attach themselves to a piece of furniture or an inanimate object.

4. Souls that are afraid to go to Heaven because they did something wrong end up rejecting God. These souls may become trapped in or consumed by the demons, and may be used by them to possess and influence other humans.

In this book, I will discuss the normal transition to Heaven. What goes wrong with the souls after the death of their physical bodies will be covered in detail in the next book.

According to my hypnotized patients, after the death of their physical body in a past life, they often became aware of a brilliant, white Light coming down from above, coming from beyond the sky and sun. It is brighter than the sun, but it does not hurt their eyes. As this beautiful Light comes closer and surrounds them, they feel enveloped in it and feel the unconditional love it radiates. They may see a religious figure, angels, or their departed loved ones who have come to escort them to Heaven. These beings are often surrounded by Light; they have loving eyes and wear white robes. Their hands feel warm and real. The departed loved ones appear young and in good health, not sick or old, as they looked before their deaths.

Those who are still preoccupied with the problems and issues of their now-ended life or who do not realize that their body is dead, often do not notice the Light immediately, or they feel it is far away. After a while, when they realize their body is dead, they resolve their unfinished business and are ready to make their transition; then they often see the Light and heavenly beings in it. According to my patients, when they are ready (and not before), they perceive the Light and heavenly beings, even though both are always there.

My hypnotized patients give different representations of how they travel from the Earth plane to Heaven. They report traveling through a tunnel, climbing up steps, walking, running, flying, floating, or being sucked up or drawn up into the Light. Sometimes they travel instantaneously, that is, they think about it and they are there. As they move into Heaven, they describe themselves as resembling a Light being. They still have the human form and identity as before, but they do not have a solid body or earthly clothes.

Here are a few reports from my hypnotized patients on how they made their transition to Heaven after the death of the physical body:

- "After the death of my physical body, my soul shoots up toward the Light because I know that is where I need to go. I see heavenly entities resembling mushrooms of white, bright, and dazzling Light. I cannot see their faces because they look like slender Light blobs and all are part of the Light. They surround me and shower me with unconditional love and acceptance. The Light is healing and there is a feeling of all-knowing and understanding. As the Light beings welcome me, the darkness disappears and all my soul parts are pulled back to me like a magnet, and then I am taken to Heaven."

- "I look down at my dead body but I don't feel dead. I am in a spirit form, which is milky and transparent. I see a bright, shimmering Light, and I am drawn to it. As I go up, first there is blue sky, and there is a line, and when I cross it, I see a lot of angels and other beings cheering me on. They are happy to see me. They seem to know me, and I them. They take me to Heaven, where everything is shimmering and glowing."

• "My spirit exits from my chest and I look down at my dead body. It is dirty, covered with grime. It looks tragic. It was a hard life. I have a remote feeling that something good will happen to me. I feel a need to watch out for my body. I wait for two days until it is found by somebody. Then I see a bright, white Light above my head. I feel I need to go to the Light. Two angels take my hands and escort me into the Light. We enter into Heaven through a beautiful, white ornate gate. It is a wonderful, loving, and peaceful place."

• "I am out of my body. I look down at my dead body. It looks old and gray. I am relieved that life is over. I wanted to be free of that life. I do not go up right away, but hang around for a while. I visit relatives and friends. They do not see or hear me. They may sense my presence a little, but not much.

"I get bored with walking around, so I try to find where I am supposed to go. I see a dark tunnel, and I see Light in it. I see angels escorting me. The angels say people are waiting for me. It is hard for me to believe that I will meet people there. I am in the Light now. I see my father. He is wearing a plaid shirt and the old-fashioned pants he wore on Earth. [Usually, people do not wear any earthly clothes in Heaven.] Later his clothes turn into Light, like a white robe. He says to me, 'What took you so long?' He is joking with me. I also see my mom, and I immediately realize she is the same person as my mother in my current life."

• "I died when a volcano erupted and the smoke, fire, and lava killed me and others. I was covered with smoke and lava, and my spirit came out of the body. Other people who died, they are here too. It is very sad. We do not know where to go. Somebody is trying to lead us away. I see a bright angel who is taking us to the Light, treating us like lost children. He is very loving and kind, drawing us like a magnet into the Light, and we float up. Light is pouring all around us and our bodies are changing. We are more refined and have Light bodies."

• "I am a twelve-year-old girl. I committed suicide by hanging myself because I felt that nobody loved me. I felt alone. I can see my limp dead body. I am outside my body and can see it hanging. I feel sad: what have I done? I do not feel dead as I wander around the house and nobody sees or hears me. I go to my funeral. There are a lot of people there, and everybody is dressed in black. They are putting my casket in the ground. I feel alone and lost.

"My parents are sad. I feel bad for what I have done. I misjudged them. I try to comfort my mom and I go into her body. I can go in and out of her any time I choose. I stay around her for a couple of months. Then I pray for help and suddenly I see Light all over me and I am glowing. This Light is coming from above and beyond the sky. A figure holds out his hands and tells me to come. He is wearing a white robe. Everything is dazzling. He says, 'Do not be afraid. Come to the Light and we will take care of you.' He seems to be in Heaven in brilliant Light and his hand stretches down toward me. I get pulled up by this hand into the Light. I see lots of children playing, and everybody and everything is glowing here. I am of Light, too, and have a transparent form."

• "I was a 'whiz' kid and became a medical doctor at an early age. I died of exhaustion during my residency at the age of twenty. I am out of my body now, lingering near it. I have unfinished business. I have to take care of somebody. Since my uncle died, I have had a feeling he is in me. My habits changed to those of my uncle. I try to move to the Light but cannot. I try to jump in it but cannot. My legs feel as if they are tied down. There are cords going down to the operating table from my legs and also to stacks of books. I try to break those cords but cannot. I pray to God to remove them. I see an angel cutting the cords. This surprises me because my God on Earth was medicine.

"I am moving up in a golden shaft of Light. I can see angels' hands and wings, but I cannot focus or turn my head. It is as if somebody put dark glasses on me.

Maybe my vision is blocked, but it seems that two people are seeing through the same eyes. I pray to God to separate us because we are attached. Maybe I should perform a spiritual surgery, but I do not know how. Maybe an angel can do it. I pray to God to send an angel to separate us. I was such a smarty-pants on the Earth, but here I do not know what to do. A strong Light comes and draws something out of me.

"I think—I think too much. I analyze too much. How do you turn your mind off? I hear my uncle chuckling because he was able to merge religion and knowledge, but I could not. I feel stupid. I was so quick to merge with the knowledge that I missed the wisdom of my culture.

"I see a spiritual ladder, as my religion teaches. Some rabbis spend a lifetime teaching how to go to Heaven by this ladder, but I stumbled upon it. How could it be so easy? I got it: all you have to do is ask God for help. And I went to school all these years to learn this? People up in the Light look at me, waiting for me to come in. Maybe I need to ask for forgiveness, but then I am not sure if I am doing the right thing. I hear my uncle saying, 'Stop thinking and keep going.'

"I see a ladder, but I do not understand its use. I cannot use it. I do not know how to do this. If I were on Earth, I would find out from books. Do they have books in Heaven? I hope they do. It is my intellectual pride, but even though I know I need to pray, I do not want to be somebody's cosmic joke. I do not know how to travel up there. I ask people who are waiting up there, 'How do I come up?' I get the answer, 'Just think it.' I think about going up and I am up. Everything is glowing here—even I am glowing."

Chapter Sixteen

Returning to Heaven (Light)

Usually people experience the re-entry into Heaven in terms of the life they just lived. The souls are still human and they do not want to go through too much of a shock. The appearance of the entry into Heaven is a duplication of what people were used to on Earth. In Heaven, they go through several steps to understand and resolve the life they just left, but they do this from the higher spiritual perspective. This happens at the outer edge of Heaven, where everything appears in earthly forms. After they have gone through those stages, the souls are ready to drop their human feelings and personality and go back to being pure spiritual beings. The order of these stages is typically as follows (although they do not always happen in this order and some are not mandatory): ventilation, cleansing, life review, and rest and restoration.

Ventilation

My hypnotized patients claim this step does not occur every time. If the life they just left was traumatic and they are still experiencing anger, guilt, or confusion, they then are taken to a place where they are allowed to ventilate their thoughts and feelings in the company of a Light being. The process is like psychotherapy, and the heavenly beings help the souls by being good listeners. Some of the examples are as follows:

- "My spirit is wandering around after the death of my body. I do not know where to go. A radiant being is asking me to come into the Light, saying I will be safe there. I start to float toward the Light. I see a man with a beard in a white robe, and he is glowing with Light. He tells me I am safe now. As we are walking, I tell him, 'I feel I have failed and wasted my life. I am nobody. I wish I had done things differently. I did not amount to anything. I should have married my girl-friend but I did not, because I was too busy feeling sorry for myself. I missed all the opportunities to change things in my life. I am angry and upset with myself. My life was wasted. I was a drunk, could not hold a job, and did not achieve anything.' The Light being tells me not to feel that way anymore. He tells me that this is Heaven and everything will be all right."

- "I go to Heaven after the death of my physical body. I sit on a rock next to a man who is glowing with Light. He asks me how my life was and encourages me to talk about everything. I feel angry about everything that happened. I tell him about my husband, how con-trolling he was, and how badly he treated me. I go on and on for a long time. The man makes a few com-ments and asks a few questions, but most of the time he just listens without judging me.

    "When I am done, he asks me to go over a partic-ular part of the story and to discuss other possible reactions my husband might have had first and that I might have had second. Like when my husband ques-tioned me about what I had said, I took it as, 'He does not believe me and he is criticizing me.' I am a little bewildered by the concept that I could have reacted in more than one way. When I look at events this way, I understand them differently."

- "I am in Heaven, sitting with a person who helped me to the Light. She sits with me, and we talk about what happened in my life. I tell her about the awful feelings I had when I was being stoned by people, because I was seeing spirits other people could not see. I am very angry with those spirits who got me killed. My death was their fault. I wish I never had seen those spirits. I do not want to see them again. The woman is very kind and listens to me for a long time."

Cleansing

Patients are consistent in reporting that every soul has to go through some form of cleansing process after entering Heaven. This often occurs at the outer edge of Heaven, before the soul enters the inner section of Heaven. Patients give different reports of how they get cleansed. Some report taking a bath or shower, standing under a waterfall, bathing in a river or ocean, or swimming in a stream. Others describe a vacuum cleaner that sucks out all their impurities, or a mechanical spinning process during which all the negative stuff is thrown off. The representation is similar to how they were cleaning while on the Earth. Patients' words and descriptions may differ, but the basic idea of cleansing is the same in every case.

Through this process, anything negative is removed from the souls. These would be things that came along with them, such as attached human and demon spirits, dark energies, and demonic devices. Negative emotions and attitudes are removed, but the memory of them is not. The soul ends up with a clean body. After cleansing, the soul feels much less human and much more of a spiritual being. After cleansing, there may be a brief rest period, like "sitting down and catching the breath." Then it goes through the life review. Following are samples of descriptions given by my patients of how souls get cleansed in Heaven:

- "When I go to Heaven after the death of my physical body, I am taken to a place where there are no walls. There are three shower circles. From each shower circle comes powerful rays that pierce and penetrate my whole being. Golden Light bombards me from each shower and cleanses me. It is a wonderful feeling how my spirit being is transformed. I can see grayish film. A river of dark energy comes out of me and goes swirling down to hell. It seems to be a very large dark one. After that I feel clean and sparkly.

"Now I go to another place with angels and other Light beings. I am in a pool or a pond. Here it is silvery Light. It is interesting that Light surrounding the silvery Light is golden, but the liquid or water inside is silvery. It seems like my inner soul (main body of the soul) gets cleansed. It actually separates from the rest of my spirit. It looks gray. As it gets cleansed by the silvery liquid energy, it gets brighter and brighter. A grayish dust comes out and it changes into Light. After cleansing, the main body of my soul comes back to my being.

"Now I go to the top of a mountain. Here, I see golden Light bombarding me from different angles. It is as if there are two balls of Light, like suns, one on each side, that are bombarding me with the powerful golden Light. They are infusing me with love, happiness, and joy.

"Then I go through a huge gate. A big, beautiful angel with wings opens it. I am going through a circular place. The walls are cushiony, airy, and fluffy as if they are made out of clouds. There is no ceiling. It is funny, the floor looks like a green lawn. There is some kind of heat coming from it. As I walk on the lawn, my feet are being cleansed and healed. There are many, many angels at the top, as if the ceiling is made up of angels."

• "I go to a place where there are baby angels. They hold me and comfort me. I am put on a table. There is a Light shining from above, and it is a healing and cleansing Light. It takes out some of the darkness from my being. Angels do some type of body integration here. They are putting my neck and back together, which were broken as a result of a fall, and they are healing them."

• "When I am in Heaven, I am taken to a place where I can bathe in beautiful blue water. It reminds me of crystal clear mountain water flowing over a waterfall into a basin. As I cleanse, black blobs come out of me. As the blobs enter the water, they transform into Light. After cleansing, I am completely lighted."

• "I stand near a beautiful waterfall. A being tells me to go into the water to be cleansed. I go into the stream and stand under the waterfall. Everything is very bright and radiant with golden liquid Light. The river has crystalline blue water, but when it comes down the waterfall, it is a whitish gold, and it radiates Light. As I go under the waterfall, I feel dark beings come out of me. They are pushed out of me as if something is pumping them out. I become brilliant and white, like a shining beacon. I am free of all my negative feelings. It is strange. I see black beings leaping out of me and going down a tunnel. They are pulled down by dark hands that grab them and take them into hell again."

• "I am in Heaven. I am taken to a place where I can cleanse myself. There is a wooden bucket and a dipper to use for cleansing. It is like what I had on Earth. It is marvelous: no matter how much water I dip out, the bucket is still full. I do not have to refill it. I cannot see anything moving in the water either, such as bugs. It is crystal clear. After cleansing, I glow. I feel good. I do not feel the anger or resentment I felt before. I feel peace."

• "When I enter Heaven, angels take me to a healing temple. I am taken to a room to be cleansed. I see a lot of pink Light. I take a shower and all the brown and other bad stuff is washed out of my being and goes down the drain. It is as if my body was filled with mud and dirt, and when I shower, it all washes out. I tingle all over. I feel a big relief, as the hurt feelings and all the emotional garbage is washed out of me.

"Now, I am in a room that is square and the walls are light emerald green. The liquid Light comes down from the ceiling as if the whole ceiling is a shower head. It is as if fiberoptic Light or beams of laser Light come down from the ceiling. Different colors of Light go through me. I feel I am going through different 'washing-machine' cycles, and I am now in the last part of this cycle, waiting to hear a bell so I can walk out.

"Different colored Lights go through me to cleanse me. The first one is white, then pink, violet, green, and blue at the end of the cycle. I hear the beautiful sound of a bell, as if informing me, 'Okay, now you are clean and you can come out.' I feel free, as if I am back to my real self. A huge sense of relief flows through me. My consciousness is getting lighter and lighter. I am all Light and transparency.

"At the beginning, everything here is as it was on Earth, because the guides do not want you to be shocked when you come here. So what I see is similar to the environment I lived in on Earth. It is a duplication of where I came from. Then, the 'solid' buildings change into buildings of Light. The transition to the higher level is a gradual one. After a while, I see things from the heavenly point of view.

"They want me to stay here so I can get a feel for where I am. They want the process to be as gradual as possible. They do not rush me. They wait until I am ready to release the feelings about where I came from. It is my decision. They honor my free will."

• "I was blown to pieces during World War II by a bomb in Germany. After I go to Heaven, I cleanse myself in a pool of water and many dark spirits come out of me and instantly change into Light.

"I see many spirits that died in concentration camps coming to Heaven. Heavenly helpers use different devices to cleanse them. Some souls are cleansed and healed by the angels by being touched with a magic wand of Light. Some are cleansed with devices like a vacuum cleaner, which sucks out the dark energies and devices from them. They also draw out different types of gases from them, which killed them in 'gas chambers.'

"Some spirits are cleansed with a power shower like a dishwasher or what you see at a car wash, in which they are cleansed from different directions, but in a gentle way. Some are cleansed with steam, and heavy, dark entities, devices, and energies are removed that way. The steam softens and makes the sticky, dark entities loosen up so they can be washed away. Many people are showered en masse as a preliminary step to their individual cleansing. This is done in a large area where there are mechanical ceiling devices that move back and forth like a big sprinkler to cleanse people."

• "I am in a healing temple. I see myself sitting in this room, and a tangible Light goes through me, pushing out a dirty, yellow substance. It is debris, or matter, I collected on Earth. I see little demons with big ears coming out, and these beings are transformed into Light. I also see that memories from different times of my life are being cleansed with the Light.

"The first Light I see is like a shower. Some of my memories are cleansed by different Lights. Some Lights clean out the debris that comes with our soul. It is a shimmery, bright, white Light, and it has a wind-like quality, whooshing and pushing out from my form dark entities and everything that is not me.

"Then comes a golden liquid Light to cleanse and heal my traumatic memories. It acts like a medicine to heal those memories. Then there is a shimmery, white, liquid Light that removes something from me that has shape and is tangible. Sometimes the mind needs to be cleansed, so it is cleansed with buckets filled with liquid white Light. There are rooms filled with a purplish gaslike substance, another form of Light. This heals the lungs. When you breathe it, you get rejuvenated.

"Some people here have a very white, pale complexion. They come from the concentration camps. They look very scary, and their eyes are hollow. They need a lot of care. They are exhausted and almost unconscious. First, they have to be cleansed of the gas from the 'gas chamber.' The angels get them into the rooms and cleanse them with some type of transparent blue gas, which is the antidote to the gas that killed them. It is a hard, long process, because their beings are poisoned from the killing gas. I see their beings become more alive as the poisonous gas is removed.

"I am allowed the general understanding of how they are healed. They need to go through different rooms to be treated in different ways. Angels who are working with them have masks and wear special robes. They also put a mask and robe on me so I can go with them to observe the cleansing. It is like a monk's attire, topped with a helmet and goggles.

"There is a liquid gas, a gauzy substance of blue color that cleanses them of certain types of debris. Then the angels get a hose to cleanse the souls with a white, liquid Light. I can see their beings get more alive as the poisonous gas is removed from them.

"Before they come to this room, the concentration camp souls are cleansed with an airy type of white Light. This has a lot of power and can remove entities and other dark things from a person. Demons and other things jump out of them under the pressure of the gassy Light, and these dark beings get transformed. This powerful airy Light pushes out everything from the person that is not part of them, such as entities, devices, and negative energy. Then the souls get treated with a golden liquid Light that looks like honey. It is a Light that can fill and heal every little crack and space. After cleansing, they feel very light."

• "I am standing in an open place and a whirlwind of energy whips around me and cleanses my body. I can feel the pulsation of a flame, like a blend of gold and green Light. It swirls around me. It does not touch the body but goes all around it and cleanses me. My body is also swirling and three or four ribbons of Light come up while I am swirling inside of them. All my pain is removed. Orange pieces come out of me and vanish."

• "I am in a big temple with a high ceiling. There is Light shooting like a lightening bolt from all around. Strangely, it is also like a car wash. Beams of Light come from all directions and cleanse me. My old body is dissolving and I have a new, shining, spirit body in its place."

• "After death, my soul went to Heaven. There I was taken to a room for cleansing. I was cleansed with a shower of white Light, but some stubborn dark entities would not leave me. They held my fragmented soul parts. So I was taken to a place like an operating room. There I saw heavenly beings who looked like surgeons, only they did not use a knife to cut. They used highly focused Light beams to push the stubborn dark entities out of me. Once out, they got transformed into Light, and my fragmented soul parts were reintegrated with me."

• "I am in a room in Heaven, where I am getting cleansed. I stand in a harmonics room. I hear the best music I have ever heard. It consumes me as if I am part of it and I resonate with it. It is as if a wave of Light and music come together continuously, as if Light and sound are one. It is all-consuming. It is as if I am retuning and realigning myself with God. It is awesome. That is why I like music so much. As these waves of Light and sound pass through me, they push out grayish debris. After my cleansing, and by giving up bodily feelings and awareness and becoming one with the Light, I am experiencing a bliss."

Life Review

After the cleansing phase, hypnotized patients describe being escorted to another "room," where they review the life they just finished with some heavenly beings. Depending on the individual's level of spiritual evolution, there can be three to five or more beings to help. They may be angels or other wise beings. If the person is spiritually at an advanced level, there may be masters and other high beings there to help.

These beings, who serve as counselors, usually have a clear understanding and a broad perspective of the nature of the Light and universe. The role of these spiritual figures is to help the person sort through the now-ended life, but not to judge them.

The souls, with the help of the spiritual counselors, evaluate their life, viewing it like a panoramic playback of every event in detail, usually in chronological order. They not only reexperience those events with all their feelings and knowledge, but they also experience the feelings of *other* people who were involved in those events. In this way they are presented a well-rounded picture of the events and how they affected *everybody*.

Souls receive more knowledge and develop more understanding while reviewing their life than when they actually lived their life. In Heaven, patients describe themselves as nonphysical beings, and there are no barriers of time and space. They can return to any moments in the life they just finished and observe the events from different points of view. They also have access to their other past lives and even their future lives. My hypnotized patients often describe this review stage as a process of self-evaluation and analysis of the life they just left. They claim it is a most difficult and painful process because it is they who took the actions, and it is they who are to judge themselves. They are their own harshest judge and jury. There is no judgment by the counselors or God.

Individuals alone interpret their success or failure in meeting the goals they set in Heaven for that life. Their feelings of disappointment and bitterness over lost opportunities, failures, and wrong actions are hard to express. Their feelings of success and triumph about the good actions and the goals they achieved are profound and equally hard to convey. In this stage, they also recognize the success or failure of their personal and group goals, and in case of failures, they also realize how this life may have set them back from their spiritual path.

During this process, the souls come to grips with the harm they did to themselves and others by suicide, murder, and other negative actions. People who lived negative and wicked lives in which they did severe damage to others and to themselves find it hard to go through this process. The full realization of the severity of harm they inflicted on themselves and others can be a terrifying experience. For most people, this is about as close to hell as they can get.

Some of the examples of life review described by my patients are as follows:

• "After resting for a long time, I am taken to a place where I review my life. Three wise-looking spiritual beings help me with the review. They have human forms, long white beards, long white hair, and white robes. We are seated at a round table.

"I see images of my life on the screen of my mind. They are in color and are shown to me in chronological order. I review my whole life, but I spend more time on the important events, such as when I fell from my pony and hurt my head. At that time, many demon spirits came into me. From here I can see that they sprayed a dark substance into a certain part of my brain, and this made me irrational and paranoid. The demons constantly talked to me and told me not to trust my family and to hit them.

"Then they took over the part of my brain that controls aggression, and this made me violent. There was an angry spirit in me that acted through me. I see how much pain and suffering I caused my family. I can feel their feelings and pain. I feel ashamed and sorry for all my negative actions during that life.

"The wise beings are very loving and nonjudgmental. They help me to see that past life, the lessons I learned and the ones I did not, and the things I needed to understand and change. In the review, I realize I had a great deal of potential, but it was blocked because of the dark influences."

• "I am taken to a room. There are three people sitting there, who resemble elders in my village, except that they are glowing with Light. They ask me to look back to the beginning of my life. I see my whole life through my mind's eye. I perceive things as other people saw them. I sense the events from *their* point of view, as they saw, heard, and interpreted them. I see what their reaction was. I understand things in a different way. I now have an insight about how wrong I was regarding how people treated me, and how dark beings influenced me to see everything negatively. I realize I assumed that whatever others did was done with malicious intent, to demean me or make me angry. But, I see now there were innocuous reasons for their actions."

• "I am in Heaven with two angels, Joseph and Raphael, reviewing the life I lived in 6000 B.C. They seem to be pleased. Angel Raphael is outgoing and warm. We review my life. It was almost picture-perfect: everything went exactly as I planned. The books were written and the information sheets with all those wise sayings were prepared; the merchants carried the news as the city grew. All the people were taught, as the old religion was replaced with the new one. We taught about an eternal being, life after death, and how people can become better through spiritual development. Things worked out extremely well. Then the angels send me on for more learning."

• "I am taken to a room to review my life. There are seven beings there. They are different ascended masters. I recognize Kwanyin. She is a beautiful woman with lots of purple around her. She has a loving heart and is very good with children. I see the goddess of liberty, resembling the Statue of Liberty; she is huge and yellowish white and gold. Then I see Nada. She has a pink-rose color. I seem to know her from a long time ago. Then I see a being with a brilliant blue form and a crown. He is young and old looking at the same time. He has brilliant eyes, and he is known as the 'great divine director.'

"I see two other beings. One is of white, green, and violet Light, and her name is Portia. She represents justice. Then there is a very tall being with green robes. He has brilliant, penetrating eyes. I recognize him as the Elohim Cyclopia. I see another female figure wearing an old-fashioned dress of green and white. She has grace and beauty: she is the goddess of truth. All of these masters have many other names, and they are all very loving, kind, and gentle.

"I died when I was a child, but I seem to be grown up now and I can understand things better. As I review my life, I see some karma being expressed here. I understand that my death at a young age was karmic because in different lifetimes children died innocently in battles because of me. It happened through the influences of dark forces. Guides are saying that I will get another chance.

• "I am taken to some counselors who are wise beings. There are twelve of them. We are in a beautiful, big room. It has a big table and beautiful chairs like you see associated with kings and queens. The counselors look solid, but they are of Light.

"Some of the beings have a crown on their heads. I see many ascended masters. I see a beautiful woman with a crown; she looks like a queen and her attire is very beautiful. They call her Queen of Light or Mother of Light. I also see Jesus. He has so much Light that I cannot look at him. I see the master of art. He knows me well and he shakes my hand. There is another figure, the master of healing, who is wearing a green pulsating attire.

"I sit at the table. Everybody looks at a movie screen. They point at some things and explain other things. I see different moments of my life, such as when I was screaming because I did not want to do something. I had a hard time adjusting to sudden changes. I was too deep in my world and did not recognize what was going on outside. Sudden shock was very traumatic. Everybody in the room is taking notes. It does not take a long time to review my life, because my life was short. Then they ask me to study different things to prepare for the next life."

• "I was tortured and killed in a concentration camp at the age of thirteen. After cleansing and healing in Heaven, I am taken to a luminescent room to review my life. Everything is glowing here. Four Light beings help me with the review. There is an opening in the floor like a review portal, through which I can look back at and review my life in the concentration camp.

"I can see how different types of physical, emotional, and mental abuse I suffered in that life created different problems for me in the current life. I starved for months, which caused the weight problem I have in the current life. They broke my nose and put metal rods in the sinuses, and this is responsible for my current sinus problems. They fed me mild poison in the food, which caused throat and stomach irritation at that time and also in this life. They broke many bones, which caused aches and pains in different parts of my body in the current life.

"The counselors remind me that I chose to incarnate in that life. In Heaven there was a foreknowledge about what is going to happen under the extreme dark influences on Earth. Higher-evolved souls volunteered to incarnate there to raise humanity's awareness. It takes something so horrific as a concentration camp to get people to stand up and take notice and learn lessons. Less-evolved souls were not allowed to incarnate and go through it, because they were not developed enough to cope with the intense trauma. It helped humanity to learn a lesson and it also helped the souls that incarnated there, because it balanced and erased much of their karma."

• "I am in a hall with records. Six wise Light beings show me a tablet or a book and say, 'Touch it and you will get the information.' They are master beings who are here to help me. This is very familiar to me. I have done this before.

"As I touch and focus on the book, pages turn and I see, feel, and relive different episodes of my life, which I just left. It is a kind of fast-forward movie. As the pages turn, I see episode after episode of that life being unlocked. Every time I turn a page, I see events in their time sequence. I am viewing it, but am not immersed in it.

"I see I was supposed to learn to be humble and to have patience. I had to learn to live two different types of life: a regular human life and a knowing life with higher knowledge. I had to learn to be careful and to not take risks. Some people will understand what I have to say and some people will not, but either way, I should not sacrifice myself.

"I think I learned these lessons in that life. I also understand that my family is important and I should not leave it, because I left my family in that life. That is a big lesson I have to learn. I see that one of the problems that came from that life to my current life is the fear of other people finding out that I have a special knowledge."

Rest and Restoration

According to my hypnotized subjects, after reviewing their lives, they go to a place to rest. If they lead a traumatic life, they are sent for rest right after the cleansing, and they review their life later. Patients give different descriptions of this "place" in Heaven. Most commonly, they describe a house with a bed, a beautiful garden, a meadow with trees and flowers. Some people describe it as like sleeping on fluffy clouds or sitting on clouds with angels or resting on the beach. Their needs govern what type of representation they see. The purpose is the same: resting, healing, and allowing experiences to integrate.

Limited activity is the main hallmark of the resting phase. Mostly, there is sleep, rest, recuperation, and preparation. The length of resting depends on the individual. If they lived a traumatic life, they require a longer time to rest. The more spiritually advanced people tend to need a longer resting period, because more work was done, and thus there is more to integrate. Here are some depictions of rest and restoration as given by my hypnotized subjects:

• "After I review my life (in which I was very cruel), I rise into a tunnel leading to layers of clouds. I spend several 'years' wandering amongst these clouds. I think about the life I just left and realize it is going to be very difficult when I have future lives because of the suffering I brought to all those people. I try to forgive myself and heal, and I hope to learn from all the mistakes I made. I walk around or float aimlessly on those clouds. When I get tired, I rest on the clouds and sleep. Not many people are around. Now and then some beings of Light come around to give me hope and encouragement, I still feel very bad about what I have done.

"I tell God how sorry I am for what I have done. As time goes on, I spend more and more time sleeping, until finally I find peace. I still have a human form. Then I go to a higher section of Heaven, where I do not have a human form. I am a ball of Light."

• "After cleansing my body, I am taken to a place where I can rest, heal, and be refreshed. This place has soft chairs and beds. One can hear soothing music, if one tunes into it. Every being has an individual room. Those resting can also go outside and rest near a beautiful garden. This is a beautiful place. The beds, chairs, and lounges are soft and inviting. They are all of Light, but they resemble earthly hardwood furniture. Many beings come to serve my needs. There are multitudes of beings resting here. I can rest as long as I need until I feel refreshed."

• "Angels take me to a place where I can sleep and rest. It is like a hospital or a rest home. Nuns in white robes tell me I have to rest and heal before I do anything else. There are beautiful hallways with cathedral ceilings. I hear wonderful, peaceful music, which takes me to another part of my being.

"Everything here is designed for rest and is planned to calm you down by the music and the way everybody walks around you. They respect your space and needs. They do not look at you or talk to you, but you can sense they send you love. They do exactly what you need. If you need quiet, they are very quiet. If you need compassion, you sense it coming from them. Elder Light beings counsel me and explain my state of being and what I need to do. I am resting up and recovering very fast, because I lived a short life."

•   "I lived a very traumatic and abusive life in which I was brutally tortured and killed. When I went to Heaven, I was suspended in a cocoon of Light, like a butterfly. I stayed in it for a long time to rest and heal."

•   "After the cleansing, I float up to a beautiful beach. Everything and everybody is white and glowing. People seem to be resting and at peace. They are very friendly. I introduce myself. Everybody has a Light body. Even I look like that now, a being of Light. I rest here for a while and then go to another place, where I review my life."

•   "I rest in fields and forest. There is green all around—green bushes and trees. They are more alive and their colors are different from their counterparts on Earth. The air is permeated with music. I walk, meditate, write, and draw pictures. I sleep once in a while, but I do not have a need to sleep much. I am mostly alone, meditating on my thoughts, planning what to do next."

•   "After my cleansing, I go to a place that is like a resort on Earth, but much more beautiful. There are lounge chairs and everything is very peaceful and tranquil. There is music, if you wish to hear it. There are Light helpers who provide services for you. They take care of everything you need. You are made as comfortable as you want to be. It is like a luxury hotel on Earth. Some souls have individualized counseling. Some are restored and made whole again. Some are in private rooms for quiet; some listen to music; some walk around outside or sit in a lounge looking at a beautiful, glowing garden."

The following are longer, more detailed descriptions from some of my hypnotized patients in which they describe the overall transition experience, like death, transition, and return to Heaven and what happens there, and many of its seemingly Earthlike details:

- "I am a king. My son has imprisoned me for many years and I feel very sad and tired. I am dying at the age of seventy of heart and lung problems. I am ready to die because I am tired of living like this. I have chest pain and breathing problems. I stop breathing and my spirit comes out of my chest. It is curled up in a ball because it is tired and sad.

  "I see gold spiral steps just like in my palace. I walk up those steps. I believe I am going alone, but as I look back, I realize I am not alone. Angels are escorting me. I did not notice them initially, because I am preoccupied with my feelings. When we reach the top of the staircase, somebody greets me. He is gracious and says, 'Welcome, king,' and takes me inside Heaven. It is like an extension of my palace, of what I am used to. Then things change, the staircase disappears, and it becomes a corridor of white Light.

  "They put me in a bathtub. The attendants appear like maid servants, similar to what I had as a king on Earth, but they are really angels. It is more luxurious than on Earth, but it has an earthly setting. I see differently colored water, but it is really energy. I see blue for cleansing, which changes to green for healing. Some black things come out of my body. Scars around my feet melt away. A black scorpion (a demon) comes off my chest; it had caused me a lot of grief.

  "Something else that is dark falls away from me and disappears. I am given something with which to dry my body, and as I do so, gold dust is rubbed on my body to heal me. Though I do not feel good about myself, the angels treat me with respect and reverence. I see Krishna, the godhead. He gives me a hug. I feel overwhelmed.

  "After resting for a while, I am escorted to a large chamber with beautiful and ornate architecture. Six beings sit on thronelike chairs. They are dressed in kingly costumes; they are heavenly kings or ascended masters. One is Sanat Kumara, another is Yam. I do not recognize the others. I also feel the presence of Vishnu, the godhead, above us, and a connecting cord going from me to him. I see that all the others in the room are also connected with Vishnu.

"The beings here have a lot of gentleness and humility. Although they are very high beings, they are also extremely humble. Yam reads the events of my life from a scroll. In a few minutes he has read the whole thing. As he reads, I see all the events in my mind's eye. I experience failure and guilt about how my son turned out; maybe I could have done something differently, I think to myself.

"Beings tell me not to be so hard on myself. They say my son was that way because of his inherent nature. I am given the understanding that this was a special life and I was selected for that role for a specific reason. After the review, I am escorted to the resting area.

"I am given ornate clothes as I was used to as a king, but these are made of Light. I am taken to a room for resting. It is like the bedroom I had in my palace. The floor is made of marble and there are marble pillars. The bed is pink and red, and the pillows are of gold. I rest for a long time because my soul is very tired."

• "I am in the womb and am about six months old. My mother is upset because she is not married and is worried about what people will think about her. She is concerned that if she has a child, she will be forced to stay home and take care of the child for the rest of her life. She does not want that, because she wants a leadership role.

"I am a male fetus in the womb, and I am aware of what my mother is thinking. She got a wire from her friends. She uses it to hurt me, and the lower part of my body gets torn from the rest of my body. I lose consciousness and die.

"I feel a lot of anger toward my mother. What she did is terrible. I remain near her for a while as a spirit.

Then I begin to be afraid of my mother. I see a bright Light and start to move toward it and it pulls me up. I still have the form of a young child.

"In Heaven, I am put on the floor of a room filled with Light, and some Light beings talk to me about my life. I seem to grow up a little and am able to understand. They remind me that I had gone into that life knowing I would be aborted and knowing that, in the long run, it would be an experience of growth for me and my mother. Thus I should not feel resentment toward her.

"While in Heaven, I planned to be aborted to make me realize how terrible abortion is. I also chose to be aborted, because in another life I was a warrior who killed a lot of children, and the mother who aborted me was one of those children. I butchered her, so in this life I planned to be butchered by her by being aborted. This would balance out my previous negative actions. It would also make my mother realize, after her death, how bad abortion is. My mother did not plan the abortion in Heaven. She made that choice when she was in life because of demonic influences.

"I am put in a bathtub filled with liquid Light. I remain in it for about forty-five minutes and get cleansed. Then I am taken to a crib by a Light being and I stay there for a long time. I grow into a young adult. During this time, I rest and reflect on my life.

"From Heaven's perspective, I see that abortion is always wrong, but given that it exists and happens, it can be used by the souls to grow or balance out their actions from past lives. It is wrong, because although a child's soul knows in Heaven that it will be aborted in life, it is not making the choice to die. So abortion is basically a murder before the child has any chance to live at all. But we need to stay away from judging the mother and other people involved. We can educate them, but it has to be a mother's free will. She will have to face her negative actions and balance them in a future life. This is the universal law and nobody escapes it. From Heaven, I see that abortion will continue for many years on Earth, until things change on our planet, when we become beings of Light, and children are seen as a blessing rather than a burden.

"After resting, I see a bridge in front of me and I walk on it and pass upward through the clouds to the upper level of the Light."

• "I am dying of a stomach infection and hemorrhage. I lived a very evil life. I was hired to torture prisoners and I did it without feeling guilty. I believed that people who break the law and commit crimes should be punished for what they do. I tortured them meticulously and professionally. I think that when I go to Heaven God will reward me.

"As I lose blood and consciousness, my spirit comes out of my body from the back of my neck. My spirit is white with dark spots. I feel burdened by the pain I intentionally caused to other people. I did not feel it while I was in the body.

"I see the Light coming. I am scared and worried how I will be judged. Dark beings behind me tell me I will be safer with them because of what I did. They tell me that I did my job well and I should be proud of that. I am trying to move away from the darkness and go toward the Light. I see baby angels. They sing softly and try to comfort me to make me less scared.

"I am brought to a platform, where I stand and lower my head as a column of Light passes through and cleanses me. All the darkness trickles out of me. All the dark beings, dark devices, and dark energy get transformed into Light. Soul parts and the spirits of dozens of people I tortured come out of me. Angels bring my soul parts back from my other lives, which were held back from me.

"I go upward to another place that has four round columns between the floor and the ceiling and no walls. There are four Light beings present, and they are expecting me. They show me my book and want me to look at it. They point out different events in my life and I see them in my mind's eye. I feel the horror of what I did and I feel the feelings of the people I tortured. The Light beings tell me I was saved from going into the darkness because of my many good past lives. In the future, I will have some lives where I will get a chance to purify myself. In the future, they suggest, I should have compassion for people who are suffering.

"Then I go off to a garden. I think about what I have done and what I have learned from it, of the difficulties I will have in future lives. After I have rested, I am taken into a higher level of the Light."

• "I am a twenty-year-old female. I find my boyfriend with another woman. I feel my life is ended. It is very painful and I feel ashamed. I believe there is no way out. I will not trust this man again. I want to kill myself and end it all. I find some drapes, go to the barn, find a hook, tie my braided hair around my neck, and hang myself.

"As I am trying to hang myself, I change my mind. I suddenly realize what I am doing. I do not want to die, but it is too late. I am trying to stop it. It is so stupid to die over a man. I want to scream, but I cannot. Everything happens very fast and it is over. As I look back, my spirit comes out from the top of my head. I see my dead body. It looks awful. My tongue is sticking out, my face is blue, and my eyes are popping out.

"I feel horrible that I did this. I think about my friends and parents. I do not know what to do. I wander around in a meadow. I am afraid and ashamed to go home, because I do not know how my family will react. I just sit here and cry. After a while, beautiful angels come and I go with them. They tell me I will be okay and I do not have to go home if I do not want to. They hold my hand and I fly with them to the beautiful city of Light.

"Everybody is trying to cheer me up because I feel so horrible and ashamed of what I did. The angels listen and cheer me up. I tell them how I idolized this person, and how my whole life revolved around him. I believed he liked me too. I was very innocent. I am surprised that he can do things like this, betray me by seeing somebody else behind my back. I was truly hurt. I felt as though my world had shattered. I feel better after I talk to those angels. Then I am taken for cleansing.

"I see a woman who talks about what got damaged

in my life and what I need to do to cleanse myself. She says that when people commit suicide, they destroy a very important part of their soul. It is as if they betray their soul. It is a self-destruction of the soul that is not easily repaired. I will have to come back again and again, maybe for many lifetimes, in which I will re-experience betrayal by a man. I will have to be strong and deal with it *without* killing myself to get my soul parts back. The first step of healing is 'self love,' she tells me.

"I am taken to another room. I feel very sad and am almost unconscious. The angels carry me, wrap me in a white blanket, and put me on a table of Light. I feel comforted and loved, and I remain here a long time. Then they take me to a shower room, where different Lights, such as blue and purple, go through my body. They remove everything negative from my body. Afterward, I feel better.

"Then my body is merged into a clear, liquid Light. It is a different form of Light. I stay in this for a while and breathe deeply. Darkness comes out of me, like a dark mist covering my soul. The angels put a robe around me.

"I go to a room in which there is a white gas. It goes into me and I feel more together. They put Light rays into my eyes and restore what was lost from them because of my hanging. I hear messages such as, 'You love yourself; everything will be fine. You will heal from a broken heart. You have to take care of yourself. That is the most important thing. No man will take your crown.'

"I see my broken heart on the floor. I pick it up and talk to it. I tell my heart that if there is nobody to love you, you have to love yourself, that nobody can break your heart unless you allow it. I put my heart pieces together using some type of glue. Then a windlike Light goes into my heart. I ask my heart to forgive me. I hear the words, 'You need to be devoted to your heart and take care of it.'

"What I see is incredible. I see my hair braid. I have karma with my hair because I used it to hang myself. I have to ask for forgiveness from my hair. I hold this braid in my hands and repeat over and over, 'forgive me, forgive me.' I have a revelation that I have to work with hair to make up for my wrongdoing. That is why I am a hairdresser in this life. I have pain and hollowness in my solar plexus because I weakened my will to live. So the angels put little crystals in there to support my solar plexus.

"Two baby angels with trumpets take me to a room after the cleansing is finished. It is a big, glowing room with a long table. Present are twenty-four Light beings, both male and female, who help me review my life. They are not formal or judgmental. As I enter the room, I am afraid and ashamed of what I did. One of the beings, who is dressed in beautiful clothes, takes my hands and tells me, 'Don't worry, we are not here to judge you.' A younger-looking being asks me what pushed me to take my life. I tell them that I felt so desperate that I would be in that pain forever, so I wanted to end it.

"As I review my life, it is as if I am here sitting at the table *and*, at the same time, can be down on Earth. I see all the events in my mind's eye and relive different events of my life. People are not surprised about what I did in that life. I have a feeling I planned that life, that I planned to feel brokenhearted and planned to want to end my life because of the intensity of pain. The beings tell me I did a lot of good things in that life. I was happy and joyful. Everything was great in my life. My parents adored me and I grew up in a beautiful environment, but the trauma of the betrayal was too intense for me.

"During the review, I am upset and feel down. The Light beings try to cheer me, but I am very hard on myself. I feel like an old woman with all these burdens. I sense I am a very high being and that I planned to have my heart broken to make myself strong. I was told I may commit suicide, but I said, 'No, I am going to be stronger. No way am I going to commit suicide. I will not do that.' I was so proud of myself that I would not do it, because I am a higher Light being. I almost went into that life knowing it might happen. Now I am ashamed about what I did and of not being able to be strong.

"I see I chose to have a broken heart during that lifetime, and that if I had succeeded and not committed suicide, I would have grown greatly because of the strength I would have achieved through the pain. I could have chosen not to have that trauma in my life. But I chose it for fast spiritual growth. But this way I have gained much more, because, by committing suicide, I had to work it out in a harder way, which will make me even stronger.

"After the review, I feel awful and ashamed. I go to a place to rest. I visit friends. Sometimes, I go to the library to study and other times I rest. This is what my soul needs. I also take some navy blue substance, like a pill, to make me heal faster."

• "I am a youth who was in the drug trade. I used to get the younger generation hooked on drugs, and when they despaired, I convinced them to commit suicide. I was apprehended and put in prison at the age of thirty-six. One of the prisoners plunged a metal rod in my chest and killed me.

"My spirit stays in the body for a couple of hours after the death of the body. My spirit is not ready to leave. After I come out of the body, I see dark beings. My first thoughts are that maybe the guys want to take some lessons from me. They tell me that all the people I pushed to commit suicide are waiting in hell to take revenge on me. I do not like the sound of this. Eventually, I pray and see glimpses of Light, and two Light beings pull me up into the Light.

"When I go to Heaven, the angels put me in a pool of Light and I remain there for a long time. They want to do the cleansing gently and to give me time to reflect on what I did. As I am in that pool of liquid Light, all sorts of evil entities, energies, and devices come out of me. The soul parts of people I pushed into killing themselves, the soul parts of the person who killed me, the soul parts of my parents—all these come out of me. Eventually, I am cleansed completely.

"Then I am taken to a room where there are two glowing Light beings. They have a book of white Light on the table. The room is like a library, but the walls and floor are of Light. The beings tell me to look at the book. They are kind and nonjudgmental.

"I see in my mind's eye all the souls who committed suicide because of me. I understand how wrong it was and how much I damaged those souls. I realize that in future lives I will have to go through similar suffering to that I caused them. As I look back at the events, I see I had a lot of dark entities inside me laughing and telling me to do different things. Also, dark demons outside of me were manipulating me. I feel terrified and in horror of what I did and experience a lot of guilt. I feel the physical and emotional feelings of the people I convinced to commit suicide.

"After the review, I am lifted into a building with lots of rooms. I go there to rest and reflect on what I did and receive counseling along with other beings. I am counseled to see how wrong the things I did were and the negative effect I had on the souls I convinced to commit suicide. The counselors tell me that if I am determined to work those actions, they will try to prepare and coach me for it. They give me strength, willingness, and perseverance. They calm me down and get me to rest a lot.

"I rest for a long time, reflecting on what I did. I feel myself called to the roof of the building. There, a ball of Light comes to me and passes into me and pulls me up into the upper section of the Light."

• "I am an African man living in a jungle in A.D. 840. I am in a tribe. We capture members of enemy tribes, blind them by stabbing their eyes, and use them as slaves. I believe that I am doing a good job for my tribe. After some time, I get caught by another tribe. They are going to decapitate me. I now seriously doubt if it was okay to torment other people. I conclude that I should suffer with vision problems for eternity.

"I am kneeling, facing the ground, as they cut off my head. It takes several attempts, and I die before my head separates from my body. I wonder where all those animals are that are supposed to greet me upon death. That is what my tribe believed.

"I feel warmth on my back. I look up and see a bright Light. I feel it is the place I should go to. So I start moving toward the Light. Most of me is very dark. I feel afraid of going to the Light, but I go anyway. I see many people whose eyes I cut out. I am shocked they are in human form and not animals, because my tribe believed most people come back as animals after their death. I am scared of them, but they are loving and help me up.

"They take me to a pool of Light and put me in it. A column of Light goes through me and pushes dark beings out of me, and these turn into Light. After the dark entities and energies are removed, I feel weak and shaky.

"I get out of the pool and walk toward a hut. It is similar to what we had on Earth, but it is made of Light. Two men stand as guards at the hut. They ask me to go in. Inside are three Light beings, who are kind and loving. They show me a stack of wooden tablets with writings on them. They say, 'This is your life.' I start to shake as I get ready to look at that life. One Light being puts his hand on my shoulder to calm me down and fill me with Light.

"I begin to read the tablets. I see the children I beat up. I see when I cut out people's eyes. I experience their feelings. I realize that I should have left the tribe rather than do what they told me to do. I decide that sometime in my future lives I will have to suffer with what they suffered. I see that my children and tribe are doing well, and I feel more ashamed, because we became strong by hurting and killing other people. I see my death, and I feel that I got much less than I deserved. I feel nauseous and sick. I curl up on the ground and hide my face with my hands. I feel guilty, ashamed, and horrified.

"After the life review, I go to the top of a mountain made up of Light. I drift on clouds, still curled up and hiding my face in my hands. Gradually, I relax and calm down and think about the things I have done. I reflect on what I have done, and I rest. I drift around on different clouds. Sometimes Light beings come to help, but most of the time I choose to remain alone. Toward the end of my rest, I am able to talk with other people. I feel hopeful that I will be able to improve my soul in future lives and that I will not be hardhearted. Then I am taken by seven Light beings up through a hole in the clouds and into the upper part of the Light."

Up to the resting phase, everything the souls see is in human terms, such as tables, chairs, gardens, rooms, palaces, huts. This takes place on the outer edge of Heaven. After resting, healing, and integrating, people let go of their past-life personality. They do not destroy it but incorporate it into themselves, making "themselves" greater than the individual personality they just lived. The experiences, knowledge, and feelings are integrated into the oversoul. After rest and integration, they lose their human form and become a pure spirit and go on to the inner section of the Light.

Chapter Seventeen

Life in Heaven (Light): Our Real Home

According to my hypnotized patients, if we can imagine the whole realm of Light, or Heaven, as a crystal globe (see figure 1 on page 22), then the outer edge of that globe is the place where people reenter the Light after the death of their physical body. In this re-entry area, souls go through the cleansing, ventilation, life review, and resting phases of afterlife experience. In this area, everything is of Light, even though things resemble their counterparts on Earth, that is, human forms, buildings, gardens, meadows, waterfalls, rivers, beaches, tables, chairs. As a result, when people come here from Earth, they feel comfortable in this familiar environment.

Hypnotized people claim that after they've rested in Heaven following death, they let go of their past-life personality and integrate it into their larger self, making "themselves" much greater than the individual past-life personality. They become a complete spiritual being. They drop their physical form and look like a spark or a ball of Light. They function with their full spiritual capacity and knowledge.

After resting, souls go to the inner section of the globe (in the global model) or the upper section of the pyramid (in the pyramidal model of the Light). Some see many pathways as they move toward the inner or upper part of the Light and go through one of the pathways, depending on their spiritual evolution. Others do not see any pathways but have an inner awareness of where they are supposed to go.

In contrast to the outer edge of Light where everything appears as things on Earth, inside the inner section of Heaven, everything is of Light. There is no earthly representation here, only "clouds" of brilliant white Light, souls floating around in different shapes such as balls, pyramids, squares, or elongated forms of Light of different sizes and vibrations. Souls recognize one another through their vibrations and forms. In Heaven, there are no barriers of time and space. People can access their past, present, and future any time they choose. Inside Heaven, souls communicate telepathically. They go from one part of Heaven to another telepathically. All they have to do is think of the place they want to go and they are there. They do not eat or sleep, and they rest only when needed.

Each soul has an inner awareness as to which part of Heaven they belong, and that is where they go. Souls that are the least spiritually developed remain closer to the outer edge of the globe of Light. More evolved souls go further inside or upward, and those that are most evolved go even more inside or upward in the Light, closer to the godheads. Souls that are the least developed have low vibrations, so they are more comfortable near the outer edge of the Heaven. Higher-evolved souls are comfortable closer to the godheads, because their vibrations are higher and they feel comfortable in the inner section.

My hypnotized patients claim that they plan for their next life while they are in the Heaven-world. They plan their personal and group goals, if they are part of a group in Heaven. As part of their individual goals, they select their parents, spouse, children, and other significant people in their lives. They choose to be with certain people to resolve karmic problems. Through the resolution of problems, they can learn to live with each other in a loving way.

Sometimes they choose certain people for love and support through rough times, or because they will be able to give them guidance so they can fulfill their purpose. Souls also decide their professions and other key circumstances for their coming lives. They choose happy events and also traumatic situations, so they can grow spiritually through the pain and suffering. They also pick the gifts and talents they will have on Earth. They select physical, emotional, and mental problems to address the unresolved physical, emotional, and mental residues from deaths or traumas in their past lives.

In Heaven, people have several meetings with the souls with whom they are going to be on Earth. If these people are already living on Earth, their souls travel to the Heaven-world while sleeping. Everything is planned mutually and with other people's permission, according to the reports of my hypnotized patients.

As I explained earlier in the book, people under hypnosis claim they plan the date and exact time of birth according to astrological calculations. There are specialists in Heaven who help them figure out what will be the best day, date, and time of birth to give them certain personality, physical, and emotional characteristics as well as particular strengths and weaknesses. Parents are also instructed as to when to conceive, although on the conscious level they usually have no awareness of this. Sometimes they succeed, while other times they do not because there are other forces influencing them. Souls also decide the time of their death and how they are going to die. They often choose to die from an illness, which will help them resolve karmic problems.

If the beings are part of a group in Heaven, they also plan collective goals and how to achieve them. Group goals are usually "higher" divine goals that will help humanity to evolve faster. Plans are made in such a way that souls can fulfill both their individual and group goals in a given lifetime.

People decide on which planet they will incarnate. According to my patients, we incarnate on other planets similar to Earth. If it is Earth, then they choose the country, culture, race, and other situations to suit their needs. Not only do they plan for the next coming life, but they plan tentatively for their future lives. According to my patients, even while on Earth, they continue to go to Heaven while asleep at night and meet with different people who are living on Earth as well as in Heaven to plan further details.

Under hypnosis, my patients claim that in Heaven they take classes, study in the library, and learn and prepare for everything they are going to do on Earth. Whatever they are going to do on Earth, they have already done it in Heaven. For example, if they are planning to research and invent something, they have already done that research in Heaven. When they incarnate on Earth, they can access that knowledge through their soul or guides from Heaven. Even as they do the research, they can go to Heaven during sleep to gather more knowledge, which they can apply on Earth the next day.

For example, those who plan to write a book have already written the book in Heaven before incarnating on Earth. Later, they receive the knowledge of the book from within or from their heavenly guides. Most people do not have this awareness consciously and do not know how much help they have from the Heaven-world. They just think they are working alone or only with people on Earth. Of course, not everything works out as we plan, because everybody, once incarnated, has free will, and the dark beings are always there trying to distract us from our purpose.

My patients claim that in Heaven they teach and help souls that are at lower levels of development. At the same time, they learn from beings at a higher level and also from the masters. While in Heaven, people claim they go to the Akashic libraries related to our planet as well as to the ones that belong to other planets. They learn and teach at these libraries. Sometimes, they make plans to work with beings of other planets to help the beings on Earth or other planets.

My patients claim their guides and guardian angels are also assigned to them in Heaven. Heavenly guides are human souls that have incarnated on Earth before and have chosen to remain in Heaven to be spiritual guides for specific people on Earth. Usually, guides choose to work with the individuals because they have known them from another life, or they may have special talents the person will require on Earth. For example, a musician or a painter may have guides with similar gifts. Guides are with us from conception until death to provide love, support, guidance, and protection, but they can change from lifetime to lifetime and sometimes even in the same life. Everybody has one to three (or more) personal guides, depending on their life purpose.

Our guardian angels are also chosen before we incarnate on Earth. They are often assigned to us, or have planned to be with a certain person to provide protection and help. People claim that sometimes they have the same guardian angels from lifetime to lifetime. As explained before, angels are spiritual beings created to remain in Heaven only and to work from there. As a rule they never incarnate in a human body and are not created for that purpose. If by mistake or in a special circumstance they incarnate on a planet, then they lose their angelhood.

Everybody has one or more guardian angels assigned to them, depending on their purpose on Earth. Angels are always with people to help and protect them, but because God gives us free will, He, the angels, and the guides cannot help us unless we ask and pray for help. Therefore, we should pray to God and request our guides and angels to protect us, guide us, and help us with our day-to-day situations and problems.

Here are some examples, as described by my patients under hypnosis, of how we live in Heaven. What is especially interesting is that many offer practical tips for spiritual living from their heavenly vantage point.

• "After reviewing my life, when I was killed because I was able to see spirits that others could not see, Heavenly counselors tell me to study more about spirits and psychic gifts. I go to the inner section of Heaven to a learning place, where I study about the spirits and the purpose of being on Earth and the meaning of the universe.

"I do not have human form anymore. I am formless, just a ball of Light. There are other souls that also look like me, and the place looks like a cloud of Light. We communicate telepathically through our minds without saying a single word. We do not walk, just float around. We think about where we want to go and we are there. We do not sleep, just rest, and we have no need to eat.

"Heavenly beings tell me that some of the stuff I am studying is what I have written myself many lifetimes ago. When I review it, I will remember it, because I was the one who wrote it in the first place. That is confusing to me. But as soon as I read it and study it, I know it. I am just reviewing it to go back to Earth and work more.

"Even in the Light, when we go back we do not remember everything until later. I see that I wrote this 'book' thousands of years ago in the Light, after many lifetimes of development and learning about how things work and through the knowledge we have gained by working for God. This 'book' is about how reincarnation works and our purpose in the Light (Heaven) and on Earth. There are many in the Light here who have no idea who they are. While in Heaven, I learn about different things I will need in the next life on Earth.

"Now I am at the Akashic Records studying about different bodies we have and about different energy systems such as chakras, meridians and Kundalini. I see a book. It is opening by itself. I see back to the beginning when we were one with God. I see the fall of Lucifer and his demons. There are multiple layers of creation. What I see are concentric spheres, the universes one over the top of the other. These are different planes of existence. God is at the center and these other planes are outside.

"I see that we exist on four different planes at the same time and we have four different bodies: the physical body, the etheric body, the astral body, and the spiritual body. The *physical body* is constructed of earthly material like minerals and other substances, but it is fed and animated by the other bodies. The *etheric body* is an invisible body that overlaps the physical body and interpenetrates it. Without the etheric body there will be no physical body. It is essentially the invisible blueprint of the physical body. After an amputation, the etheric body still exists and is responsible for the feeling that the amputated part is still there. The *astral body* exists just above the etheric body. Our negative emotions and feelings can affect our astral body. The *spiritual body* lies above the astral body. Disturbances in the spiritual body can affect the astral body, which, in turn, can affect the etheric and physical bodies.

"Each of these bodies has a cord, and they all merge into a single cord, which is our connecting cord to God. Lucifer and his demons can attack us through any of these bodies, but most commonly through the spiritual body. It is difficult to stop these demons on the psychic or spiritual level because they exist on that level. There are other sets of planes that interlock with ours but that do not touch them. They exist on different planes. They belong to other dimensions.

"I see interaction with people on the physical level like conversation and physical contact. When two people's physical bodies interact with each other, the other bodies (etheric, astral, and spiritual bodies) interact as well. We can affect people's etheric, astral, and spiritual bodies just as we can affect their physical body. When the attempt is made to heal at the physical level, healing occurs on the other levels as well. Human beings are affected positively or negatively by the presence of others. We cannot damage others without damaging ourselves. We need to tell people how things work. Most of the religions teach this, but they do not provide any framework for people to understand.

"I see my astral body is being put out of shape and needs healing. My spiritual body is pretty well developed, but it needs some healing.

"When we heal the spiritual body, this healing will bring changes to the etheric, astral, and physical bodies as well, resulting in an improvement in general health. This understanding is very important in healing a person. From Heaven I see that in the future you [Dr. Modi] will develop more understanding and techniques to heal your patients at all levels of their being. You will heal and activate many people spiritually and you will teach and train other medical professionals.

"I see that a handful of people (five to ten), through their daily prayers and mediation, can cause a medium-sized city to change positively and reduce the crime rates. Imagine what can happen when everybody prays. I also see that by praying for Lucifer and his demons, we can reduce their power. Lucifer and his demons do not want us to know this. That is why they are trying so hard to stop you from doing this work, because they do not want you to give this knowledge to the world through your books. From Heaven, I also see how the demons try to manipulate your patients to quit therapy, so they do not heal and fulfill their purpose. Unfortunately, I see that they are succeeding with a few of your patients who end up leaving without completing the treatment. They are being manipulated by the demons and they do not even recognize it.

"I am in Heaven in a classroom, learning about different energy systems of the human body like chakras (energy centers), meridians, and Kundalini. They are all located in the etheric body and are designed to spread the Light energy through the body. *Chakras* are wheel-like energy centers, which are located in the etheric body along the spine. There are seven major chakras located along the spine, from the base of the spine to the top of the head, which distribute Light energy to seven endocrine glands. These energy centers are the gateways between different bodies. There are many minor chakras all over the body. I see that the higher four chakras are more active in a highly evolved person.

"I also see that we also have different channels throughout our body called *meridians*. They are located in the etheric body and allow Light energy to flow through them. They link up with different parts and organs of the body and allow energy to flow into them and balance them.

"I see that *Prana* is an all-persuasive life force all through the universe, while *Kundalini* is a much more specific energy associated with the sun and the solar system. It is not the same as Prana, but it is definitely related to it. Prana is a key to unlocking Kundalini and using it. Kundalini is a serpent-like energy coiled at the base of the spine, near the first chakra. In most people it is inactive or sleeping. When awakened, it moves

DIFFERENT BODIES AND CHAKRAS

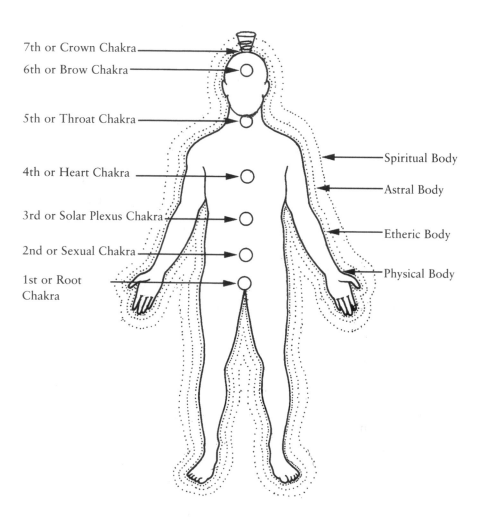

7th or Crown Chakra

6th or Brow Chakra

5th or Throat Chakra

4th or Heart Chakra

3rd or Solar Plexus Chakra

2nd or Sexual Chakra

1st or Root Chakra

Spiritual Body

Astral Body

Etheric Body

Physical Body

Figure 9

like a serpent around the chakras until it reaches the crown chakra at the top of the head; then it moves back down the spine to the base chakra. As it moves through the chakras, it causes them to open up and become bigger.

"In 90 percent of people, Kundalini is not open and it remains inactive. Kundalini should be opened to obtain grace of God, to facilitate spiritual development, and for enlightenment. But if the Kundalini is open, it does not mean that the person is enlightened. A person has to be spiritually developed before opening up the Kundalini.

"Kundalini can be opened prematurely or accidentally as a result of physical or psychic trauma, that is, an injury to the back, trauma during delivery (causing postpartum psychosis), or in response to the use of hallucinogenic drugs, which can cause severe psychosis.

"When the person is spiritually ready and Kundalini is 'boiling' on its own, it is much easier to open. It cannot be active unless a person asks for it. It can be purposefully opened through vegetarian diet, fasting, meditation, and deep breathing. Spiritual study and working with another spiritual person can also help to open it. We can also activate and open the Kundalini and chakras through prayers and by asking God to open it when ready, because God does not make mistakes. If it is opened in one life, it is easy to open in the following lives.

"As I look at my Kundalini, I see it as boiling lava, tossing and turning. I am at the point of opening my Kundalini, and when it happens I will change from being lethargic to a ball of fire, and everything will change very rapidly after that. I see you [Dr. Modi] developing different methods to heal, by healing the chakras, Kundalini, and different bodies in the future.

"It is interesting that the *Earth* also has four bodies, chakras, meridians, and Kundalini—like the human body, because Earth is a representation of us. There are major and minor chakras (energy centers) all over Earth, and they are known as sacred places on Earth. Churches, temples, and other holy places are built on these energy centers, so people who go there can be rejuvenated.

"Various bodies, chakras, meridians, and Kundalini in humans and on Earth can be infested by the dark entities, energies, and devices, thus creating blocks in them, which can cause physical, emotional, mental, and spiritual problems for us. So we should regularly pray for their cleansing, healing, and shielding for us and for Earth.

"Now I am looking at the *psychic antennas* in human beings. They are pieces of etheric energy condensed together and projected into the astral body. These antennas are all over the body and are of various shapes and sizes in different people. Everybody has these antennas and uses them from time to time, such as when having an intuition about something or somebody. But most people are not consciously aware of them. The more we use them, the more they develop.

"Different psychic antennas have different functions, depending on where they are located in relation to the body. For example, the antennas for psychic vision (clairvoyance) are located in the back of the head and are connected to the occipital lobes of the brain, while the antennas for psychic hearing (clairaudience) are projections around the ears and are connected with the temporal lobes of the brain. There are also antennas for the olfactory (smell) senses present at the root of the nose, and antennas for tactile (touch) sensations are present all over the body.

"These antennas receive and gather information from outside and funnel that information to the chakras. The chakras interpret the meaning of that information, which is then received through the appropriate sensory organs. The psychic antennas can be infested by dark entities, energies, and devices, and they can feed false information from the dark side. We should therefore regularly pray to cleanse, heal, and shield those antennas.

"I also study about *meditation* in Heaven. During meditation, when the soul concentrates on the Light and God, it becomes more spiritual in its own nature and its manifestation on Earth and becomes more directly connected with God and the Light. That is the great benefit of meditation. It frees the spirit from being too closely bound to the physical body and earthly concerns, so that the spirit can achieve its spiritual goals more easily. Our physical goals on Earth are simply to maintain our existence and to reproduce. This is about all the physical body has to do.

"The spiritual body, on the other hand, has many things to deal with on this Earth, such as Karma, balancing, spiritual development, and passing on and enhancing spiritual messages to other generations. Only when the soul is freed from the concerns of the physical body, can things work at their highest level.

"During the early stages of meditation, in which there is really no focusing, only the intent, the progress is very slow, because the spirit is never free of the body. At the highest level of meditation, there is complete focusing, concentration, and a very strong will directing that attention. At this level a person can ascend to the spiritual realm.

"In hypnosis, we focus, but the purposes are different. Hypnosis is an aid and, in the ordinary form, it does not have any spiritual focus. But hypnosis, which you [Dr. Modi] are using with your patients in conjunction with spiritual focus, is also a form of meditation. Attention is focused on spiritual matters for hours at a time.

"In Heaven, I also learn about a *vegetarian diet and fasting*. They can remove the blocks from different energy systems like Kundalini, meridians, and chakras, so that the Light energy can flow unimpeded through them.

"I remember that when I used a vegetarian diet and fasted a few years ago in this life, I had the most unusual effects inside my body. I felt jolts, a sense of electricity running through my body, and 'slams and bangs,' as if there was some great force moving through me, running into the obstacles and removing them.

"While I am in Heaven, I go down to lower levels to teach and also go to higher levels to learn from the masters. I plan my personal goals for the current life and also group goals with my group for making spiritual changes on Earth. I choose my parents, my wife, and children to resolve karmic problems and also for their support.

"I choose my profession. I even planned to come to you as a patient. By treating me with these therapies, you will activate me spiritually, so I can work toward my spiritual goals. I see us meeting in Heaven and planning how we are going to meet and do the work. I plan the details of the day, date, and time of my birth. I choose some gifts to be born with and others I will develop while in the body."

• "I have prepared my life blueprints and have planned my personal and group goals. Preparation goes on for a long time. I have many meetings with different people and groups and go to libraries to study about what I am going to do on Earth.

"I am meeting with a group of forty people called the 'perseverance' group. Our goal is to gain the knowledge of Light through perseverance, hardship, and difficulty. The main goal is to learn about the Light and bring it to people and the planet. I recognize two people in this group. One is a student I knew and the other is Gandhi. We discuss how to bring Light to the world and how we must keep our faith in God to give us the necessary strength. We will do it by teaching and by being examples. People can disagree with our points of view, but they cannot deny our example.

"I meet with a science group of twenty people. I do not know them in this life. We discuss the internal struggle that people of science and spirit go through; we discuss to what extent we measure and observe and still hold a spiritual belief. We realize the benefits science can bring to humanity, as well as the dangers.

"It is a privilege for people of science to seek truth through experimentation. When we go into science, most of us will be teased for being too intellectual. We hold the responsibility of sharing scientific knowledge and not distorting it, which would damage humanity. I study information in the Akashic Records written by other scientists and myself. This is to prepare for the research I will do on Earth.

"I am in a big group meeting of people of my generation. There are several million people in this group. A master is speaking, saying we are going to be an important generation but we must try always to be humble. We should try not to give into despair, yet we should recognize the real dangers on Earth. We must have hope and realize that human beings will prevail. We must always look to the Light and resist the seduction of darkness. We must not use the excuses of our ancestors for not doing better. We should try to pray often and ask for guidance.

"I also meet with my godhead, Master Jesus, to whom I am connected with a silver cord. He tells me to have strength and be in peace. As he puts his hand on my forehead, I see a blazing white Light coming from his hands, bringing me peace and strength. I also meet Master Buddha, who gives me the attributes of patience and discipline."

• "We learn and prepare things beforehand in Heaven that we will do on Earth. Whatever we are planning to do on Earth we already have done in Heaven. I am in a library, reviewing what has been done in the past, refreshing myself in the knowledge I will take to Earth. Very little is available for my waking consciousness; instead, the information is stored in a compartment of my mind. When I need it, I can access it.

"It is a type of university here. We go through different lectures and classes. When somebody teaches you something, you not only mentally grasp it, you also gather it through all your senses. You experience 100 percent of the teacher's thoughts. You feel it in the deepest level of your being; it is a total communication and much faster than anything on Earth.

"I see myself going through different classes on learning how to move the body. I see myself doing martial-arts exercises. They are not fast movements.

They are more like pushing and moving the Light against a resistance. You can create a weight with your consciousness. You can lift or move it, telling your mind you are moving a heavy object.

"One of my classes is about movie making. I am learning the technique of deepening the hypnotic state that is produced by movies, enabling people to be 100 percent in touch with their higher reality. This is done through images, audio techniques, and suggestions at different levels of awareness. It is interesting to realize that we are sitting in a movie theater and are experiencing that which we are supposed to reproduce later on Earth. I sit in a theater watching a movie, and I receive an awareness of all the possibilities.

"I see a class on jewelry making, and it is very different from making jewelry on Earth. The concept here is the use of metal and crystals to trap Light. You focus a greater-than-normal amount of Light into a crystal for a specific purpose. The jewels are receivers and transmitters of a particular energy. I sit at a jewelry maker's bench as an instructor walks around, guiding the process. He is a master of the art.

"I am at a group meeting of about three hundred people. My wife is here; you are here, Dr. Modi; and there are many more people here whom I know. A Light being is speaking. We are seated in a circle around him. I experience the feelings I get at a graduation ceremony. Tears come to my eyes as I focus on this. Such profound love, understanding, and wisdom come from this being. He is a master, and we feel an overpowering oneness with him. I feel warmth coming from his heart.

"He tells us, 'We need to focus on bringing everybody into oneness on Earth. You people can do this. You all have been specially trained for this. You will go through some hardships, but you will pull through and be victorious. Many golden angels will assist you; they are very powerful angels. [I see a group of angels marching side by side in line like an army.] Remember, the greatest power lies within you. If you ever get lost, look inside yourself and you will reconnect with your purpose. All the information is hidden inside your soul. Pray and meditate and you will be on the right path.'

"The master talks about liberation from darkness. He explains some of the dark tools and techniques that will be used against us during our time on Earth. He explains everything from rock-and-roll music to electronic manipulation of energy and information. We need to develop a sense of universal laws, neighborly laws, and the laws between mates. We can express those laws by loving those closest to us. It may be difficult at times. This will be a strengthening process, to deliberately love those people who are hard to love. If we can contact the heart of that person, the love will flow between us.

"The master says that it is important for us to experience joy and buoyancy as much as possible every day. The mind is the gateway to higher consciousness. Focusing on our higher purpose will take us upward like a ball pulled through a tube. Certain books will bring unity and will bring the group members together. I do not know if it is one particular book, like your first book, Dr. Modi, which brought so many people to a higher awareness, or if it will be many books.

"Next, the master tells us that we need to look beyond the imperfections in our spiritual community. The information that was originally brought through is high and pure. The consciousness of people in different religions may go up and down, depending on the degree to which they are affected by the darkness. People should look beyond those imperfections and forgive those affected. It is more important to focus on the truth.

"He further says, 'Many people will judge you in a negative way for what you are doing because they are not on your level. This will be temporary. Try to avoid these people as much as possible, while you try to become close to those who share your purpose and mission.' Many people will contact their higher purpose through hypnotherapy, which you [Dr. Modi] are using. In the future, hypnotherapy, which you are doing, will be called 'Light therapy.'

"Next I see a brush and get the sense that the 'tubes'

need to be cleaned out often. These tubes are our connecting cords to God and are other channels of communication with our higher selves, guides, and angels.

"There are certain chairs and recliners here that are very soft, and when people sit on them, they feel as if they are floating. The chair is made out of a buoyant white material. There is nothing like it on Earth. When you are in this chair, you can contact the higher reality almost instantly. This chair will be on Earth in the future.

"We also need to examine our physical body, feeling for 'kinks' that will be receptors for negativity, and block the flow of Light. I understand that while on Earth, we can place certain objects within our houses and offices, a picture or statue of a master like Jesus, Shiva, Buddha, Krishna, or whomever you believe in. Every time we look at or touch one of these objects, it will act as an instant connection to our higher source. We can have as many objects as we want. Since there are so many things on Earth that can trigger negative energies, we have to have things that will trigger positive energy and Light.

"I see that I planned to come to you [Dr. Modi] for treatment, and to work with you later on. I see us sitting in a room in Heaven with about twelve people around a table. I do not know who the other people are. We are discussing our plans.

"I see myself in a group in which I teach 'love and communication.' These people are at a lower level than I am. I also go to beings on the higher levels. I visit the masters. Just being in their energy field imparts vibrations of their essence to me and a realignment of energy occurs. I feel a golden radiation coming to me from the masters.

"I meet with my godhead, Shiva. I can see my connecting cord going through him to God. He looks like such a high, mighty, and holy being, yet innocent and childlike. I feel lots of love coming from him. He is saying, 'There is a vast universe inside you. Learn to play and have fun and be joyous, and the demons will leave you alone.' Shiva is very happy and joyful, radiating this everywhere."

• "While in Heaven, I have made plans for my coming life. I am in a laboratory learning about vibrations. This is an instructional laboratory in which heavenly beings are teaching us, impressing on us that vibrations can be healing at one level and destructive on another. They give demonstrations of using vibrations in different mediums.

"At another time in a classroom, I learn about color therapy from a master being. He is talking about the effects of different colors. He says that color, sound, and vibrations are tied together and work similarly to different types of music. Some kinds of music will relax you, while other kinds will jar your nerves. Similarly, different sounds and vibrations affect the body in different ways. Color and sound therapies help bring the body into balance and heal different parts of the body. When the body is in balance, it can repair itself.

"I am at the Akashic library studying about sound, vibration, and color therapy. It is like refreshing myself in what I already know, but it is also learning new knowledge to use on Earth. I realize I have written a book on vibrational therapy in one of my past lives.

"I am also reading a book about sound therapy. This therapy shows ways to stimulate areas of the body that are out of balance and to counteract those imbalances. If there is a weakness in the body, it is more susceptible to disease; sound therapy at the proper frequency can correct it.

"I teach souls at the lower levels about colors. I talk to groups about sound and vibration, telling them how different sounds have a broad spectrum of effects."

• "I am in Heaven making preparations for my current life. I have chosen my parents, husband, and children because we have to resolve problems from past lives. I have chosen the time of my birth.

"I am meeting with the ascended master, Saint Germaine. He wants me to serve for freedom. He gives me the gift of violet flame, which has the power to transmute dark energy and dark beings. In life, I can call for the violet flame and release it to our planet and people. [For more about the violet flame, see chapter 19.] Over time, it has the power to transform dark beings and negative energy and to free our planet and humanity from them. I will talk about the violet flame to people and they can also invoke it for themselves and the planet. Saint Germaine also tells me I will have a lot of opposition, but I will be given protection.

"I am choosing different gifts, such as the ability to communicate with people, love for music, the drive to find the truth about God and creation, organization, endurance, courage, strength, and adventurousness.

"I meet with my group. We will work together on Earth to disseminate the ascended masters' teachings. I see myself spending hours doing decrees to mitigate all the bad predictions. I am in another meeting in Heaven with about four hundred people. We discuss what we are going to do to make people on Earth respond to our calls, because they do not seem to hear them. We send them signals to hear the voice of truth, but they do not respond. They listen, but the message does not sink in. A being says we have to create a new group to spread the truth. We need to tell people to pray more.

"I am in another group meeting. I do not recognize the leader, who talks about healing. He says that we have to give people different ways to heal. There are new ways that are easy. We have to give that knowledge to people so they can live longer lives and stay young longer. We can also raise the vibrations of the planet.

"I am meeting with a smaller group of twenty people. I know some of these people. We are planning to have a big center similar to a mini 'golden age city' in which everybody will be great in mind, body, and spirit. It will be an anchor for Light on Earth. I receive the gift of violet flame and of being a person of Light that people will look up to me as an example. I am also meeting with you [Dr. Modi] to plan how we will meet on Earth.

"I see myself with my godhead, Buddha. A connecting silver cord goes from me to him. He is full of golden Light. He is very wise, kind, loving, and joyful —like a child. He gives me his Light and tells me that he loves me, saying, 'I am happy that you chose to do decrees every day. I will keep you illuminated with my Light, so you can fulfill your purpose. Be the Light for this new city on Earth.' I feel warm, joyful, and humble in his presence.

"I study the different masters and their teachings in a classroom. I also study meditations that enable you to clear yourself and receive illumination. I learn about prayers and different ways to pray. We can pray quietly or out loud. I learn about the power of speaking the words out loud. When we say the words out loud, the presence of God in us also says them and that is how the words become powerful, but we must be conscious of doing that. We should pray in an affirmative way. It is very powerful because in this way we affirm the power of God.

"Repeating the same phrase over and over gives it more power, but there are three steps to this. The first time we say it, this magnifies the power of God; the second time we say it, we center it in our heart; and the third time, we send it out where we want. If we repeat prayers faster and faster, this activity accelerates the vibrations and accelerates the action of the power of God, provided this comes from the heart and not only from the mouth. We need to be grateful and thank God before we begin to pray.

"We should voice our petition, and whatever we ask for ourselves, we should also try to disseminate over the world so everyone can benefit. For example, always ask at the end of the prayer that whatever you have asked for also be given to anybody who needs it. Praying in groups is more powerful than praying alone. The more of us who pray, the more powerful prayer becomes. If three instead of one pray, it is not only multiplied by three, but multiplied by nine—multiplied exponentially.

"I learn about the violet flame, which is a great gift given to the world. It is one of the rays of Light coming from God. It can transform all darkness to Light. Whatever we put into the violet flame, the darkness in it gets transmuted to Light. We can make this life our last life by using the violet flame, because it can transmute our karma. Without it, it will take a long time before we can finish working out our karma."

• "I am in Heaven. After the review of my life, I rest and go inside the Light. My consciousness is rising and my body is getting lighter and lighter. I could probably fly if I wanted to. I feel like I have wings on my back, because I am in a spirit form. My outline looks like a physical body, but it is transparent.

"I see a bright sun in the distance and I feel many people are headed toward it. It is as though here you are on an upward journey toward this bright sun, to a brighter place on a higher plane. I sense the energy rising in my body. It starts in the lower part and rushes upward into higher vibrations. I move through the 'clouds' of Light as if I am on an escalator of Light. That is the closest thing I can compare it to. I am rising forward and upward.

"There are other people of different frequencies here, and the only way I can see these other beings is by tuning into their frequencies. As I tune into them, I see a crowd of people in the same process. We are all going up higher. There are other people who are not on my frequency, and when I tune into them, my frequency is lowered and I feel heavy, as if I carry a backpack that pulls me down. I am going to tune them out now. Now it is like being on an elevator, moving faster than an escalator. If you want to, you can go as fast as a supersonic jet.

"Higher up, there are three temples: a healing temple, a learning temple, and I do not know about the third temple. I am hungry for knowledge of the higher awareness. I can hardly wait for the knowledge. I need to go to the learning temple, which is golden. It looks like some churches on Earth. It has many different sections and lots of rooms and places of learning. But there is one circular temple at the end to which people go to worship God or to become transformed into higher vibrations.

"In this building, beings sit around and watch what is going on in different parts of Earth. They are in another realm, watching a full-scale replica of what is happening on Earth, as if on television. They are working on a project that has to do with Washington, D.C. These beings have golden threadlike connections with people in Washington, D.C., and they send down the correct information so that the government can run properly. This is a very holy temple; everything here is golden, reflecting wisdom. They are guiding people on Earth, saying that what is going on on Earth is very important at this time.

"I do not know why, but this is very emotional for me, because I am so connected with what is going on. It is like my soul knows this and is profoundly happy. The feelings are so powerful that I cannot express them in earthly language. My chest is expanding with the Light. I hear beings say we have to prepare Earth for the golden age. I realize there is a network of people working on Earth, and although we are connected and we know one another out of our bodies at night in Heaven, it is important for us to meet in the physical world. It will be an awakening for these people to know who they are. The heavenly beings say we have a lot of work to do. Many trials and tribulations will affect mankind. People in power will see the errors of their ways and turn around. This will greatly increase the efficiency of the process of transformation to a higher vibration.

"Most important, transformations in the consciousness of people on Earth will happen when they start to look inward and upward instead of outward and downward. In times of meditation and prayer, we need to focus on our higher purpose and reflect on why we are here in this time in history.

"I keep feeling there is a special kind of healing that needs to take place. Once it happens, everybody will be able to have more direct connection with their higher self and Heaven. I see people in the future will have this ability and that it will come to them easily because of the violet flame that helps remove some blockages so people can reach for higher levels of awareness.

"On Earth we are programmed to believe we cannot go to a higher level. It is a belief placed here by the dark forces. The great healers of the future will work almost exclusively with the consciousness of people, individually or in large groups, and also through books. Your first book, Dr. Modi, is affecting many people in different ways. For some it is like an electric shock. It is almost too much power, yet people in their souls know it is the truth. Other people cannot pick it off the shelf because of dark influences in and around them, and they are afraid of it. There are still others who are reading it, and for them it is like finding water for the first time after walking across the desert. Your second book will open people up even more, with the realization that they are part of God, and it will help them connect with God.

"Beings are saying that it is very important for people to learn to meditate and that every house should have a temple. I see a square room symbolizing a temple in the house. Houses on Earth should be duplicates of houses in Heaven, such as this golden temple. It has a work area and a library. It also has a very sacred place, where people go to meditate or pray, and in which it is easy to connect with God.

"The room in Heaven is circular, but it is not practical for most people to have a circular room on Earth. They can build a circle inside a square room. On one side of the room there can be an altar, similar to a desk with sacred objects on the top. There should be a circle made up of Light or a white circular cloth in the center of the room. This can be used as a meditation place; the person can sit in the middle and pray or meditate. The circle acts as a protective device.

"Above the center of the circle, on the ceiling, there needs to be some type of special crystal, conical or pyramidal in shape. It can be like a cap on a pyramid. The room is the base of the pyramid and the crystal is the top of the pyramid, like most temples, churches, and other holy places have those pointed or conical structures. It points consciousness to Heaven, or God.

"The next thing people can do is make a golden cross of cloth to be set inside this circle. As you look down on the circle and cross, one straight line should point at the altar, one behind the person, one to the left, and one to the right. The person sits in the middle of this cross.

"I see people sitting on pillows cross-legged, doing breathing exercises. Breathing is the most direct connection with the Light and God. It pumps more Light and energy into the body for healing and lets the body tune into higher frequencies. The people seated in this room state their purpose, their intention, and why they are here, saying in effect, 'I am here and I give my intent to connect with a higher reality, to be an instrument of God this day and through all the days I remain on Earth.' They pledge to do their best to acknowledge when God is talking to them so that they can be a pure instrument.

"Beings tell me that people have to be more aware of the objects in their homes, because objects are connected to a thought form and many other things. People need to understand that although some things have sentimental values, they also attract negative energy. For example, when people keep heirlooms and antiques from diseased parents, grandparents, and others, entities and negative energy may still be connected to them. When people keep these objects in the house, they attract more negative energy, and sometimes this holds the people back from progressing spiritually.

"People need to understand the significance of symbols, colors, and words. Each color represents a spiritual vibration. When somebody is living in a dwelling of dark, brown, gray, black, or muddy colors, it restricts the Light flow into that place and brings in dark influences. While certain colors attract negative energy, other colors, like white and pure and bright pastel colors, can attract Light and increase the vibrations of the people who live there. Almost any color can be distorted by adding black, gray, brown, or other muddy colors to it. Pastel colors in pure form can be gentle and healing for the soul. They are more similar to heavenly colors, so the soul is very happy to be surrounded by them, because it realizes, 'I remember what Heaven looks like.'

"The words we use have a great impact on us. When people use words that symbolize high ideals, high vibrations, and good and positive things, they attract positive energy to them and increase their vibrations and the vibrations around them. If people use negative words such as curse words, vulgar and obscene words, and profane language, they attract negative energy and demons, and they lower their own vibrations. We should all try hard to rid these words from our vocabulary. They are inspired by darkness and open our shield so darkness can come in. Someone like a president or a leader talking to the world in a positive, loving, and uplifting way creates positive feelings and raises their vibrations. What we say and think and how we act become the reality.

"Now I am at the Akashic library learning about sexual relationships from the spiritual point of view. Sex is a spiritual as well as physical experience. It is an experience in which we can be connected to the ecstasy of God. When we have an orgasm, we have a glimpse of Heaven and God.

"During *loving heterosexual intercourse,* from the spiritual aspect, love flows between the heart chakras, which begin to vibrate faster. The vibrations and Light from the heart chakras spread up and down the spine, waking and vibrating the chakras, from the top of the head down to the base of the spine. It speeds up the body's vibration, increasing the flow of the Light. In sex, Kundalini rises slowly, going up to the head and the third eye, then comes down again.

"As the excitement increases, there is an intensification of Light within the chakras of both partners. The chakras get brighter and spin faster. As the excitement increases, the energy of the chakras intensifies and spreads throughout the body. Their energy centers get in alignment with each other and eventually blend together with the climax. There is no fragmentation and no dark influences. From the Akashic plane, they look like two balls of Light pushing and pressing against each other.

"I see a bright Light coming down. It becomes a deep spiritual level of communion between man and woman. In heterosexual sex, the vagina is like an electromagnetic center or a tunnel of Light, and as the penis goes into that tunnel of Light, this connects the male and female at many different levels.

"During *intercourse without mutual love* and desire or when done with force, both partners can lose soul parts and become vulnerable to dark influences. The vagina is not charged with love and Light and there is no spiritual communion between the partners.

"During *oral sex,* when the man is standing up and the woman is sitting down, the man's energy comes down to try to match the woman's energy. I see gray energies all over their energy centers. It looks like a draining out of the Light from both of them, as the Light is replaced by the dark beings.

"The different chakras have to be lined up between two people. During oral sex, there is no alignment of the energy centers. They are all messed up. It is like the person is giving her energy to the other person for his pleasure and not receiving anything in return. When people are focused strictly on oral sex, they continue to lose their Light (soul parts), and then the gray and black entities come in.

"I see darkness around and inside people engaged in oral sex. People who are giving oral sex often lose their soul parts from their lips, tongue, and throat, and these parts are often replaced by darkness. Also the Light is drained from the person receiving oral sex. It is often replaced by the dark entities and energies, which in turn give them more desire for oral and other types of deviated sex. Oral sex is also a degradation of the woman. It is putting her on a much lower level than the man. It is putting the woman in a position of a slave, and there is no spiritual communion between them.

"From Heaven I see a lot of darkness around the *homosexual relationship* too, because there is no alignment between their energy centers. The partners lose their soul parts, which then are replaced by darkness. Demons hang around homosexual clubs to tempt and manipulate people. From Heaven, I see reasons for homosexuality and gender identity disorders as follows:

1. Possession by a spirit of the opposite sex or a soul part of a living person of the opposite sex who desires sex with the person of the same sex as the host.

2. A spirit or a soul part of a living person who has homosexual tendencies that are transferred over to the host.

3. Sometimes a soul that has been in a male body for many lives feels awkward in the female body, and vice versa. So they are not comfortable with the partners of the opposite sex or want to have a sex-change operation.

4. Souls that were created from the male essence of the energy ball at the beginning may not feel comfortable in a female body and vice versa. They feel like an alien in the body of the opposite sex. They have anger and resentment about having to live in a body that is of the opposite polarity to their soul. So they try to misuse, deny, or destroy the existence of those organs. Some people even have a sex-change operation. It is like a rebellion against God.

5. Sometimes it occurs for karmic reasons, where in another life they made fun of people because they had a lifestyle that was out of the norm. So in this life they chose to balance that negative action by putting themselves in the similar situation and going through the similar suffering.

6. In women, sometimes it is a result of being abused by men, making them develop hatred toward men. Instead of resolving the problems, forgiving them, and moving ahead with the heterosexual relationship, they choose the homosexual lifestyle.

"During male or female *masturbation,* what I see is that there is an escape mechanism or a self-abuse mechanism. It can result from a psychological imbalance. It is not the best way to go. During the act of masturbation, the soul can fragment and go to the person of their fantasy. They become less and less themselves each time because of soul fragmentation and soul loss, and these parts are replaced by dark beings, who give them more desire to masturbate. Masturbation depletes their Light and opens their shield, which becomes weaker and they become more vulnerable.

"I see that *group sex* is often inspired by dark entities that surround and influence people. These dark beings are also having sex with each other through people. It is not protected, because there is no love and commitment in the couples and there is no divine flow between them. It is an abuse of sexuality and is not from Heaven. It is a perversion introduced by the dark beings.

"*Prostitution* also causes soul fragmentation and opens people up to dark influences, because there is no love and commitment. It is not from Heaven. There is no divine flow and no protection between two people.

"During *rape* and *inappropriate fondling*, both the abuser and victim lose soul parts and dark beings come in, creating more problems, because there is no love, no divine flow and, as a result, no protection."

Chapter Eighteen

Structure of Light (Heaven) and Its Beings

Throughout this book, my hypnotized patients have provided glimpses into the structure of Heaven and the kinds of beings who dwell in it. This information is very intricate and hard to comprehend for us who are on Earth. In this chapter, I will attempt to describe the simplified version of the "structure of the Light and its beings" and how everything works there, as described consistently by my hypnotized patients.

If we imagine Light (God and Heaven) as a crystal globe, we enter and depart from the outer surface or edge of it. (See figure 1 on page 22.) This is on the surface of the globe. The resting area is just inside the re-entry area, which in appearance seems like the planet we lived on when we were in an incarnation. Here beings coming up from a life on Earth or other planets are transformed into spiritual beings. They drop their attachment to the body and to their ways of being in the physical world. This place is part of Heaven, but it is planetlike, that is, it has buildings, tables, chairs, gardens, rivers, waterfalls, etc. As a result, souls feel comfortable while they rest. After resting, reflecting, and integrating their life experiences, they become pure spirits. Then they move on to the inner section of the Light through a passageway. Since there are no barriers in the Light, it is not really a passageway; it is merely a space their awareness takes them through.

Picture a globe created by stacking many pyramids together. This is God as a whole containing multiple pyramids. Each pyramid is a godhead, and over the top of each godhead is God. (See figure 2 on page 23.) After resting, we return to our pyramid (godhead), through which our silver cord passes on to God. Under each godhead are multitudes of individual souls that belong to that godhead. When we are in Heaven, there does not appear to be any real division. We can pass through any area of Heaven and learn in any part, but while entering and leaving, we generally go through our godhead. It does not have to be that way; it is just more convenient, because we are connected to *that* godhead and to God with a silver connecting cord.

My patients describe the Light and God as having various shapes, depending on how wide or narrow the patients' viewpoints are. If they are looking from inside the Light and have a narrow focus, then their viewpoint is limited. It is as if they are in a space they perceive as limitless in all directions. They think there is an up and down, with the entry portal "beneath" their feet, and God "above" them. It is as if they do not perceive the shape of the Light as a whole.

If souls have a wider viewpoint, then they perceive Heaven as a pyramid, with the entry and departure area at the bottom, the space where souls live between lives is higher, and then godheads with God on the top. If the point of view is still wider, then the person sees the Light in a spherical shape that contains multitudes of pyramids (godheads). In this spherical model of Heaven, the entry and departure areas are at the "outer edge" of the globe, and souls go "inside" the Light after resting. Then, as we go inside, there are godheads, and then God at the core of the globe. So, in the pyramidal model souls go from the bottom upward, while in the spherical model, they enter Heaven at the outer edge and then go inside.

The least-developed souls tend to congregate around the outside layer, just past the resting area, but not too far "in" or "up." The more-developed souls tend to move closer to the godhead. The souls that are less developed can also go toward the godhead and God, but they are not comfortable there because their vibrations are slower. As we move upward toward the godhead, the vibrations are faster and Light is more intense. So souls tend to stratify in layers from the least developed at the bottom to the more developed moving upward toward the godhead, while the most developed are near the godhead.

Godheads: Pathways to and from God

Under hypnosis, people say that the godheads were created automatically by the pathways, which were originally created by God to transfer His energy from the core out into space to create universes. One effect these pathways had was to divide energies around the core of God into many different sections; these later became the pyramid-shaped godheads. Then God created small bridges over these tunnels from one godhead to another so the souls from one godhead could go to other godheads. These are the connecting cords between the godheads.

As God was creating different universes, He saw the convenience of these sections. That is, God saw how these sections could represent an energy area for each of the universes. These energy areas could be used as oversouls for various universes. These godheads are located between two pathways and extend between the core of God to the outer edge of the globe of God. The core of God is not divided. The energy in the godheads is not as condensed as in the core of God. The further away from the core, the less condensed it is, and the nearer to the periphery, the more porous it is. Everything except the core is godhead energy.

Each section between two pathways became a pyramid, a godhead separated from the core of God. It is a large, well-developed section of God, which serves as an intermediary layer between God and the universes. It serves as a protection between the Light and the ordinary soul. It is not the most refined part of God. In the sense that the godhead is the part that is separated from God, it is similar to a created soul. Godheads are discrete and separate entities, distinct from one another. They are situated close to each other, but they are not contiguous. There is one godhead in each pyramid.

When we were created by God, our energy was separated off from God. As a result, we have gone through a great deal of "first forgetting." Similarly, godheads have also gone through some forgetting because of the division of energy, but compared to us, their forgetting was much less. They know they are part of God and they understand their role. We have forgotten that. Even the souls in the Light have forgotten it to some extent.

According to my hypnotized patients, a godhead associated with a pyramid may populate dozens of universes. Souls from one godhead may have lives in ten to fourteen different dimensions at the same time. We incarnate on other planets connected with the same godhead we are connected to. The wider the spread, the more difficult it is for the godhead to keep track of the souls. The concept of incarnating into fourteen different universes is called a "span of control" and represents what one godhead can efficiently manage. This may overlap with areas controlled by other godheads, so that there may be souls incarnated in the same universe from three or four different godheads.

There is no dimension that does not have a godhead over it. Even that dimension in which Lucifer and his demons exist, which they think of as "hell," is under the control of a godhead. We normally do not incarnate in the universes that have a different godhead, unless our souls are at the "border," close to the next godhead. Even so, we can go to different godhead pyramids to teach and learn when we are in Heaven and when we are sleeping on Earth.

Multitudes of created masters go into one godhead after their creation. Then after a while, their energy permeates through the whole godhead energy. In that sense, the godhead can be known by the name of these masters, some of whom we know on Earth as religious figures or deities and many we do not know.

A godhead has many functions. It serves as a partition between God and the universes; it assists God in planning and helps souls on the planets, and it acts as an intermediary between God and the beings on the planets. The godhead serves as an administrator to make sure the universe continues to function properly and that the demons do not mess it up. It also provides teaching and healing functions for beings on the planet.

According to my hypnotized patients, demons also came from many of the godhead pyramids, but they left before God was subdivided. Lucifer is the largest being, the head demon. There is one Lucifer, but there are other large demons who serve under him called Satan or Devil and by other names in different cultures. They are not part of Lucifer, but they work under him. Lucifer is not Satan but is a separate being. Satan is a common name for the large-sized demons that serve under Lucifer. They are next to Lucifer and are assigned as leaders for different dimensions. They can function on planets and dimensions with lower vibrations, but they cannot go to the universes with higher vibrations, because they cannot tolerate the higher frequencies. Lucifer, with one of the equivalent Satans, also works on our planet Earth.

Masters: Holy Partners of God

According to my hypnotized patients, masters are highly developed souls, created to be nearly perfect. They work primarily in the Light and occasionally take incarnation on the planets to help humans and other beings. There are multitudes of masters created around God, and there are many masters created for each godhead. After their creation, all the masters underwent the "first forgetting," but they did so to a lesser extent than angels, humans, and other souls.

After the creation, masters were sent to their respective godheads, to the topmost layer. After a while, their energy permeated the godhead. In that sense, they became the godhead. The energy of many masters permeated each godhead, so there are many masters who represent one godhead.

According to the heavenly beings, created masters go through a growth process while in Heaven, but it is not as extensive as the process the souls in the universe go through. When masters incarnate on planets from time to time, like us, they also go through the growth process. They also have a connecting cord to their godhead and God.

Some of the human and other souls on other planets can and do grow, perfect themselves, and evolve into master status through repeated incarnations on the planets. These are called the "ascended masters." They were not created as masters but have achieved masterhood by evolving and perfecting themselves.

Next to God, masters have the most powers. They are the spiritual agents for their respective parts of the universe and are responsible for overseeing the spiritual development of intelligent life. They are responsible for coordinating the dispersement and reception of the souls. They are recognized and worshipped as religious figures and deities, and our prayers reach God through them. The masters have all the attributes of God, but each master has specific functions and attributes that are uniquely theirs. They are partners and helpers of God, intermediaries between God and the souls on the planets.

Angels: the Holy Helpers of God

My hypnotized patients state that angels were created as spiritual beings who will remain in the Light. They do not incarnate on the planets as corporeal beings, but remain in Heaven as God's holy helpers, messengers, communicators, and intermediaries among humans and beings on other planets, godheads, masters, and God. They protect the universes and the beings who dwell there, and they guard Heaven. They provide a buffer zone between Heaven (Light) and the universes.

There are a wide variety of angels: large, medium, small, male, female and androgynous, with two, four, six and more, or no wings. Some have well-defined forms, while others do not. Different angels have various functions and purposes. Some are archangels, who are like masters of the angels. Some angels remain near God as His companions and act as intermediaries between Him and other angels. Some angels teach, guide, protect, and heal, while others act as messengers and communicators between God, godheads, masters, and souls on the planets. Some are art angels, like the classical Muses who were assigned to inspire art, such as music, painting, and sculpture. "Baby" angels (cherubim) bring joy and happiness to those who are sick and in despair. According to the angels, they also go through a growth process, but it is nothing compared with the growth process of souls who live on planets. Angels are created differently for different planets, depending on the vibrations of those planets.

Higher Self or Oversoul:
Our Perfect Self or Christself in Heaven

The higher self, or oversoul, is a person's pure self, or Christ self. It remains in Heaven and does not come down to a planet. It is a step down from God and is perfect, while the lower self, the soul within us, is in "school" on the planet. The lower self incarnates again and again to learn and grow. The higher self is our main soul, which is in the Light and has thousands of individual souls living and evolving on Earth and on other planets at the same time. The lower selves on the planets have free will, which their higher self cannot interfere with.

According to my hypnotized patients, when our soul is created in God from the original ball with male and female aspects in it which divides into two separate souls, before or after going into its godhead, or later after incarnation. These two souls then incarnate on the planets repeatedly as separate souls, living separate lives, learning and growing with each

SOUL PYRAMID

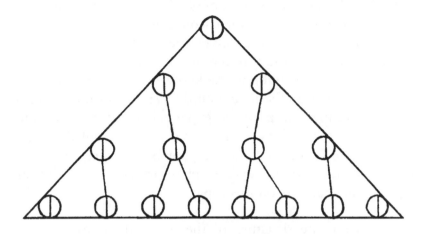

Figure 10

life. When these two souls have grown to a certain size, they split again and become four souls. It is as if they take their gifts and put them into two separate packages to develop more efficiently. Then all four souls live separate lives, learning and growing independently on different planets. When they grow to a certain size, they divide again into eight souls. This process goes on and on, creating a pyramid of souls. (See figure 10 above)

Not all soul divisions proceed at the same speed and, as a result, they do not split at the same time. Everybody's soul pyramid looks different. Some patients call this splitting of the soul a "soul twinning" and call the first twins a "twin flame." The parts that split afterward are called "soul mates" or "soul partners."

According to the heavenly beings, the purpose of soul twinning or splitting is to enable a soul to evolve faster by living many separate lives at the same time. These are called "parallel lives." After a certain growth period of the soul, its vibrations become fast, and all of it cannot incarnate in a body having slower vibrations. If it does, the body will burn up.

This is another reason why each soul has to split in order to incarnate and grow.

If you look at a soul pyramid, you see that the top of the pyramid is like our higher self, or oversoul, overlooking the growth and evolution of multiple soul partners. It is our soul's space in the godhead, and it is connected to God. There are connecting cords from the soul partners to the higher self, and we have access to God through our higher self.

It is in the oversoul that the knowledge, information, and personality of a life is integrated during the resting phase in Heaven. All the soul partners' experiences and lives are integrated with their oversoul. It is as if the oversoul is a filing room in which the souls' developments are categorized and fitted into the overall scheme. Here are some descriptions given by my patients on this topic:

- "I see the structure of the pyramid of my soul. First, I see one soul split into two, then two into four, four into eight, then eight into sixteen. They keep dividing and now there are thousands of souls at the bottom of the pyramid. I see different people, some male and some female. We are all living and learning through our different lives. These people are of various races and different ages. Some are living on Earth, others are on other planets, and still others are in Heaven between lives. Some of my soul partners are in hell. I get glimpses of these lives. They (soul mates or soul partners) are all parts of my soul, living different parallel lives at the same time."

- "After its creation, my soul looks like an orb of Light that begins to move. I become aware that there are two sides of me, like two sides of a coin; these begin to separate and to gradually define themselves. I become more aware of 'we' than 'me.' We gradually separate, and there are now two orbs connected with a cord between us.

    "We are together but have moved apart. The feeling of being separate is exciting, like there is another one of me. We cling to each other, because it is part of me and I do not want to let go. Gradually I adjust to this and then it is okay.

"Then as we incarnate on the planet again and again, we split into four, then eight, and so on, creating a pyramid containing hundreds of balls at the bottom of the pyramid. The growth and splitting of each soul is not the same, so the pyramid is not symmetrical. Everybody's pyramid does not look the same."

• "The pyramid of my soul appears bright and high, made of hundreds of lighted balls. On the top, there is the original soul, which is the brightest and largest. It divides into two, two into four, four into eight, and on and on. All the parts grow and split at different times so the pyramid does not look even and proportional. Hundreds of my soul mates live separate parallel lives in different places all over the universe. Many of my soul mates are living separate lives on Earth. I do not know any of them. As I look from the Akashic Records, I see many cords going from me to Earth in Africa, the Far East, Europe, England, Scandinavia, the United States, and Canada. A few also are on other planets. Some are in Heaven, between lives, and some are in hell.

"I see the growth of my soul. I have grown to about two thousand times the size I was originally. The reason a soul splits is to evolve and grow faster. Another reason is that as our soul grows through different incarnations, our vibrations grow. After a certain amount of growth, the vibrations become too fast to enter a human body on Earth. So we divide and incarnate in two bodies, and this goes on until we have perfected ourselves."

Sometimes, my hypnotized patients use the words "oversoul" and "higher self" in different ways. For example, our inner self, the soul within the body, can be our higher self; our higher self in the Light can be our higher self; our godhead can also be called our higher self; and ultimately, God is also our higher self. Similarly, our higher self in Heaven can be called our oversoul, a godhead can be an oversoul for everybody in it and under it, and God can be the oversoul for everything in the creation.

Most often, our soul in Heaven is identified as the higher self, Christself or oversoul, for all our soul partners. Through growth and evolution, all our soul partners can perfect themselves and go back to our oversoul and become one. Then we do not have to go through the cycle of incarnation anymore because the oversoul has evolved to perfection. As all our soul partners grow, our oversoul grows, and in turn our godhead and God grow. According to the heavenly beings, humans and beings on other planets are responsible for most of God's growth.

After all the soul partners have joined the higher self, we have several choices. We can go into our godhead and become one with it, or we can remain outside the godhead in the Light and help different souls on the planet to evolve. Other times a completely evolved and perfected soul may choose to incarnate on the planet, not because it has to, but to help people. The created masters do this from time to time. If we draw an organization chart, it will show God, godheads, masters, oversouls, individual souls, and angels. There are many godheads in God, many masters and oversouls in one godhead, and many individual souls in one oversoul.

God: Describing the Indescribable

My hypnotized patients describe God as a brilliant golden orb of Light at the core of the globe of Light (in the spherical model) or on the top of the pyramid (in the pyramidal model). (See Figures 1 and 2 on pages 45, 46) God is the initial spark of Light, the "parent" ball at the core of the big globe from which all the other energy balls came before the creation. Patients described this parent ball at the core as having plus and minus or male and female aspects in it. It is a golden creative energy force, an infinite intelligence constantly growing and expanding. It is the source that has grown and diversified and become more complex.

God is the creator of the whole creation. Plants, animals, humans, and other beings for other planets, universes, inanimate material, angels, masters, godheads—everything and everybody in the creation, including Lucifer and his demons, all came from God and are one with Him. They are all tied together in one system, one being called God. God encompasses everything in the creation. Everything in creation is connected to Him with a silver cord. This means we are never separated from God.

Everything and everybody in creation is continuously growing and expanding. Therefore, as we grow, God grows. Under hypnosis, people claim that at the very beginning God was just a spark of Light with a vast void around it. Now God and all the universes and everything in creation has expanded tremendously and has filled most of the void. Even the pieces of God that broke off and were thrown away in the void before creation have grown. Multitudes of them grow all around God and look like planets, and they all have a connecting cord to God.

According to my hypnotized patients, God (including the universes) has grown and expanded tremendously and very little void is left around God and the universes, which look like dark edges around them. Soon God will expand and fill the whole void, and we all will grow and evolve and become one with God. That is the ultimate goal: to "de-create" the creation.

Chapter Nineteen

Methods to Transform Ourselves
and Our Planet

Here we have the story of our soul: who we are, where we come from, how and why we were created, why we are going through this revolving door of life and death, what the reason is for this pain and suffering we go through, and what our role and purpose is in this vast universe. I hope this knowledge provides comfort and hope to all, especially to those who are sick and in despair, knowing that we all come from God and are pieces of God, and that there may be a reason why we are going through the pain and suffering.

We are living in an exciting time. A time of change, a time of healing and transformation of humanity and our planet. Everybody has an opportunity to do something to make a difference. Although we are experiencing a lot of darkness on our planet, there is also much more Light from Heaven at this time because of the spiritual awareness in more and more people and because of their prayers.

According to the heavenly beings, our planet is one of the darkest planets in the universe because of the heavy demonic influences, and we all have to work hard to transform it. While doing this work for fifteen years, I have been advised by heavenly beings through different patients of actions we can take to transform ourselves and our planet, so we can go back "Home" to God sooner. I wrote some of them in my first book, *Remarkable Healings*. But since not everyone will read that book, I am mentioning them here again along with other suggestions. They are as follows:

Dedicating Our Lives to God

According to the heavenly beings, during prayer we can form an intent to accept the work of God and achieve God's purposes by dedicating our lives to God. Many people are afraid that if they dedicate their lives to God, they will have to give up their possessions and loved ones and go to a remote place to pray and meditate like some saints did in the past. This is not true. When we dedicate our lives to God and God's purposes, this establishes a strong connection and ensures constant communication back and forth between us and God. This means we will always be in the Light and will be guided by God and the heavenly beings in the right direction every day.

When we dedicate our lives to God, we are also giving our permission to Him and the heavenly beings to help and guide us in the right direction. God gives everybody free will. As a result, unless we ask God and heavenly beings for help, they cannot help us. By dedicating our lives to God, we exert our free will. However, this will not mean that all our actions will be correct and all our thoughts will be noble. Because of our human frailties and the dark influences, we will still be prone to make mistakes, but by asking for God's help, we can be protected and directed toward the right path. Here is a prayer to use to dedicate our lives to God:

"Dear God, I intend to dedicate my life to you from this day on. Please protect and guide me every day, so I can fulfill your will. Please keep me on the right path and help me in achieving the goals and purposes I planned for this life. Thank you."

Intent to Become a Channel for God, as a Group

One of the suggestions given by heavenly beings is that we can speed the evolution and transformation of ourselves and our planet by becoming an instrument for God's love, Light, power, and healing. According to them, everyone is special to God and can become a tool for His love and healing. He is waiting for us to ask Him to become His instrument, which will help us and other people around us, including those people who are blocked from God by dark influences.

To become a channel for God, first we have to give an intent to God. It has to be pure and inspired by love to help others. If we have anger, hate, jealousy, fear, ego, and pride, which are often the result of dark influences, then as a channel we can become blocked by darkness and God cannot work through us. If we feel that for some reason we have become blocked, then we should meditate and pray to be free of these blocks, so we can become a loving person and eventually become a successful channel for God's work.

A minimum of three people are needed to form an intent to become a channel for God. If there are fewer than eight people, we need to hold hands. If there are more than eight, then there is no need to hold hands. Then one person in the group can pray for everyone out loud, while others can repeat the prayer silently or out loud. In the prayer, we need to give our intent to become a channel for God's love, Light, power, and healing. This is to benefit everybody forming the intent and all the human beings and to allow us to serve as His instrument as long as our souls exist to overcome the power of Lucifer, his demons, and humans and other beings under his influence who are working for him.

People who form the intent together remain connected with one another, although they may live far apart. Through their connecting cords to God, they create a wider channel between each other to permit more Light to come through. For example, if three people living in New York, Miami, and Los Angeles form an intent together to become a channel for God and then go to their homes, they, with their connecting cords to God, create a triangle between them. Through their silver connecting cords to God, together they create a wider channel and more intense Light can come through the triangle to help all those around them and between them. So the Light is coming through them, around them, and between them. Most of the Light is where the channels are, but people who are geographically encompassed between the channels get filled with the Light of God as well.

When we dedicate our lives individually to God, it is an individual act and is beneficial to ourselves only. Forming a channel for God as a group is beneficial to all who are in the group, and it spreads to other people around them and between them. It is a group act. Here, God is the main actor and director. Following is the prayer that can be used to form an intent to become a channel for God:

> "Dear God, please permit us to serve as a channel for your love, Light, power, and healing for the benefit of ourselves and for all human beings and the planet. Allow us to serve as your instrument to overcome the power of Lucifer, his demons, and those human and alien beings who serve him. We seek to do this as long as our souls shall exist. Thank you."

Reiki Attunements

According to heavenly beings, through Reiki attunements we can become an individual channel for God to heal ourselves and others. Reiki is a Japanese word for the Universal Life Force Energy. The word "Rei" means universal, and "Ki" means vital life-force energy. "Ki" is similar to the word "Chi" of Chinese acupuncture or "Prana" from India. It is similar to "Light" energy that I have described in my books as coming from God and Heaven. We all have this energy in us. During a Reiki attunement, people's energy centers and channels through which God's Light flows in us are opened up by a Reiki master, who removes the blocks in them. Through the

Reiki attunements, people get connected with God and their higher selves and guides, and as a result, increased amounts of healing "Light," or "Ki," energy can flow through their crown chakras down through their hands, which can be used for self-healing or healing others. When God's Light flows through the person's hands to the other person, it can transform dark entities and energies and thus can heal aches, pains, and diseases.

There are three degrees of Reiki attunements that can be given by a Reiki master. When we intend to help others through Reiki, we are also healed automatically. During Reiki healing, it is really God who is healing with His Light, and the person only acts as a channel for that Light. It is not a religion or faith healing and does not require any belief system. There are Reiki centers in almost all big cities. It is similar to what we call hands-on healing, or touch therapy. Many people are born with healing hands, and cosmic Light energy flows without any difficulty through their energy centers into their hands.

Taking Care of Ourselves and Our Families

According to the heavenly beings, one of the most important things we can do to evolve is to take care of ourselves, but not in a selfish way at the cost of others. If we do not take care of ourselves, nobody can. By taking care of ourselves, we are also taking care of our spirit, the piece of God within us. Our body is like a temple for our soul, and we have to be good to ourselves by doing things that will promote our physical, emotional, and mental health. We need to stay away from drugs and alcohol and other self-destructive behaviors. We have to do an honest self-evaluation and recognize all our positive qualities, which can make us feel good about ourselves and raise our self-esteem. We also need to know our negative characteristics, so that by recognizing them, we can work on changing them and thus make ourselves better people.

We should not spend our time in criticizing and judging

others, because it is not constructive and is a pure waste of time and energy that we can use to do something positive. We have to remember that we cannot change anybody except ourselves. Everybody has to do their own changing. We can help others if they allow us, but they have to do their own changing. If we all can work on changing ourselves into better people, we can change our society in no time. We alone are responsible for our actions, and we should not point at others for our problems and behavior. Similarly we should never allow anybody to blame us for their actions and never let anybody accuse us of being somebody we are not, which will destroy our self-esteem. We cannot stop them from blaming us, but if we know who we are, then we can ignore their accusation and not take it to heart. Once we feel good about ourselves, then nobody can shatter our self-esteem and inner peace.

We also have to know that our happiness does not depend on other people or materialistic possessions, and we should not search for happiness outside ourselves. Happiness comes from within. Only when we are happy and healthy and at peace with ourselves can we be helpful to our family, friends, and society. We should pray, meditate, and be spiritual in our nature and day-to-day life.

Then we have to take care of our immediate family. We have to act and behave in a way that promotes love and harmony in the family. Many spouses are driven by their professions and making money. They do not make time for their spouses and children. Families are the main source of our support and have to be the priority in our lives.

Children follow what they observe. If children see their parents showing love and affection and treating each other and their children with love and respect, youngsters learn to treat their parents and others the same way. If they see their parents being happy and secure with each other, they feel safe and protected with them. This is the best way to bring up our children.

If parents constantly dominate and control each other, argue, scream, and yell at each other, call each other names, and insult and humiliate each other in front of their children, this does the greatest damage to the kids. It is like living in an emotional battlefield with kids being the biggest casualties in that battle. Here parents are the ones who are acting like two-year-olds, throwing temper tantrums. How can they tell kids that it is wrong to scream and yell when they act the same way all the time. These kids grow up feeling insecure and learn to treat others around them in the same manner. No two people are alike, so when two or more people are together, it is natural to have a difference of opinion between them. This can be resolved by proper communication.

According to the demon and earthbound (human) spirits, they crowd around couples, families, and others who are constantly arguing and fighting, and these spirits continue to create more fights between them. They dwell and thrive in those places. After fifteen years of engaging in spirit releasement and soul integration therapy, I was amazed to find out how many people had fragmented soul parts (inner child) in them from their childhoods, who were still hiding under the bed or in a closet with their fingers in their ears because they did not want to hear their parents arguing and fighting. These soul parts, or little ones, are often covered and trapped by the demon spirits who continue to manipulate them, causing them to feel scared, angry, and untrusting toward grown-ups.

Children of divorced parents become innocent victims who do not have any choice or control of their lives. They feel split between parents. When a divorce is bitter, parents use kids to hurt each other. Children lose their self-identity and do not feel whole again. Sometimes they blame themselves, "If I had not cried that day, my dad would not have left" or "If I had listened to my parents or studied harder, my parents would still be together." Youngsters do not understand that their parents had their own problems and that they are not responsible for their parents' divorce.

After divorce, many of these children grow up in a single-parent family at or below the poverty level, or with stepparents and siblings, being confused about who they are and where they belong. They feel unloved and disconnected with everybody. Some of these children become depressed and anxious with a lack of self-confidence, while others become angry, hateful, and rebellious toward authority, because the authority figures in their lives were irresponsible and did not take care of them.

With the high divorce rate in our society, the majority of our children are growing up in broken families and are struggling to fit in, they have trouble developing relationships and follow the same behavior as their parents, and this goes on from generation to generation and gets worse with each generation. And we wonder why our kids are becoming more rebellious and violent. We are living in an "I, me, and myself" society, where many people are preoccupied with themselves and make decisions based on what will make them happy. Spouses are as disposable as old clothes or furniture.

Even in a loving family with both parents working, parents do not have enough time or energy to guide their children in the proper direction. Children grow up with various baby-sitters, TV, video games, and computers with little supervision and guidance. We have to understand that kids did not ask to be here; we brought them into this world and it is our responsibility to take care of them and treasure them to the best of our ability in a loving environment. We have to rise above "I, me, and myself," and our children have to be the priority in our lives. We have to teach them how to respect and love themselves and others by being role models and showing love and respect to our spouses, children, and others around us.

We need to cleanse our vocabulary and get rid of toxic words such as obscene, profane, and curse words, because they are used to insult and degrade another person, and they do not say much about the person who uses them and are inspired by the dark side. We should also free ourselves from toxic behaviors such as screaming, yelling, fighting, criticizing, judging, humiliating, and insulting others. They attract negative energies and entities in and around us and block us from God. "Thank you," "please," "I am sorry," and "I love you" are the most healing words and attract positive energies and Light in us.

We need to teach our children communication skills.

Parents and children should learn how to communicate properly and resolve problems without screaming and criticizing each other. Each school should have compulsory courses in communication. I personally like "Transactional Analysis," a technique enabling us to understand ourselves and others and how to communicate with each other. I find it extremely effective and use it successfully in individual, family, and marriage counseling.

Doing Things to Promote Love and Harmony on the Planet

Many of the world religions teach the law of cause and effect: "every action has a reaction," "as you sow, so shall you reap," "what you send around, comes around." All these statements underscore the boomerang aspect of human interaction. On a much greater scale, "as you sow, so shall you reap" has some staggering ramifications. Under the guise of freedom of speech, expression, comedy, and the press, some of the video games, Internet programs, music products, radio programs, television shows (including some of the violent wrestling and boxing shows), and motion pictures, which are filled with violence, nudity, and illicit sex, can desensitize our children and make them violent, indifferent, apathetic, and hardened to other people's feelings and suffering. Children absorb everything without discrimination.

Also, when we make fun of other people in the name of a joke or comedy, we are hurting those people. Pain is pain no matter how we rationalize our actions. Our actions and behavior create consequences. These facts present a challenge to those writers and producers of radio, television, motion pictures, music, video games, and Internet programs. They can make or break our society. The choice is theirs, and that choice will have positive or negative consequences for our society and for them, depending on their actions.

Indeed, what we send around comes around, individually,

as a society, as a nation, and as a planet, in this life or hereafter. Our good deeds will have a positive effect on our lives, while our negative actions will have a negative consequence for us. We will have to suffer with the similar problems and symptoms we are causing for others. There is no way out. It is the universal law. Instead of pointing fingers at others, we have to look at ourselves honestly and see how we are affecting others.

I have also seen the effects of "as you sow, so shall you reap" during past-life regression therapy. Many of my patients have found the source of their physical, mental, and emotional problems in one or more past lives when they hurt others through their actions and behavior. Now in this life they are suffering with problems similar to those they caused others in their past lives.

Choices we make have a profound effect on us, our family, our society, our nation, and our planet. Our words, actions, and behaviors, reflect who we are. Whatever we do and say affects others in a ripple effect. We need to know that no matter how we strive to rationalize our actions, the results and consequences of those actions remain the same, pain is pain, no matter the reason. Rationalizing our actions may help us feel better for the moment, but the long-range damage is done to everyone concerned, including ourselves. It is as though, once we set the karmic wheel in motion, the wheel goes where it goes and we cannot change that. We have to remove all the toxic products and behaviors from our society to promote love and harmony on our planet. Only love can heal and that is the only thing that really matters.

Drug and Alcohol Use

I mentioned in my first book about how damaging and deadly both drugs and alcohol are for everybody. They have devastating effects on individuals, families, and our society, and they carry far-reaching consequences. They are both progressive killers. They destroy individuals, taking away money, self-esteem, health, and jobs. They also damage relationships and break up marriages and families. Like a ripple in the water, the consequences are ever widening.

When children grow up in families torn apart by alcohol and drugs, they build equally sick habits and relationships based on the physical, mental, emotional, and sexual abuse they endure. This leads to a vicious cycle that passes from generation to generation, and ultimately our society becomes weak and sick and fails to survive.

We are given confusing messages. We restrict our youths from drinking until the age of twenty-one because it is so dangerous, but at the same time we glamorize drinking for adults. No party, wedding, or elegant dinner is complete without alcohol. We associate gracious living and high society with "cocktails." All the "in" people have a wet bar and know how to mix all the fashionable drinks.

Through my patients, both demon and human spirits have repeatedly bragged about their ability to latch on to drug addicts and alcoholics. Sometimes only one drink can open people up by weakening the energy shields (aura) around them, allowing the spirits to come in. These demon and earthbound human spirits often claim to hang around in bars and places where alcohol is served, waiting for a chance to move in on an unsuspecting host. Once inside people, they cause arguments and fights, break up marriages and families, and promote the desire to continue to drink. What a deal for the entities who have nothing to lose; they get their drink and the hosts pick up the tab with loss of job, marriage, family, and home. Most of the alcohol and drug addicts have "spirits of drug and alcohol addicts," who are satisfying their addictions through their hosts. As long as these addict spirits remain in a person no treatment will work.

It is time to take responsibility for ourselves, our families, and our society. It is time to recognize that the abuse of drugs and alcohol lies in the darkness. Even for the nicest people, consuming drugs and alcohol creates an open invitation for the human and demon spirits to come into their bodies, leading them to the path of destruction.

Listening to Harmonious Music

Over the years, heavenly beings have consistently advised us to use harmonious music, like classical music, devotional songs, and music which vibrates positively in our energy centers and has the potential to heal. This music raises our vibrations and affects us positively. It opens our hearts and connects us with God and the Light. This is why devotional songs and music are part of worship in every religion. Harmonious music creates positive energy in us and in our surroundings by attracting and bringing more Light. According to heavenly beings, loud, disharmonious and invasive music lowers our vibrations. It dissipates the shields around us, making them as porous as cheesecloth. This allows demon and human spirits and negative energy to come in and around us, creating different problems.

Removing the Racial and Religious Conflicts and Wars

Throughout human history, people have quarreled and waged wars in the name of race and religion. This is just as true now as it has ever been. Even within the major religions there are points of contention great enough to cause divisions, all in the name of God and in the defense of religious beliefs.

Heavenly beings, through hypnotized patients, have repeatedly told us that scriptures of all the religions are gifts from God. But these scriptures contain subtle influences from Satan and his demons. Because the scriptures were received by humans and written with human hands, they were also subject to human errors. Demons often brag about influencing humans to change the words and, consequently, the meaning in translations, resulting in conflicts, fights, and wars in the name of religion. Over the ages, all the scriptures have endured much dark influence. As readers, we must use our judgment in accepting the information that feels right and set aside what does not feel quite right.

When we believe, "My religion is the only correct religion and the religious figure in whom I believe is the only one who is real," we are bringing our ego and arrogance into our beliefs, which have no place in the truth. As mentioned throughout this book, we are all linked to God through our godhead. All godheads and masters work in perfect harmony with God and with one another to help humanity. Why then can we not live and work harmoniously with each other, worshiping one God and believing in all the masters?

As described in this book, we all are part of the same body of God and thus part of each other, connected to each other. When we hurt another person in any way, we are hurting the whole body of God, including ourselves. We cannot damage others without damaging ourselves. We have to understand this and treat each other with love and respect regardless of race, religion, and nationality. Everybody has a right to believe in what they want to, and we have to be more respectful and tolerant of other people's race, religion, and viewpoints. Only then can we preserve the whole.

It is time for us to recognize the dark influence at the core of all our strife within ourselves, our families, our communities, our nation, our religions, and the world. It is time for one worldwide religion, whose adherents believe in one God and all the masters, and for one world in which every person contributes prayerfully to the good of us all.

Forgiveness

Our world is full of anger and hurt. When we are hurt, it is easy to become angry and resentful. Unresolved feelings of hurt grow quickly into bitterness and vengefulness. We desire the opportunity to "pay back." Yet there is another avenue of response open to us—that of forgiveness. When we forgive, we free ourselves from anger, hate, resentment, and the desire to take revenge; thus we heal ourselves. Those we forgive are also healed, as our forgiveness releases them from guilt and anguish.

Through past-life regression therapy, I have seen the healing and regenerative power of forgiveness. During a past-life regression therapy session, a patient who is able to forgive the person who hurt him or her in a past life often reports being completely free from that problem now. Even the other person who hurt the patient in the past life (and who is also here with the patients in the current life) heals, without ever coming for treatment. Forgiveness is one of the most important parts of the therapy.

What we do affects all those around us. When we generate anger, hate, hurt, or any other negative feeling and behaviors, like a ripple effect, we affect many people far more than we realize. When we give or receive forgiveness, those wounds can heal. Only through forgiveness can we let go of the hurt and pain and ensure our healing. Then the energy of the universe will remain positive and in balance. Positive energy heals—not only the person who generates it, but all the souls it touches.

Physical Exercise

According to the heavenly beings, exercising regularly between a half hour and an hour each day not only can make us physically fit, but it can also give us mental clarity and connect us with our spirituality. They often recommend slow-moving exercises like yoga, tai chi, and various martial arts. These exercises can open up our energy centers, different channels like meridians through which the Light can flow into us, and also can open up the channels of communication with God, our higher self, guides, and angels. Exercise can increase the flow of the Light energy into the body and push away the darkness by a combination of slow physical movement and willpower. With slow exercises and breathing performed at a certain rate, people can get access to another dimension or another level of their being.

Quietly walking every day between a half hour and an hour can be a meditation. Many times while I am walking I have mentally received information about what is going to happen the next day or further into the future, which I have no way of knowing otherwise. I have also received knowledge about a particular problem or situation for which I was praying for guidance. This information usually comes to me as my own thoughts, and I initially have a tendency to dismiss it as "just my own thinking." But the information has often turned out to be true. Later, during a session, my heavenly guides often confirm they were the ones giving me the information that came to me as "my" own thoughts or intuitive feelings. According to these heavenly guides, each of us should trust our intuitive feelings or thoughts, because they may be the whisperings from our guides, angels, higher self, inner self, or God.

Vegetarian Diet

Over the years, heavenly beings have often stressed a vegetarian diet to enable us to connect with God and the Light. According to them, a diet that includes meat makes us more grounded in the physical world and blocks us from our spiritual nature. Our bodies have many energy systems, that is, meridians, energy centers, and Kundalini. They are designed to spread the Light energy through the body. They can be slowed down or blocked by meat in the diet. By eating meat, emotions of the animals such as fear can be transferred over to the person. Red meat creates more problems than white meat does. The health-giving effects of vegetarianism do not result from eating more vegetables, or from having more fiber, minerals, or vitamins. A vegetarian diet permits Light energy to flow unimpeded in us and allows us to connect with God and the Light.

Fasting

According to the heavenly beings, fasting also removes the obstacles to the flow of spiritual energy (Light) in our body. It is like performing spiritual cleansing. While fasting, we should direct our mind to the purposes of fasting. This creates a spiritual expectation in a person. With fasting, the obstacles to the energy flow in our bodies can be removed and energy can move in a more dramatic and forceful fashion through the body.

There are many ways of fasting as advised by heavenly beings. For the average person, taking one small complete meal during a day can be helpful. This can be done for an extended period of up to thirty days after which a thirty-day break can be taken. This can be repeated indefinitely.

Fasting by eating a small amount of vegetables and fruits is also beneficial for most people. Fluids should be taken freely with this fast. This can be maintained up to five to seven days, depending on the person's constitution. It can be done several times a year.

Another type of fasting is to drink water, and occasionally, fruit juices. This can be damaging to the body if done for a long time. It should not be extended beyond three days and should be done very sparingly.

The most effective way to fast is the complete abstinence from all foods and drinks except some water. This type of fasting can be damaging to the physical body when it is done for an extended period and should not last for more than a day. It should be done sparingly, unless you are trying to accomplish a higher spiritual objective.

There are other special ways of fasting, but these are only for some special purpose by certain people who are trying to attain a higher spiritual goal. They should not fast for less than seven days and not more than ten days. In this fast they should take nothing by mouth except some water. This type of fast should be done maybe two or three times during a lifetime, and it is not advised for most people.

There is always a spiritual improvement with fasting. The extent of the improvement depends on the individual's mental and spiritual preparation. When people go through fasting simply as a formality, without really preparing for it mentally and spiritually or without examining the effects during and after the fasting, they do not achieve the full benefit. We should also pray and meditate during fasting for achieving more spiritual benefits.

Surrounding Ourselves with a Pleasing Environment

According to heavenly beings, we should create a positive and pleasing environment by creating a loving environment free of fights and arguments and also by wearing and surrounding ourselves with pure, brilliant, and pastel colors, because they attract Light. We should try to stay away from black, gray, brown, dull, and muddied colors, because they block the Light and attract darkness. They also suggested that the black attire of nuns and black robes of judges should be changed to pure white, which can attract more Light and keep the darkness away from them, so that they can be guided by the Light to do the right things and make the correct decisions. Many demon and human spirits in my patients have claimed that they had difficulty entering or influencing nurses and doctors who were wearing a white coat or uniform. This is also true for every human being.

Heavenly beings also claimed that surrounding ourselves with plants and live flowers, flowery fragrances, and incense can raise the vibrations of our surroundings. Demons do not like incense, flowers, and flowery fragrances and stay away from them. That is why flowers are so important in funeral homes.

If possible, we should create a meditation or worship room in our homes filled with pictures, statues, or illustrations of different masters, angels, other heavenly beings as well as other sacred and positive items that can attract Light in us and our homes and that can protect us. We should also keep these items in our workplaces for more Light and protection and to keep the darkness away from us.

Discernment

We are living during an exciting time in history. There is an explosion of spiritual information coming from different sources. Most of the information is from the Light, but some may be coming from the dark side. There are many religious and spiritual leaders, gurus, and teachers. We should listen and learn from different sources, but we should not follow anything or anybody blindly. We especially should not follow anybody who claims to be the only one with the special knowledge and tends to dictate how a person should live and what he should know and do. Any type of control, domination, or self-righteousness comes from the dark side, and we should learn to discern that.

We have to remember that we have the greatest source of knowledge within ourselves, that is, our soul—the piece of God within us. It is our greatest teacher. We also have our angels, heavenly guides, higher self, and God, who are always with us to guide us in the proper direction when we ask for it. It is crucial that we learn to discern right from wrong, either from within or from above—from Heaven. When in doubt, we should pray and meditate for guidance. We should follow only what feels right in our hearts, and souls and set aside what does not feel right.

Meditation

Over the past fifteen years, heavenly beings have consistently advised us through different people to meditate daily. Sometimes patients were advised by heavenly beings to do slow, deep breathing (like in meditation) to achieve healing. During deep breathing, we allow God's Light to flow through us, which has the potential to heal.

When we pray, we speak to God. But when we meditate, we allow God to speak to us and guide us. When we are in deep meditation, our consciousness can ascend to and become one with Heaven. During the highest stage of meditation, we become immune to demonic attacks, because we literally become part of the Light (Heaven). Through meditation, we can also get in touch with our soul—that piece of God that is in each of us and that is a storehouse of knowledge and wisdom. It is our inheritance, and through meditation we can tap into that knowledge, which no book, science, teacher, or guru can teach us.

Prayers

I have found time after time that all prayers are heard, no matter how superficial they are. Sometimes they are not answered right away or the way we want because there is a lesson to be learned from what is going on in our lives. The answer to a prayer depends on our life plan. God granted us free will to learn the lessons and to grow spiritually, but God does not interfere with our free will. Asking for God's help is an exercise of our free will. God is all-knowing, but He will not intervene unless we ask.

All communication between us and God passes through our silver connecting cords. When we pray, our prayers ascend through our cords to God. God hears and answers all our prayers through this "cosmic umbilical cord." Information is always flowing through this cord whether we are aware of it or not. I am thoroughly convinced that it is very important to pray for protection and guidance daily. While individual prayers are important, group prayers have incredible impact. It is very important for families to pray both individually and together for protection and guidance for themselves and for all the people in their lives. Praying for other people sometimes is more powerful because it is selfless.

As controversial as the subject is, prayers are especially important in schools. When we pray, a column of Light and love floods from God to us and our surroundings through our silver connecting cords to God. The demon spirits are afraid of the Light and cannot come close to it. If we can keep our children and schools filled and illuminated with God's Light through prayers, they can be protected from negative, demonic influences. It is important to remember that where there is no Light, darkness will rule. This is what is happening in our schools without prayers.

According to the heavenly beings, this is one of the most

important reasons why our children are becoming rebellious and violent, and why they are indulging in drugs, alcohol, and self-destructive and antisocial behaviors. Through prayers in schools, our kids can remain clear of all the dark influences that plague them. It is particularly important to teach our children these protection prayers, not out of fear, but out of awareness.

We must keep our children clear of dark influences through prayers and thereby keep them away from drugs, alcohol, violence, and other self-destructive and antisocial behaviors. This way we can build a loving and peaceful society. Prayers are our open line to God. God will protect us and guide us and will listen to and answer our prayers, but we must ask. Instead of creating conflicts about which prayer to use and which religious figure to pray to, why not pray to one almighty God or supreme being most religions believe in rather than not praying at all and allowing darkness to rule us, our schools and children.

With prayers, we can also transform the demons into the Light and send them to Heaven. Thus we will have fewer problems to deal with. As explained in this book, demons are also part of the same body of God. They are the lost souls and need our prayers and help for their transformation.

According to heavenly beings, we should also ask God to bless all food and drinks before we consume them, so they can be cleansed and energized to benefit our mind, body, and soul.

I have prepared a protection prayer given by different heavenly beings, through many patients over the past fifteen years, as follows. It is explained in detail in my first book, *Remarkable Healings*.

Protection Prayer

Sit in a comfortable position and take several slow, deep breaths. Then you can either read this protection prayer out loud or record it on a cassette tape and listen to it every night before sleeping and in the morning after you wake up.

"I call on the power and presence of God and all the masters, higher selves, guides, and angels of all human beings, including mine, to be present to help as I pray for everybody.

"I pray to God and request the protector angels of the Light to cover with the blanket of Light and to destroy all of Satan's command centers, communication centers, and any other centers he may have, all of his dark devices of every shape, size, form, and color, and all the negative energy. Cut their dark connections with each other, with Satan and all of his demons, and with everybody and everything in creation, including the whole Earth and all human beings, other living beings and their homes, workplaces, and cars, and destroy them totally and completely.

"Scrub and scour, take away any residue that is left over. Plug all the holes and tunnels throughout the creation. Please cleanse, heal, fill, shield, protect, and illuminate the whole creation and everything and everybody in the creation, including the whole Earth, and each and every human being, other living beings, and their homes, workplaces, and cars, with the brilliant, dazzling, white, liquid Light, reflective mirrors, and rays of shimmering, white Light.

"Please create multitudes of communication centers made of Light, all over the creation, including above the Earth; each nation; each state; each city, town, and village; and each and every building and everybody and everything in them, thus protecting and guiding them.

"I pray to God and request the protector angels of the Light to collect in the net of Light and remove all foreign entities, dark shields, dark energies, dark devices, dark blocks, and dark connections from my body, aura, soul, energy centers, meridians, Kundalini, psychic antennas, and connecting cord to God. Also from my family members, friends, coworkers, all my soul partners, and each and every human being's bodies, auras, souls, energy centers, meridians, Kundalini, psychic antennas, and connecting cords to God, and from the whole Earth and all our homes, workplaces, cars, places of recreation, and everything and everybody in them and miles and miles around them. Collect them in the net of Light, lift them up, help them to the Light, or bind them in space. Cut their dark connections. Scrub and scour, take away any residue that is left over.

"Plug all the holes and tunnels in all of us and in all our surroundings. Please cleanse, heal, fill, shield, protect, and illuminate all of us and our connecting cords to God, and all our homes, workplaces, cars, places of recreation, and everything and everybody in them and miles and miles around them with the brilliant, shimmering, white, liquid Light. Cover these shields with reflective spiritual mirrors and rays of shimmering, blinding, white Light.

"Do the same for the whole Earth and everybody and everything on the Earth and all the interdimensional pathways.

"Please locate all our missing soul parts which we lost in this life and in all our past lives from the beginning of time and bring them back to us. Cleanse them, heal them, fill them with the Light, and integrate them with our souls. Clamp the cords to the soul parts that cannot be brought back at this time. Please cleanse, heal, fill, and shield our souls with the white Light.

"Also, locate and remove all the soul parts of other living people from us, cleanse them, heal them, and fill them with the Light and integrate them with whom they belong.

"Please cleanse, heal, balance, and open up all of our energy centers, Kundalini, meridians, psychic antennas, and all the channels of communication with God, our higher selves, innerselves, angels, and guides as needed and cover and protect them when not needed. Do the same for the planet Earth, all the dimensions around it, and each and every human being and other living beings.

"Put the triple net of Light and metallic shields around us and our homes, workplaces, and cars, and around the whole Earth when needed, and remove them when not needed. Please stay on guard around us in this dimension and in all the other dimensions twenty-four hours a day. You have our permission to take any action on our behalf to protect us as long as our souls shall exist.

"Please help all the earthbound spirits who are stuck on the Earth plane, in hell, or anywhere else and take them to Heaven.

"I request the protector angels to create blinding, white, protective bubbles or shields of Light covered with spiritual reflective mirrors and rays of blinding, white Light around each and every universe, extending around their connecting cords to God, creating tubes of Light around them. Put similar protective shields or tubes around each and every galaxy; each and every planetary system; each and every planet, sun, moon, star, comet, and asteroid; each and every continent in each planet; each and every country; each and every state; each and every county; each and every city, town, and village; each and every building in each city, town, and village; and everything and everybody in them and miles and miles around them, including each and every human being, living beings and their homes, workplaces, and cars, and everything and everybody in them, thus creating concentric shields inside shields. Please, put the triple net of Light and metallic shields around these protective shields when needed and remove them when not needed.

"I pray to God to please let your love and Light flood like a waterfall through the connecting cords to all the dimensions throughout the creation and all the beings who dwell in them, including the whole Earth and all the human beings and other living beings in it, including in me.

"Only I have a right to live in my body and shield. If anybody or anything tries to enter into my shield and me, I will be aware of it, even at subconscious levels of my mind, and I will say no to them. Instead of allowing them in my shield, I will direct them to the Light or where they belong.

"I also pray to God to cleanse, energize, and bless, all food and drink before I consume them, so they can be beneficial for my mind, body, and soul.

"I form an intent not to be possessed and influenced by any spirits and to reject all the works of Satan and his demons as well as humans and aliens under their influences. I also form an intent to accept the works of God and achieve God's purposes and to achieve the goals and purpose that I planned in Heaven by dedicating my life to God. Thank you."

As you pray, imagine or visualize it all happening. Whatever you imagine becomes reality in the spiritual world. Imagine the protective, concentric shields being created around the whole creation and the love and Light of God pouring like a waterfall all over the creation, through the connecting cords, including all over the Earth, and in all human beings, other living beings, and their homes, offices, work places and cars.

Then visualize or imagine a brilliant, dazzling, shimmering, vibrant, white, liquid Light coming from God, through your connecting silver cord from above your head and going through your head, pushing out of you everything that is not you, and filling and illuminating your whole body, from the top of your head to the tips of your fingers to the tips of your toes, cleansing and healing every part, every organ, every cell, and every strand of DNA of your body. Imagine this Light spreading an arm's length all around you, below your feet, above your head, in front of you, behind you, both sides of you, and all around your connecting cord to God, up to the Light, creating a wonderful tube or shield of brilliant, white Light around you and your connecting cord to God. Now imagine this tube of Light covered with reflective, spiritual mirrors and rays of brilliant, vibrant, white Light.

Just imagine or visualize yourself, your family members. friends, coworkers, and all of your homes, workplaces, cars, and places of recreation looking like a blinding, hot afternoon sun several times a day so that the demons cannot come close to you because they are afraid of the Light.

For centuries there have been many predictions about the overwhelming destruction coming in the future. It has been prophesied in many religious scriptures and by many well-known and not-so-well-known prophets. Sometimes, with some people, I do what we call God's work free of charge. During these sessions, we work with heavenly beings and are allowed to tap into any knowledge we want or the heavenly beings want us to have.

During one of these sessions, as one person under hypnosis went to the Akashic library in Heaven, he was given a book by heavenly beings who were there to help. It was a book about what can happen in the near future. As he focused on the book, he began to see images of massive destruction all over the Earth, to the extent that the whole geography was changed. Many parts of the world were completely destroyed. Where there had been water, there now was land, and where there had been land, there now was water. He saw that more than half the population of the world had been wiped out and there were no modern facilities like transportation, electricity, and different communication media. Before this, many of my patients, under hypnosis, also gave similar descriptions of the future.

It was very discouraging to hear how bad it could get. So I asked the heavenly beings who were helping us why they wanted us to know this information at this time and why God could not stop the destruction. They said it is time for human beings to know what can happen in the future and what we can do to change it. They claimed that none of the destructiveness is caused by God but can be prevented with the help of God through prayers. Some of the destruction results from the Earth's changes and shifts, leading to natural disasters like earthquakes, hurricanes, tornadoes, and other changes. Some of these disasters result from planetary karmas, and others are meant to be lessons to us. During these times, dark beings will influence and make everything worse. The heavenly beings said that when we have everything and there are no problems, we do not pray or pay attention to other human beings around us who are suffering. But when there is a disaster, we turn to God for help. During that time, we can also see people getting together to help each other.

According to the heavenly beings, what happens in the future is in our hands. We have to know that with the help of

God through prayers, together we have the power to prevent the massive destruction. The choice is ours, and God and the heavenly beings cannot interfere with our free will. We should all pray and meditate regularly and include God in our daily life and not just when there is a tragedy.

Violet Flame

According to heavenly beings, one of the most awesome gifts given by the grace of God to every human being who desires it and to our planet at this time is the "violet flame." It has the power and potential to heal and transform us and our planet and even the whole universe. If we can visualize the white Light of God under a prism, we can see the seven colors of a rainbow. Each color has a different vibration, quality, and function. The violet color has the highest vibration and has the power to transmute and transform the negative energies and entities. It is described by my patients as the "flame of mercy," "flame of freedom," "flame of forgiveness," "flame of love of God," "flame of transmutation," "flame of transformation," "a fountain of youth," "antidote for negative energy and disease," "flame of the grace of God," and so forth.

According to the heavenly beings, violet flame can transmute and transform the dark entities, dark shields, dark devices, dark blocks, and dark energies from inside us and around us. Gradually, in time it can absorb and dissipate all our negative thoughts and feelings; that is, anger, hate, jealousy, pride, ego, and arrogance, and it can eradicate all the violent and negative behavior. It can heal our emotional, mental, and physical problems. It can dissolve all the karmic imprints from our DNA and from our planet and thus free us from our personal and planetary karmas (actions), from this life and from all the other lifetimes from the beginning of time, and it can purify us and our planet. It has the potential to reverse the aging process and conquer death. Then we would not have to die from disease or old age, which are often the result of karma. We can live as long as we want to, and we can choose to leave the planet, still looking young and healthy, when our work here is done.

Violet flame can also ward of the planetary upheavals, earth changes, and all the future predictions of nuclear cataclysm and Armageddon between Light and dark. We can raise the vibrations of ourselves and our planet and we can be closer to the Light and God. We can live and function as pure Light beings, free of any and all dark influences. Violet flame is God's love, grace, power, and healing in action.

According to heavenly beings, God has promised to dispense this astounding power of violet flame to transform the human race, Earth, and the whole universe, but we must exert our free will and ask for it—not just a few people or a few spiritual groups here and there, but each and every person regardless of who he or she is. It does not matter who we are and what we have done, this gift is given to all without discrimination. Just ask for the violet flame and watch it create the miracles for us, our planet, and the whole universe. It has unlimited potential.

It is a golden opportunity given to us by the love and grace of God. For some it can be a one-way ticket to eternal life. We can enter into the golden age free of all the dark influences and ills of our society. All we have to do is pray and ask for it, and God will do the rest. We have nothing to lose.

Prayer and Meditation for the Violet Flame

Sit in a comfortable position, in a place where you cannot be disturbed. Do some slow, deep breathing. Then you can either read the following prayer or record it on a cassette and listen to it before sleeping at night and after waking up in the morning.

"I call on the power and presence of God and all the masters of the planet Earth and all the other dimensions throughout the creation to be present with us. I pray to God to fill the whole creation and all around it with the violet fire, like a violet lava, nonstop twenty-four hours a day, penetrating and permeating all the dimensions and everybody and everything in them and miles and miles around them, including the whole Earth and all the human beings, other living beings and their homes, workplaces, and cars. Let this violet fire blaze into intense flames twenty-four hours a day nonstop and let it transmute and transform all the human and dark entities, dark shields, dark energies, dark devices, dark blocks, dark connections, karmic imprints from our DNA, and all the negative thoughts, behaviors, and all our personal and planetary karmas (actions).

"I also pray to God and masters who work with me to let the violet liquid fire pour through my silver connecting cord to God, like a waterfall, permeating and penetrating through my mind, soul, and every part, every organ, every cell, and strands of DNA of my body, and in my home, office, workplaces, and cars and in everything and everybody in them and miles and miles around them. Let it blaze into intense violet flames nonstop twenty-four hours a day and let it transmute and transform all the dark entities, dark energies, dark shields, dark connections, dark blocks, all the karmic imprints from all my DNA, and all my negative thoughts, behaviors, and karmas (actions), and my mind, body, and soul, thus healing all my mental, emotional, and physical problems, and my day-to-day problems and issues.

"Remove what needs to be removed from me and my home, workplaces, and cars. Please let it transmute and heal all my karmic problems with my family members, friends, coworkers, and other people in my life, and anywhere else, so we can live with each other in a loving way. Do the same for my family members, friends, coworkers, other people in my life and each and every human being, other living beings, and their homes, workplaces and cars.

"Please bring my missing soul parts back from people, places, darkness; cleanse them, heal them, fill them with the Light and integrate them with me. Do the same for every human being. Thank you."

Now imagine a violet liquid fire like violet lava pouring from God, like a waterfall through the silver connecting cords to all the dimensions throughout the creation and everything and everybody in creation and all around it, including the whole Earth and everything and everybody on the Earth and all around the Earth, including each and every human being and other living beings and their surroundings, and blazing into intense flames nonstop twenty-four hours a day. Visualize the violet flames dissolving and dissipating all the negative entities, energies, thoughts, feelings, relationships, and daily problems and behaviors, gradually transforming the whole Earth and all the human beings and living beings on it.

Picture a globe of Earth dipped into and filled with violet liquid fire like violet lava that is blazing into intense violet flame, nonstop twenty-four hours a day. If there is some part of Earth facing special problems like war, disaster, or famine, then focus on those areas and fill them with the concentrated violet liquid fire and violet flames for a longer time, several times a day until the problem is resolved.

Then imagine violet liquid fire pouring like violet lava from God through your connecting silver cord in and around you like a waterfall, penetrating and permeating your mind, soul, and every part, every organ, every cell and strand of DNA of your body and igniting into intense violet flames, spreading in and around you, all through your home, workplaces, cars, and everything and everybody in them and miles and miles around them, nonstop twenty-four hours a day.

You can also invoke the violet flame for your family members, friends, coworkers, people who did harm to you, people who you did some harm to, and even your enemies. Anybody and anything you choose can be put in that violet fire, including your day-to-day problems and issues and all your physical, emotional, mental, and relationship problems, and they can be resolved and transformed. Imagine that violet liquid fire pouring continuously, and blazing into intense flames nonstop twenty-four hours a day.

You can also imagine your body made up of transparent crystal and through it you can clearly see every part and organ in your body. Then visualize that violet liquid fire coming from God through your connecting cord and going down through your whole body. As this liquid fire penetrates and permeates through every part, every organ, every cell, and every strand of DNA, it ignites into flames, blazing through your mind, body, soul, connecting cord, energy field, and surroundings. Imagine all the dark energies, entities, and problems in the body being transmuted and dissipated, thus healing your mind, body, and soul.

If you have any special illness in any part of the body, then focus on the violet liquid fire going through that part or organ continuously and blazing into intense flames. Imagine the problem or disease just dissipating and healing. This exercise can be used as an adjunct to traditional medical treatment.

Imagine the violet fire going to all your missing soul parts through their connecting cords to your soul. Watch all the dark energy in the missing soul parts and their connecting cords being transmuted and changed into the Light. Then imagine those soul parts being pulled back into your soul like a rubber band from people, places, and hell, and integrated into your soul. Or request your angels to bring them back and integrate them with your soul after cleansing and healing.

Do this visualization faithfully, while breathing slowly and deeply, at least two times a day for twenty to thirty minutes. As you visualize the violet flame, repeat out loud or in your mind over and over, "Violet fire blaze through me, violet fire heal and transform me."

According to heavenly beings, if we do not pray and meditate regularly, or if we indulge in negative behavior, this violet flame can be held back from us because of our free will, which will decide how much of the violet flame can be dispensed in an individual and how much healing can occur. So we have to be very consistent and positive in our prayers, meditation, and day-to-day lives.

Pray for this violet flame to remain ignited, nonstop, twenty-four hours a day. Just keep this vision of violet liquid fire and flames blazing in you and around you and throughout the Earth and the whole of creation.

Many of my patients have reported while under hypnosis that they saw the violet flames in and around them after they began to pray for the violet flame.

About the Author

Shakuntala Modi, M.D. is a board-certified psychiatrist practicing in Wheeling, West Virginia. She is a writer, speaker, and trainer in the fields of psychiatry and hypnotherapy. Her first book, *Remarkable Healings,* describes a new theory for mental and physical illness.

Index

Hampton Roads Publishing Company

. . . for the evolving human spirit

Hampton Roads Publishing Company
publishes books on a variety of subjects including
metaphysics, health, complementary medicine,
visionary fiction, and other related topics.

For a copy of our latest catalog,
call toll-free, 800-766-8009,
or send your name and address to:

Hampton Roads Publishing Company, Inc.
1125 Stoney Ridge Road
Charlottesville, VA 22902
e-mail: hrpc@hrpub.com
www.hrpub.com